**W9-AND-013**

# Contents

# PART
# ONE

## WRITING PHILOSOPHY

# 1

## *Love and Anger*
### (1989)

~

In 1973, the movement that had begun in the 1960s was still a force. I was working in Chicago with a community-organizing group that was part of the original Rainbow Coalition—blacks organize blacks, browns organize browns, whites organize whites. "The Leadership" of my group asked me to write a book to publicize the organization and to help raise money. I completed over a dozen oral-history interviews with working-class members, but before the book was completed—or even properly begun—the Movement had lost its force and the organization closed down. As the introduction to the book, I had written my own "oral history."

~

I was born in Providence, Rhode Island, during the depression. We lived in a little house my great-uncle built after the family came here from Ireland. It was across from the railway switching yard. We used to sit on the curb in front of the house and wave at trainmen in the cabooses and read the names off the boxcars, "Lackawana Trail," and "Phoebe Snow." Sometimes a bunch of us went over and broke open a freight and stole watermelons. All the men in the family, and the unmarried women, worked in the woolen mill. Fletcher's Mill, on the other side of Olneyville Square.

I grew up angry. Angry at clerks in the public dental clinic who treated my mother with contempt. Angry at people who kept my father in fear of losing his job. Angry at the high school principal who treated me like a slut. Angry at the fraternity boys from Brown who came over to my side of town to find a girl to lay. Angry because my people, my neighbors, my family were defeated by a sense of powerlessness. Defeated by their own respect for the men who ran the woolen mill and for the men who ran the city's Democratic machine. Defeated by their own respect for the clinic clerks, the high school principals, the fraternity boys at Brown. Defeated by their own lack of respect for themselves.

I left Providence when I was twenty, but I didn't begin leaving the world I grew up in until I started taking night classes at the University of Houston. I was twenty-four then. Eleven years later, Stanford University awarded me a Ph.D. in philosophy. It was a proud day for my father. His daughter had made it.

I'd made it into a world where people didn't know much about railway switching yards or woolen mills. I'd made it to a place where the kind of life I had lived was an unusual one. It's an easy step from there to believing that you're an unusual person, and that the life you lived and the hardships you faced were unusual, too. It's such a flattering thing to believe. Flattering but false. My life was just a life.

I grew up in a working-class world, and by going to a university I "made it" into a middle-class world. That's the main way of moving from the working class to the middle classes, by going to a university. It explains why the educational level of working-class people is lower than that of middle-class people. Once he or she goes through a university, a working-class person moves into the middle classes, no matter what sort of job there is after college.

By going to a university, working-class people learn the life-style and values of the middle classes. They get the credentials they need for moving into the white-collar, managerial, and professional jobs of the middle classes. The English they speak becomes middle-class English. They learn to devote a lot of time, thought, and energy to their careers. They learn to see their lives as slopes that rise as they go up the ladder of success. They learn to read the latest books on child care. They move to a neighborhood that has safe streets and is in a good school district. They leave home behind.

The lives of the people in this book are just lives. They are lives of working-class people who didn't leave home behind. Lives of people who grew up angry. If these people are different from other people, it's because they learned what to do with their anger. They learned how to begin to change things. They learned how to turn the anger outward and to make it creative. Understanding that means understanding that the lives of the people described here are just lives. If my life, and the lives of others in this book, were unusual, then there might be no need for revolution. There certainly would be no hope for it. But the lives are not unusual. Our growing up angry was not unusual. Revolutionaries are not adventurers. They come out of ordinary lives and want to make a revolution to change ordinary lives . . .

~

This little autobiography was written to make a point, and, of course, it leaves out many important things.

My sisters and I grew up in a little house my great uncle had built—my father's side of the family, carpenters and builders in England and Ireland. The women worked in the mills—my father's side of the family, skilled Irish-Catholic women who earned more than some of the men. My mother's side of the family was different. Her mother was the youngest child in a large family of Irish-Catholic farmers. Her father was born in England into a coal-mining family. In the mills of Lawrence and Providence, he worked as a mule spinner, running back and forth on a narrow walkway between the looms, untangling yarn and releasing jams in the pounding machines. "Risky," they called him. Mule spinners were known for their missing fingers and amputated arms. He was never a regular worker, and the family story is that he would regularly appear home at midmorning and his wife, my grandmother, would say, "Jacked up your job again, huh Jim?" She worked her fingers to the bone as a cleaning woman, to keep food on the table. Unemployed, he was used as an errand boy by other adults.

My mother's family owned no home. They fled Lawrence with landlord and creditors at their heels, abandoning whatever furnishings they had. In Providence, this beloved grandmother lived in fear of authority. As a toddler I was continually scolded if I ran the water too long when I got a drink, for Mrs. Landlady might hear and threaten eviction. This grandmother lived in fear of the police, though she and her family led totally honest lives. She lived in fear of the priests, though her heart was as Christian as a heart can be. She was the first thoroughly good person I knew.

The class differences between my mother's family and my father's family were the major class differences present in my early childhood. My mother's family was respectable, in the sense that they were honest and "poor but clean." But less than a block from the house my great-uncle built was Oak Street, not (like our house) across the street from the switching yard but alongside it. Oak Street was full of tenements, which were said to be full of roaches and were certainly full of children. Irish-Catholic families sprawled all over the stoops and shouted and gossiped. The women wore their stockings rolled down around their ankles, and their threadbare, black coats were sometimes pinned together at the front. On Fridays they would pound on the door of the men's bar (all the bars in the neighborhood were men's bars). They would yell the name of their man, and then, "The children are hungry!" They would tell their man to pass out his pay envelope so they could buy makings for supper.

My mother would never pound on a barroom door. She was beautiful, green-eyed and red-haired, with an elegant air to her. It was my mother who read us Shakespeare when we were tiny, my mother who scraped pennies to buy *Classics of Victorian Literature*—offered, in a matched set, at an

Olneyville drugstore for thirty-nine cents each (three for a dollar). But on Fridays I sat with her at the window of our second-floor flat in the house my great-uncle built, looking down the street toward the men's bar, waiting until Daddy came home of his own accord.

My father's mother, my other beloved grandmother, treated my mother and her family as if they lived on Oak Street. She had worked her fingers to the bone (and the fingers of her son and daughter) to keep the distance between her family and Oak Street. The first disrespect of others that I knew was this class disrespect between one side of my family and the other, between one side of my street and the other.

How is love to bridge the lines between one side of my family and the other? Between that father of the men's bars and that mother of the window seat? Between myself now and those beloved people of my childhood? Those beloved people of my life?

In my work as a philosopher, a sociologist, and a feminist theorist, I swim in the sea of those questions. How do love and anger turn outward and become creative?

~

It was out of love and anger that teachers in my neighborhood school lavished opportunity upon me—opportunity they purloined from my little classmates. They practiced a classroom favoritism that has since been scientifically discovered and stamped out in the name of equal opportunity. They worked within nature's hard principle by which the first gets the feed and the runt withers away. By passing me on, teacher to teacher, in their serial subversion, they chose me as one who would leave the neighborhood and go into the world. One of their own would make it. Once out, I would not forget my own. It was the tried-and-true method by which we had already gained control of our neighborhood schools, the metropolitan police forces, and the Democratic machines. The older brothers and sisters of my own generation were to give us a presence in the arts, the social-service agencies, the legal system, the universities, and the Presidency. But "us" here means us Irish Catholics, in all the tensions of both sides of the family, both sides of the street, both sides of the tracks, both sides of the gender war—all those stretch marks of bringing to birth those of our own who would make it and not forget their own.

At the appropriate time I was torn from my neighborhood and sent to Classical High School, the public school that claimed to be as good as Boston Latin and was rumored to be full of middle-class, WASP and Jewish grinds tunneling molelike toward college. The rumor was as true as such things can be. We had neither beauty queens nor star athletes (not even gym for girls after freshman year). What we had was quarterly publication of the most minute rankings of the honor role that a five-letter system allows—"All A's," "All A's but one B," "All A's but two B's," and on down the line, stopping tastefully short of ranks that would cause embarrassment to our few dunces. I ranked high when I paid attention. But I soon became a misfit in whom anger conquered love. I exploded. I became a truant. I wanted no more to do with schools. I graduated only under duress. I wanted no part of college scholarships. In romantic terms, I was a primitive rebel—but a female one, and what a difference that makes.

It took about five years to convince me that the life of a primitive rebel was suicide to body and soul. It could never become grand opposition, it would only be impotent deviance. My neighborhood teachers had not chosen me for such an end, and I certainly did not want it. Prudence forced the anger down. In the family tradition, I began working my fingers to the bone to feed my own family, eking out a bachelor's degree first in night school, then at last as a full-time student with a half-time job. Freedom, and some time to spend with my two daughters, came with a Woodrow Wilson fellowship to graduate school. After my other jobs, graduate school was an easy way to make a living.

At that time, in the mid-1960s, in my graduate years at Stanford, philosophical truth was the province of professional philosophers, just as scientific truth was the province of astrophysicists, microbiologists, behavioral psychologists, and all the members of the multitudes of disciplines and subdisciplines of the sciences. In philosophy there were great constructions of semantic systems, and great investigations into the forms of moral reasoning. The admired talents were crackerjacks who constructed clever, hypothetical counterexamples ("But what if a nuclear bomb is rigged to the elevator button, and in intentionally pressing the button, I destroy the city of New York?"). I had done my undergraduate honors thesis on Nietzsche and Heidegger, and these gymnastics left me out of the intellectual ballpark. Fortunately, my view that philosophy was an appropriate occupation let me accept the athletic training, and I soon became good enough. I had the chameleon abilities of the upwardly mobile who come into the Garden after everything is already named.

There were also, always, the love and anger. I saw, and argued, that the ethics classes had nothing to do with life as it was lived in my neighborhood or anybody's neighborhood. I saw, and argued, that at best it was a WASP ethics fit for intellectuals playing games. Professors and students explained to me how I was mistaken.

As time passed I moved through the childhood of my professional career. My last year as a graduate student began with the Free Speech movement at Berkeley. My first years as a paid professor were years of antiwar and civil-rights marches, of riots and police brutality, of shutting down the universities and organizing the neighborhoods. Until 1972, when I joined the community-organizing group, the only explicit politics I had came from a few stories my father told of working with Ann Gerlack and "the Communists" to get a union into the American Woolen Company (the effort drove the mill owners into the arms of the AFL-CIO). I had a romantic political sense that came from reading books in my early twenties: Hemingway's story of the Spanish Civil War in *For Whom the Bell Tolls*; Steinbeck's stories of dust-bowl farmers in *The Grapes of Wrath*. These gave the barest wisp of political definition to that love and anger. But the politics I acted on suited my location in the academic, professional classes, and those politics were not yet mine (except insofar as it was I who acted with others). That changed, and the change showed in my work and action, but it is the story of Part Two of this book. Here in Part One, the story is one of making philosophy out of love and anger.

I read "Nietzsche and Moral Change" (Chapter 2) in May 1972 at the first meeting of the newly formed Society for Women in Philosophy, at the American Philosophical Association Conference in Chicago. I expressed then what had rankled me since the first class at Stanford: In claiming to give a neutral analysis of reason in ethics and science, philosophers in fact give a narrow, parochial definition that leaves out life in all its tensions, and, in so doing, preserves dominance of an old order. I framed the questions in terms I thought suitable for the first meeting of a feminist society: What morality does the revolutionary act under? It is a question that is still not resolved, of course, and I still think it is not taken seriously enough within academia or outside it. I used Nietzsche to talk about some new moralities. I said that a new morality must be created, and if you can't argue for the new morality in a way the old guard demands, well, too bad for the old guard. When I finished, a famous member of the old guard stood up and asked, "Why do you call what you are proposing 'morality'?" He found none of my answers philosophically acceptable.

The vision of my mother and me standing at the intake desk of the free dental clinic is still vivid. The clerks were peremptory and would not hear what she was trying to say. I could feel outrage radiating through her silence. It is a vision that stands duty for experiences I have shared with my own—and over time, with its help, I gathered into my own many other peoples. What angered me in this silencing of my mother wasn't the personal rudeness of the clerks. It was the preempting, the blind, institutionally effected preempting of my mother's humanity, and through her, of my own humanity and my family's and my neighbors'. Our humanity was preempted by clinic personnel who upheld and were upheld by the professional powers of medicine and dentistry, which upheld and were upheld by the ruling apparatus (as Dorothy Smith calls it). My mother's outrage radiated through this many-layered preempting, though she had no "political analysis." I knew it by a child's simple perception.

I met the preempting many times in my life. It was most painful in Classical High School and in the years of my "primitive rebellion," when I had little authority of my own. But I meet it to this day. It is this vision that gives the passion to "Moral Revolution" (Chapter 3), which I wrote in 1977 for the Prism of Sex Conference, organized by the Women's Research Institute of Wisconsin.

By 1977 I had not only had a political awakening with my radical neighborhood-organizing group, I had already done some sociological fieldwork in the symbolic interactionist tradition (in connection with Howard Becker's field methods seminar at Northwestern). In "Moral Revolution," I use interviews with members of a feminist abortion collective to argue that philosophers define the moral aspects of social problems and so silence those who use other moralities. In doing so, I develop the distinction between moral reform and moral revolution that I made in "Nietzsche and Moral Change." The essay speaks of the authority by which professionals make official definitions and preempt the meaning we may give to their actions and our own. In doing so, they continually define the issues in a reformist direction that preserves their own position of authority in the status quo. In that essay, I am particularly concerned with the contribution of professional authority to creating and maintaining hierarchies of class, gender, age, and race.

In "The Man of Professional Wisdom" (Chapter 4), I discuss this professional power in terms of cognitive authority in science. That essay was published in *Discovering Reality*, the first original collection on feminist epistemology and philosophy of science, edited by Sandra Harding and Merrill Hintikka. Cognitive authority allows some people to make official definitions of our common world—definitions that are taught in the public schools and used in setting public policy. Scientists exercise their cognitive authority as "neutral experts." Philosophers try to exercise their cognitive authority in the same way. In "Moral Revolution" and "Moral Passages" (Chapter 5), I use reproductive issues to show that philosophers preempt our moral meanings and our solutions to our social problems.

The definition of abortion as a conflict of rights delineates the moral problem of abortion in a way that prevents some people from expressing their moral concern over abortion—for example, that it is intimately connected with moral understandings about human life, human living, and the place that children have in the living. But the philosophical definition does not simply affect other people's ability to express their moral opinions. The philosophical definition goes hand in glove with the political definitions made by the dominant organizations in the abortion controversy. Together the professionals and dominant activists, lobbyists, and politicians define the social problem of abortion, and, in doing so, they define the range of solutions to the problem. The solutions are cozily nestled in the hands of the courts and legislatures—the issues are those of deciding constitutionality and of passing laws, and "the people" are limited to actions of somehow joining in interest groups to affect the decision makers. But not all solutions fit within this range. In "Moral Revolution," I discuss the abortion service "Jane," whose solutions require a grassroots feminist movement offering real, practical alternatives for women as they make their lives and the lives of their families and communities. The solutions of the "pro-life" group Birthright do not fall within the range of the conflict-of-rights definition, for they too require grassroots support in making alternatives for women—in their case, alternatives that allow having the child rather than having an abortion.

The most disastrous effects of the definition of the moral problem of abortion as a conflict of rights lie in the fact that the definition gerrymanders abortion off from the other life issues of procreation. These include current "front page" social problems of teen pregnancy, AIDS, crack babies, population problems, latchkey children, sexuality, homelessness, working mothers, child care, and even destruction of the environment. It also gerrymanders abortion off from the lives we live in our communities and societies and the ways that authorities enter to define our lives and ourselves. One of the ways that the professional definition operates is to define abortion so that only the woman and the fetus are relevant moral individuals. In this moral problem of abortion, the cast of characters is limited to two. But in real life, where we face the personal and social problems of procreation (including abortion), the cast of characters is enormous. It includes the woman and her intimates—parents, siblings, partners, children, friends, neighbors. It includes authorities and officials in her social world—bosses, high school teachers and principals, government and bureaucratic functionaries, professionals of all kinds, and so on. Philosophers are included in this cast of characters, and so are activists, justices, and politicians.

In "Moral Passages," I expand the cast of characters to show how actions, virtues, and the self are defined officially, and that the method of definition differed (in the late 1960s) for white teens of the middle classes and black teens of the ghetto. That essay offers a different way of approaching philosophical ethics.

The basic insight that came from my political experience and my sociological work is that the social order is created and maintained through human social interactions. Each person contributes to the meaning of the process, but some people have the authority to define what is happening.[1] Symbolic interactionism has served me both as a philosophical method and metaphysics, and as an articulation of a moral standpoint of respect. It was clear to me that by becoming an academic professional, I ran an almost unavoidable risk of preempting other people's humanity—in the classroom and in my research. Like others I struggled with teaching methods in the classroom. In my research the anthropological methods of symbolic interactionism held out a hope of letting others speak for themselves (though it would be overly sanguine to think the hope can be satisfied in our hierarchial institutions). My conclusion was a double one: Philosophers should use an empirical, not a conceptual method; philosophers and all academic professionals should develop an understanding of responsible work that takes into account their authority to define and their risk of preempting.

The closing essay of Part One, "Why Philosophers Should Become Sociologists (and Vice Versa)," was presented at the Stone Symposium of the Society for the Study of Symbolic Interactionism in May 1988. It was written for and read to sociologists, and it is the most compact statement of my philosophical opinions that I have been able to write to date. In it I try to demonstrate how philosophy might become more empirical.

## Note

1. This understanding is implicit in "Nietzsche and Moral Change," which I wrote at the very beginning of my most important activist work, and several years before I came to sociology. From my present vantage point, I find the last endnote of the essay very interesting (see Chapter 2, n. 13, on Michael Walzer's discussion of oppressed minorities). In "Nietzsche and Moral Change," I am writing as a member of a political group in a time of mass movement that included the academy in a central role. I take a vanguardist position: The revolutionaries show the way to the new paradigm under which the oppression of the people can be seen to be *oppression*. For this to make sense, the revolutionaries have to be deeply in contact with their constituencies, and among the people "like the fish in the sea," as we then said (following Mao). In my later essays in Part One, I am less concerned with revolutionary authority than with the oppressive authority of professionals of the traditional order. By the late 1970s, the mass movement was gone, and academics no longer had the activist place they had had in the early 1970s. These themes arise again in Part Two, in which I fuss about the authority of academic feminists.

# 2

## Nietzsche and Moral Change
### (1972)

What is moral change? An answer to this question is necessary if we are to answer the question, What is essential to morality? But among moral philosophers, Nietzsche stands almost alone in trying to examine the full structure of moral change.

There is a reason for this. The main body of tradition in ethics has occupied itself with the notions of obligation, moral principle, justification of acts under principle, justification of principle by argument. When moral change was considered at all, it was seen as a change to bring our activities into conformity with our principles, as a change to dispel injustice, as a change to alleviate suffering. In short, moral change was seen as moral reform, with no other sort of moral change acknowledged or even imagined.

But moral reform is not the only sort of moral change. There is also moral revolution. Moral revolution has not to do with making our principles consistent, not to do with greater application of what we *now* conceive as justice. That is the task of moral reform, because its aim is the preservation of values. But the aim of moral revolution is the creation of values.

The traditional view in ethics has been unable to see this because moral creativity cannot be understood when the theory of morality is exhausted by the notions of obligation, principle, and justification. Nor can certain types of morality be understood, those that do not concern themselves (or those that concern themselves very little) with the notions of obligation, rightness of act, justification of principle.

---

Reprinted, with changes, from Robert Solomon, ed., *Nietzsche* (Garden City, N.Y.: Anchor Press/Doubleday, 1973), 169–93, by permission of the author. Copyright 1973 by Kathryn Pyne Addelson.

By paying attention to moral revolution, Nietzsche was able to understand some of these things. I would like to work with his insights and develop some of the points I think he was trying to make. This means that I will not be doing "Nietzsche scholarship" but trying to apply some of his insights to theoretical and practical problems that face us. Given his views on the interpretation of literature, I do not believe this is against the Nietzschean spirit.

I will argue that the narrow focus of traditional ethics makes it impossible to account for the behavior of the moral revolutionary as moral behavior. In seeing this, we shall see that the traditional view misrepresents that structure of morality, and why a Nietzschean typology of morals offers us new moral notions that are more adequate. In the end, we shall be able to distinguish moral revolution from moral reform on the basis of his typology and have a greater insight into moral phenomena.

Nietzsche's views on morality are closely associated with his epistemological views.[1] This is essential, because the traditional views on morality go hand in hand with certain traditional views on the objectivity of science. Because of this interdependence, I will consider a position held by Thomas Kuhn in *The Structure of Scientific Revolutions* (1970). Kuhn's epistemology bears strong resemblance to Nietzsche's, and the arguments he gives against traditional views in philosophy of science parallel arguments I will give against traditional views in ethics. But unlike Nietzsche, Kuhn does not stress the interrelationship between morality and science, and so his work will be of only limited use to us. But that limited use is essential because he offers fairly clear suggestions on an epistemology, while Nietzsche's remarks are scattered and incomplete. In addition, Kuhn's notion of a paradigm (or of individuals working under a paradigm) will be useful in discussing structure of moral revolution.

I will argue from a particular case of moral revolution—the women's revolution in the nineteenth century. This is one of the clearest examples of a moral revolution, and it offers ideal illustrations of some of the moral phenomena Nietzsche discusses.

In using this example, I will go beyond Nietzsche—and perhaps in a direction he would not endorse. This is not because it is a *women's* revolution. Despite its name, it was a human revolution, affecting men, women, and children. And despite his remarks, Nietzsche was no simple misogynist. His distaste for women was a distaste for the slavish character shown by nineteenth-century women. It was this slave morality in women that the women's revolution hoped to overthrow.

But the women's revolution was a revolution of the people, and

Nietzsche looked sourly upon such things. His highest moral categories are aimed at capturing moral revolution in the *individual*. However, I think that these categories can be used to understand the individual moral revolutionary and, through him or her, moral revolution itself. In the end, I think such a use of Nietzsche's categories reveals the phenomena of morality in a way he himself was unable to reveal them.

Section I below considers Kuhn's claims that traditional views on science misconstrue both scientific revolution and "normal science" or science in stasis. Section II takes up some central arguments given by conservatives and revolutionaries in the nineteenth century to show that the traditional views in ethics cannot account for the behavior of the moral revolutionary as moral, while section III suggests a new understanding of the women's revolution in light of Kuhnian and Nietzschean explanations.

Section IV considers a typology of morals based on certain Nietzschean distinctions. With the aid of the typology, a separation is made between moral revolution and moral reform in section V, and it is suggested that Nietzsche is correct in taking the essential parts of morality to consist in creation and self-overcoming.

# I

"Truth" is not something there, that might be found or discovered—but something that must be created.

—Nietzsche, *The Will to Power*

There is a certain traditional philosophical view of science that goes hand in hand with traditional views in ethics. In sketching this view, I am mainly leaning on positivist accounts, but not only the positivists hold the relevant principles.[2] The most fundamental thesis of this view is that science is "objective." What that means to a traditionalist is that there are certain observable facts and regularities in the world, and it is the job of science to formulate theories accounting for them.

Science explains the regularities. It explains them by postulating theoretical principles from which statements expressing the regularities can be derived. Ultimately, it is in terms of its ability to explain observable regularities that a scientific theory is justified.

The matter, however, is somewhat more complex than this. One theory may be better than another because it is more general, that is, it explains more of the observable regularities. A very general theory will receive justification because it "explains" less general theories, that is, less general theories can be derived from it (given suitable connections between theoretical terms). For example, Newtonian celestial mechanics was a very general theory because it explained many observable regularities, and part of the justification for it was that the Galilean laws concerning freely falling bodies near the earth could allegedly be derived from it. Again, a narrow theory may be justified by being subsumed under a more general theory. Thus the Galilean laws receive some justification in allegedly being derivable from the Newtonian.[3]

Given this interpretation of objectivity and justification, the traditional view on the growth of science simply follows. Science grows by accretion. Any new theory introduced must be consistent with the principles of those old theories that are in accord with observation. We progress in science by retaining that part of the older principles that really captures the phenomena, and we proceed to a new theory that is more general in explaining *more* of the observable phenomena, while still explaining what the old theory explained. With luck, this new theory also allows more exact prediction of the observable.

In *The Structure of Scientific Revolutions*, Kuhn suggests that there is a great difference between "normal science" and "revolutionary science." If we look at science in periods of change—revolutionary science—we can see that, not only is traditional philosophy of science too narrow in dealing with only one kind of scientific activity, it also misconstrues even that sort in its myopia.

Kuhn says that science proceeds as "normal science" until some crisis is reached. Perhaps some problem that was supposed to be solved by the theory resists solution even though the best minds in the field have struggled with it. Perhaps difficulties arise in accounting for observable phenomena that can be taken care of only by tinkering with the theory until it turns into a "monster," as the Ptolemaic theory did.

The traditional view would say here that the old theory can no longer explain observable regularities and that a new theory must be developed, one that preserves those old generalizations that are supported by observation, one that explains the observable regularities that the old theory could not. Kuhn disagrees. He claims that what is involved in cases of scientific revolution is "a reconstruction of the field from a new foundation, a reconstruction which changes some of the field's most elementary generalizations as well as most of its paradigm methods and applications" (Kuhn 1970, 85). Elsewhere, he adds:

At times of revolution, when the normal-scientific tradition changes, the scientist's perception of his environment must be reeducated—

in some familiar situations he must learn to see a new gestalt. After he had done so, the world of his research will seem, here and there, incommensurable with the one he had inhabited before. (Kuhn 1970, 112)

In fact, this is why schools of scientists holding different theories usually seem at cross-purposes.

The suggestion here is that science does not proceed by accretion but by leaps and bounds, and the leaps are to a new perspective. The whole world looks different. "Each theory creates its own experience."

It is not my aim in this chapter to examine Nietzschean epistemology. As I mentioned above, Kuhn's epistemology is far more easily accessible. But it is worth noting that in his opposition to the "objectivity" claimed for science by those who think "naturalistically," Nietzsche's opinions closely resemble Kuhn's. He says, "Forgive me as an old philologist who cannot desist from the malice of putting his finger on bad modes of interpretation: but 'nature's conformity to law' of which you physicists talk so proudly, as though—why it exists only owing to your interpretation" (Nietzsche 1966, 22).

It is our human way to rationalize the world through science. Science does not describe the "objective" reality, it *creates* the world of science.[4] Then it looks at its creation and says, "This is what is. This is fact." Seeing that, one sees that the traditional, "naturalistic" account is thoroughly and fundamentally mistaken. We ought not to talk in terms of a world of observable regularities "out there" that science slowly captures. We need a new way of constructing even normal scientific activities.

Instead of taking theories and observations as fundamental in explaining the structure of science, Kuhn prefers to talk in terms of "paradigms." There is much unclarity in the Kuhnian notion of a paradigm. But in the idea of a *scientist working under a paradigm* is a notion that will be useful to us.

Scientists working under a single paradigm are trained in the same methods of research and experiment, often in schools and laboratories having historical and social connections. They take as exemplars the major experiments or written works. For example, Newton's *Opticks* (especially the *Queries*) was studied as giving prime examples of experiment construction by eighteenth-century scientists, and his *Principia* exemplified scientific reasoning. Scientists working under a single paradigm accept the same theories and principles. They agree on which problems their theories are expected to solve. They agree on which sorts of observable regularities are relevant as evidence, and they agree on how observations are "properly" made.

But theories and principles are not simply sentences that have their meaning given in Plato's heaven. They are statements that are *understood* by the scientists in terms of their training, their exemplars, the observations they take as relevant, the problems they see *as* problems. All these enter into scientific understanding of theories and principles.

This does not mean that, once the new paradigm comes into existence, there is no comparing its theories with theories and principles of the old paradigm. But before the comparison can take place, the new paradigm must come into being, and more important, the univocality judgment and the comparison must be done from the point of view of the new paradigm.

So it appears that the key features of normal science are not quite what the traditionalist said they were. In fact, looking at normal science in a Kuhnian way, we might say its key features were these:

1. Observable regularities, which are relevant to the science, to the testing of its principles and to the judgment of its generality, are determined by the paradigm.
2. The problems that theory faces, and which it may be expected to solve, are determined by the paradigm.
3. Thus justification of scientific principles is strongly influenced by the paradigm, since this justification is in terms of ability to account for observable regularities and is (sometimes) in terms of support by other scientific theories within the paradigm.
4. The task of the scientist doing normal science is to solve the problems determined by the paradigm, to articulate the theories and principles of his or her field (thus achieving greater generality, greater justification), and to develop better instruments, yielding finer methods of measurement of phenomena, which are determined to be scientifically relevant by the paradigm.

What is important here is this: If scientific behavior is construed only in terms of normal science, then the scientific revolutionary is going to have to proceed "unscientifically." Depending on how revolutionary he or she is, that person will be unable to justify his or her view. The revolutionary will take new principles to be important and will see the world differently, taking new regularities to be important, while reconstruing the relevance of some old ones. In rejecting the old paradigm, the revolutionary cannot give justification in its terms. Moreover, since paradigms are embedded in tradition and training, and since theories are understood through that tradition and training, the revolutionary's theories will be *incapable of full understanding and justification* until a new paradigm comes into being. In scientific revolution, embracing the new theory resembles conversion rather than change of conviction by rational argument.

## II

[Morality] works against our acquiring new experiences and correcting morality accordingly, which means that morality works against a better, newer morality.

—Nietzsche, *The Dawn*

The traditional philosopher of science explains the structure of science in terms of theories, scientific principles, observations, and, in addition, all scientific methods of justification, which he is at pains to explicate. The traditional moral philosopher explains the structure of morality in terms of moral principles, as well as all the moral methods of justification, which he is at pains to explicate. In both cases, change is said to take place by reform.

According to the traditional view, it is through moral principles that situations are categorized as morally relevant or not. For example, the principle "One ought to tell the truth" selects those situations in which I am reporting facts to *others* as morally relevant, but it leaves other situations (such as when I am alone and eating supper) as morally neutral. This means that moral principles enter into our activities in two ways. They enter *internally*, in that I categorize the world of my possible actions in their terms and act in accord with them or not. They enter *externally* in that others see and judge my acts in their terms, and I justify my own acts to others in part by their means. It is a fundamental assumption here that morally proper behavior must be morally *justifiable* behavior.

Moral principles themselves must be justified. Sometimes this is done in terms of higher-level moral principles. But there are *very* high-level moral principles ("One ought to act so as to bring about the greatest happiness") that require metaphysical or philosophical justification.

It is important to look at moral justifications, which are actually given to see how all of these elements enter. I will do this in some detail, to show that the conservative fares well and the revolutionary fares very poorly indeed under this traditional view of morality.

During the nineteenth century in the United States, there was an attempt to bring about a moral revolution—an attempt that was in part successful. The main attack was on those values that operated to keep women in a morally, culturally, and socially subordinate position, as well as a legally subordinate one. That is, the thrust was against a *humanly* subordinate position of women, against a double standard of humanity, one that adversely affected the moral being of *both* men and women. The organized part of this moral revolution deteriorated into a movement toward mere reform as the twentieth century began, with the increased emphasis on women's suffrage. So its earlier phases are the ones of interest to us. But these earlier phases constitute one of the clearest examples of moral revolution, and they offer admirable illustrations of some of the moral phenomena that Nietzsche emphasized, but which philosophers in ethics generally overlook.

An argument presented by Senator Frelinghuysen of New Jersey shortly after the Civil War captures the essence of the conservative position against the women's revolution:

> It seems to me as if the God of our race has stamped upon [the women of America] a milder, gentler nature, which not only makes them shrink from, but disqualifies them from turmoil and battle of public life. They have a higher and holier mission. It is in retiracy to make the character of coming men. Their mission is at home, by their blandishments and their love to assuage the passions of men as they come in from the battle of life, and not themselves by joining in the contest to add fuel to the very flames. It will be a sorry day for this country when those vestal fires of love and piety are put out. (Flexner 1971, 147)

Eleanor Flexner, a historian of the women's rights struggle, says that emotional arguments like this characterized all debates before 1919, and that no rational argument was able to make a dent in them (Flexner 1971, 150). But she is mistaken in dubbing this a mere emotional argument. It is a perfectly rational justification of the moral claim that one ought to oppose the attempts of women's rights workers, and there are reasons that the moral revolutionaries could not make a dent in it. Let's look more carefully at the argument.

1. Senator Frelinghuysen's justification uses the scientific claim that men differ by nature from women. We might call this the "Aristotelian claim," after an earlier espouser of it. It is supported on the one hand by a vague, "Aristotelian" scientific theory (still held in the nineteenth cen-

tury) about the natures of individuals and how these relate to their natural capacities. One's nature attaches to one as a member of a kind. For example, all women have the same nature in this sense.

The claim that women differ by nature from men is overwhelmingly supported by differences in their behavior. In ancient Greece, nineteenth-century America, and even twentieth-century America, women did not display abilities to command or to reason, which men showed. They were in fact timid and dependent, better followers than leaders. Of contributions to human development deemed worthy of report to history books, virtually all were made by men. What great women statesmen, scientists, musicians, painters, religious leaders, or philosophers does history show? Such data not only support the claim that there is a difference between men and women, they show what the difference is.

In addition, the claim for the difference was supported on religious grounds, for example, on the basis of standard interpretations of Genesis. A woman's place, and her tasks, were taken to have been intended by "the God of our race."

2. Senator Frelinghuysen's justification presupposes the moral claims that *one ought to act according to his or her nature.* This claim is essential, since some women showed better abilities to lead and reason than the senator did.

This moral principle was essential, and it was considered generally impeccable down to our time. It has been used, for example, to justify condemnation of sexual deviates and to justify monstrous treatment of homosexuals on the grounds of "unnaturalness" even in our own day.

The principle can be given religious support: We ought to act as God intended. But even in the nineteenth-century, it was given other support. It is *harmful* for a person to act against his or her nature.[5] As a worthy group of Massachusetts ministers said in attacking the Grimke sisters' efforts toward women's liberation, "We invite your attention to the dangers which at present seem to threaten the FEMALE CHARACTER with widespread and permanent injury" (Schneir 1972, 39). This indicates that Senator Frelinghuysen's case rests ultimately on the high-level moral principle that one should act so as to promote the highest moral character in oneself and in others.[6]

Through the senator's argument itself, we see that the traditional view would classify his activity as morally relevant, and it appears that he has justified his behavior. But what of the moral revolutionary? We need to look at her behavior through the glasses of the traditional moral philosopher. I would like to take Sarah Grimke as my protagonist here and consider some of the moral reasoning and argument she used in 1837, in her *Letters on the Equality of the Sexes and the Condition of Women* (Grimke 1972). Like Senator Frelinghuysen's arguments, hers involve claims that were put forward throughout the nineteenth-century.

In brief, Miss Grimke argues that what appear to be natural differences between men and women are due to differences in education, training, and expectation. She claims that "women are educated from childhood to regard themselves as inferior" (Schneir 1972, 44) and that "our powers of the mind have been crushed, as far as man could do it, our sense of morality has been impaired by his interpretation of our duties (Schneir 1972, 42). She argues directly against the interpretation of the Bible used to support the "natural difference" view, saying that Genesis actually shows that God created men and women as equal.

There is also an egalitarian principle underlying the argument in her *Letters*, one that is clearly present in her argument in favor of equal pay for equal work (Schneir 1972, 45–46). We might make it explicit in John Stuart Mill's terms from *The Subjection of Women*: "The principle of the modern movement in morals and politics, is that conduct, and conduct alone, entitles to respect . . . that, above all, merit and not birth, is the only rightful claim to power and authority" (Schneir 1972, 177).

These remarks now seem aimed directly at conservative arguments against the women's movement. Living in the 1990s, most of us would accept them. But that fact is not at all to the point, for the question is whether they constituted arguments that could serve as a justification for Miss Grimke's behavior in 1837, and whether they could serve as a basis for counting her behavior as moral behavior—much less morally *proper* behavior. I shall argue that they could not so serve, that they are at best calls for a new paradigm.

1. Miss Grimke's claim that nurture, not nature, determines the difference in behavior and ability in men and women is meant to undermine the claim that the Aristotelian theory is data supported. The form of argument here is exactly correct: To undermine the empirical support for the Aristotelian theory, the data must be reinterpreted, explained by a different scientific theory. Unfortunately, Miss Grimke was ahead of her time in her scientific as well as her moral views.[7] There was no scientific theory to support her interpretation of the data. This point is important, but perhaps difficult to grasp in this case because we now accept a scientific view properly interpreting her hypothesis. But merely putting a scientific hypothesis into words does not constitute giving a justification.

If the hypothesis is understood against the background of the conservative paradigm, then "education" and "nature" will be understood as interpreted under that paradigm, and evidence for the hypothesis will be construed as it is construed under the paradigm. What Miss Grimke needs is an alternative theory on nature and education and their effects on human capacity and behavior. Her argument at best *suggests* that a scientific justification for her position can be developed. It is not itself a justification but a call for a new scientific paradigm.

One might object here that the Aristotelian type of theory is subject to a direct test that does not require development of an alternative theory. Miss Grimke herself suggests such a test:

> All I ask of our brethren is that they will take their feet from off our necks and permit us to stand upright on that ground which God has designed us to occupy. If he has not given us the rights which have, as I conceive, been wrested from us, we shall soon give evidence of our inferiority. (Schneir 1972, 38)

Such a "direct test" would no more falsify the Aristotelian theory than it did the more recent Freudian one. Freudian theory postulated a difference in nature for men and women too, a difference that was strikingly similar to that postulated under the Aristotelian theory. Women's behavior that might falsify the theory was accommodated by altering the theory slightly, to admit that some few women had "masculine natures" (and were thus natural anomalies). But the vast majority of women were supposed to have natural feminine natures. Aggressiveness and "unwomanly" behavior among these are explained by saying that they are driven by penis envy into a neurotic emulation of men. Such emulation was judged to be an illness requiring treatment to bring the woman to accept her nature. To change the educational process so as to develop these unnatural characteristics in all women would be, in Freudian eyes as well as in the eyes of the Massachusetts ministers, "to threaten the FEMALE CHARACTER with widespread and permanent injury" (Schneir 1972, 39).

But in asking that "our brethren . . . take their feet from off our necks," Miss Grimke is not merely suggesting a test for the conservative theory. She is making a call for the moral revolution.

2. The claim that merit, not birth, is the only rightful claim to power and authority is aimed at overthrowing the moral principle that one ought to act according to one's nature as it limits the participation of women in the society. However, rather than relying on that principle as it is understood under the moral paradigm, Mill is suggesting a *reinterpretation* of it. For that principle was understood to mean that birth into a particular social class should not disqualify an adult male. The principle cannot support Mill's position because it presupposes his position on women. Again,

we have merely a call to bring about the revolution, and an example of how a particular moral principle would be reinterpreted under the new paradigm.

For legal principles, we have a formal structure (the court system) to take care of interpretation of their meaning. An examination of the changes in interpretation of the Bill of Rights, for example, shows how paradigm-dependent our legal and governmental principles are for their interpretation. My claim here is that an analogous situation exists with regard to scientific and moral principles, even so-called trans-societal principles. It may be less well noticed only because we lack a formal structure to take care of their interpretation.

There is, however, one principle that does not seem quite so paradigm-dependent for its understanding, and that is the hedonistic act-utilitarian principle.[8] The principle might be stated roughly in this way: One ought to choose that act that produces a greater surplus of happiness over unhappiness than any alternative act. What makes people happy before and after the revolution will be different. But a utilitarian would hope for psychological tests of happiness, which are independent of the *moral* paradigm at least.

There are general difficulties in applying this principle, since a comparison of possible acts and their possible consequences is necessary. This is particularly difficult in the case of moral revolution, because calculating the consequences of the revolutionary's acts requires knowing what would make people happy after the revolution as well as calculating their degrees of happiness.

These difficulties are not the major ones. It is more important that there is scarcely a person who would hold the unmodified hedonistic act-utilitarian principle, because the resultant *quantity* of happiness is at best only one element with which we are concerned. Fairness in the distribution of happiness is also important. The methods used to bring about the happiness are important. To be acceptable this utilitarian principle needs to be "restricted" by other principles, particularly a principle of justice. But other principles, *particularly* the principle of justice, are heavily dependent on the paradigm for their interpretation.

If revolutionaries wish, they may give some justification to their actions by using the hedonistic act-utilitarian principle. If they cannot accept that principle unsupplemented—and I am sure that there is scarcely one who will accept it—then there seems to be no way for them to give a justification.

Revolutionaries must, then, proceed without proper justification. But this is not all. Most philosophers holding the traditional view do not feel that moral principles merely enter after the fact, merely enter in giving a justification. One does not act willy-nilly, then fish about for some principle that will justify the act. One assesses the situation morally before acting. But even to assess the situation as moral requires the use of moral categories, thus principles of one sort or another (or so it seems, in the traditional view).

Moral revolutionaries cannot do this. If they are to be seen as acting under principles at all, these must be principles interpreted under the new paradigm. Principles as understood under the old paradigm will not properly characterize the moral features of the current situation. But the new paradigm is not yet in existence. So even revolutionaries cite principles, even if in saying the words, they have only a limited understanding of those words. Let me support this with a quotation from Paul Feyerabend:

> One often takes it for granted that a clear and distinct understanding of new ideas precedes and should precede any formulation and any institutional expression of them . . . [but] we must expect, for example, that the idea of liberty could be made clear only by means of the very same actions which were supposed to create liberty. Creation of a thing, and creation plus full understanding of a correct idea of the thing, are very often parts of one and the same indivisible process and they cannot be separated without bringing the process to a standstill. (Feyerabend 1970, 24)

The arguments of a moral revolutionary constitute a call for change, not a justification. But even as a call, they are not statements of principles interpreted fully under the new paradigm but a *hint* at a direction in which to go in the creative process.

### III

> That the value of the world lies in our interpretation . . . ; that previous interpretations have been perspective valuations by virtue of which we can survive in life, i. e., in the will to power for the growth of power
> —Nietzsche, *The Will to Power*

Some traditional philosophers will not be surprised that moral revolutionaries cannot justify themselves and, if revolutionaries are seen as acting morally at all, they are seen as being evil. A contemporary Hobbesian might grant that revolution is sometimes necessary (while seeing any such revolution as political). But since the only way to judge rightness and wrongness and obligation is under the laws and rules of the existing system, revolutionaries must be traitors or subversives. It is only after the revolution that they can justify what they have done—if the revolution is a success, that is. Here, as with Nietzsche's morality of custom (*Sitte*), change is immoral (*unsittlich*) (Nietzsche 1969).

But this is unsatisfactory so far as moral theory goes, and it is certainly unsatisfactory if we try to apply moral theory to practice. It allows no adequate explanation of the structure of moral revolution *as moral*. And it sacrifices whatever light may be shed on normal morality and the traditional view itself by the phenomenon of moral revolution. We should recall that Kuhn suggests that the traditional view on science be overthrown in the light of the structure of scientific revolution.

Seen in a Nietzschean light, moral revolution contains what is essential to morality in a way that morality in stasis does not. In focusing on morality in stasis, and especially on morality as it concerns justification and principle, the traditional philosopher is "human, all too human." He offers the rationalization that is necessary to the herd, the rationalization that operates *against* creation and change. This will become more evident in section IV. Here, we might look again at the women's revolution to put traditional ethics in perspective.

I mentioned in section II that the data supporting Senator Frelinghuysen's conservative view on women were *facts*. Women understood themselves and their lives in terms of the way they were characterized under this view. Miss Grimke saw this when she said that women are "educated from earliest childhood, to regard themselves as inferior creatures . . ." (Schneir 1972, 46).

This picture of women was not one that was imposed from outside by a sexist science. Kuhn would say that the science created the world picture and created its facts. But the adequate characterization of the situation is given far better by Nietzsche than Kuhn. For it was Nietzsche's insight that our science does not operate independently of our morality—since science and morality work together not only in giving us a picture of a world but also in creating that world and the human beings in it.[9] I think that this is evident from the discussions in section II. But those discussions were concerned with principle and argument, and there is more to the matter than that.

Throughout written history the structure of the family has been closely integrated with the structure of the society, the one supporting the other. Revolutionaries and conservatives in the nineteenth century used two radically different analogies in describing the family and the relationship of husband and wife within it. Revolutionaries saw the family structure as analogous to tyrant-slave or master-servant relationships ("The Subjection of Women"). Conservatives saw it roughly as analogous to a parent-child relationship. The husband protects the weaker wife. There is a biological basis for the parent-child relationship, and they saw one in the relationship of husband to wife.[10]

The family was seen by conservatives as a unit made up of individuals with specialized functions—the social closely following the biological. Each individual must fulfill his or her function, because that is necessary for the survival of the unit. And the survival of the family unit is necessary for the survival of the society. Conservatives argued that the whole theory of government and society presupposes this view of the family, in terms of this division of functions.[11]

Women were different from men in their capacities and personalities because it was *necessary* for them to be different from men. The survival of the family and state depended on it. This offers a striking confirmation of Nietzsche's claim that whatever is necessary for our survival we see as truth—though to take something as truth does not make it true. But Nietzsche remarks on this: "'No matter how strongly a thing may be believed, strength of belief is no criterion of truth.' But what is truth? Perhaps a kind of belief that has become a condition of life?" (Nietzsche 1968b, 532).

Without departing from Nietzsche, we might say that what is necessary for our survival *becomes truth*. Theory follows fact, and human facts of this sort follow need. The traditional view has stood the matter on its head.

The way our principles are embedded in fact makes it clear that a moral revolution cannot be one based on principle, with its major struggle one to make act conform with principle. That is at best the task of moral reform. The women's revolution had to proceed by making the facts different. The revolutionaries had to proceed by bringing a new paradigm into being. Principles followed. They followed as they always have, as a rationalization of what is and what is necessary. Traditionalists overlook this because they focus on "normal morality," morality in stasis. Of that, Nietzsche says, "Whatever lives long is gradually so saturated with reason that its irrational origins become improbable" (Nietzsche 1969). But what seems improbable may nonetheless not be.

A moral, social, and scientific paradigm (the paradigm of a conceptual scheme) is not merely something through which we see the world. It is something that shapes the facts of the human world. The traditional view deals only with a certain kind of post hoc rationalization, taking this rationalization as what is essential to morality. Accepting it as the whole story, we cannot understand the moral revolutionary, and we cannot understand normal morality either.

To understand these things, and to understand how morality might be liberated from necessity, we need to look at other views on morality, or rather, other moralities alternative to those picked out by the traditional view. In Nietzsche's writings, we find alternatives.

## IV

*The* beautiful exists just as little as does *the* good, or *the* true. In every case it is a question of the conditions of preservation of a certain type of man.

—Nietzsche, *The Will to Power*

Nietzsche's interest in psychological and developmental aspects of morality, his emphasis on transvaluation of values and on self-overcoming make him one of the few philosophers who have put "normal morality" in perspective. But in understanding this, it is important to put aside the dogmatism of the traditional view. Otherwise the transvaluation is seen merely as the replacement of one set of values by another (all encapsulated in principles), and the self-overcoming is seen merely as self-discipline of the usual moral sort.

If we look at a (somewhat) Nietzschean categorization of different varieties of morality, I think it is possible to understand the varieties of moral revolution and of normal morality more fully. In doing this, I would like to consider "slave morality," "morality of the person of conscience," and what I will call "noble morality" as varieties. [12] Using these notions to pick out varieties of morality requires leaving aside negative or positive connotations of "slave" or "noble."

What might slave morality be? A slave's life, *qua* slave, is full of duties. Freedom is essential to any moral agent, but the slave's freedom consists in a freedom to obey or disobey. Because there are sanctions, which follow upon disobedience of a rule, the slave must be able to *justify* what he or she does. Sometimes the sanctions are external. If the slave cannot give an acceptable justification, punishment may come through the law courts (a political sanction) or through the ill opinion and acts of the slave's compatriots (a moral sanction). But sometimes the sanctions are internalized, and conscience and feelings of guilt are the instruments en-suring obedience. In fact, the primary value in slave morality is obedience, and it is axiomatic that the moral person is the obedient person: obedient to the moral rule.

It should be evident that what Nietzsche calls "slave morality" comes very close, as a *type* of morality, to what I have been calling "morality on the traditional view."

Nietzsche felt that a fairly widespread type of morality that grew out of the Christian tradition was a slave morality—a morality of the weak, with their fear of strength and their resentment. Women constituted slaves *par excellence* in this sense, and that fact may explain some of Nietzsche's diatribes against them. It was this sort of slave morality that the women's rights workers had to root out of themselves. But for our typology, it is better to abstract from these characteristics and see slave morality as one involving principle, rule, and justification, with acts taken as the basic moral units and with obedience to rule the cardinal virtue.

What I will call "noble morality" differs essentially from slave moral-ity, not in being a morality of the strong, but in being a different *type* of morality. It happens that strength of one sort or another is required in this morality, and that the weak find protection under slave morality, and this is morally and psychologically important. But more important to us is the difference in their structures.

Within noble morality, there is no concern with rules, obedience, and justification. The person, not the act, is the basic moral unit. Nietz-sche says, "It is obvious that moral designations were everywhere applied to *human beings* and only later, derivatively, to actions" (Nietzsche 1966, 260). But this should not be taken to mean that in noble morality it is the *person* who is judged or justified instead of the act. "The noble type of man experiences *itself* as determining values; it does not need approval" (Nietz-sche 1966, 260). This noble person apprehends himself as worthy and confers values in his acts.

I have called this sort of morality "noble morality" rather than "mas-ter morality" because, in Nietzsche's discussions, master morality is some-times not clearly distinct from what I will call "the morality of the person of conscience." It is not clearly a type that Nietzsche himself set out, al-though some readers of Nietzsche seem to interpret his master morality in this way.

In discussing the noble distinction "good-bad" (which contrasts with the slave distinction "good-evil"), Nietzsche explicitly mentions the very ancient Greeks (Nietzsche 1969). These "noble ones" do not have a noble morality in my sense because they have not attained the necessary, partial "self-overcoming" (see their behavior in Nietzsche 1969). But we might take a later development of this morality, as exemplified by some ideals in classical Greece, to represent noble morality.

Here, the noble person sees himself as worthy (see Aristotle's "great-souled person"). He confers value in his acts. He has overcome himself in the sense Kaufmann stresses: by triumphing over his impulses (Kaufmann 1968, chaps. 7 and 8). He is disciplined, so much so that his triumph and discipline flow from his nature. He is not a slave to a moral code. In fact, on a somewhat Aristotelian analysis, his valuations are the *foundation* of values for the society. A just act is one that the just person would do, and to act justly is to do such an act as the just person would do it.

There is a third type of morality, the morality of the person of conscience (following Nietzsche 1969). This individual is "master of a free will." He is free not to obey or disobey, as the slave is free. Like the noble person, he is free from the slavery to the moral codes and opinions of his society. But in addition, he is free to create.

The person of conscience creates values, but only by creating himself. Here, I think self-overcoming has a different import from that which it has under noble morality. Noble morality involves only a partial self-overcoming. Self-overcoming in the person of conscience requires a self-disciplining, it is true. But it cannot properly be described as reason overcoming impulse, as Kaufmann describes self-overcoming (Kaufmann 1968, 235). Instead, an overcoming of the *entire* old self is involved, of the old ways of perceiving oneself and the world, of the old ways of *being*. It is an overcoming that is necessarily a creation of oneself. It involves, in part, a phenomenon analogous to what is currently called "consciousness raising." One overcomes the old self that is structured within the old paradigm and becomes "the sovereign individual, like only to himself" (Nietzsche 1969). In this self-overcoming, one creates oneself anew and creates values.

Given these unfortunately sketchy remarks on types of morality, we might use them to look at moral phenomena.

First, we might see (as Nietzsche did) that different societies emphasize one sort of morality over others. Greek society emphasized noble morality. Nineteenth-century Anglo-American society emphasized slave or rule morality. It is only a myopia induced by the traditional view on morality that would bring us to see these differences as a mere difference in moral code.

Second, we might use the typology to investigate different kinds of moral phenomena that occur within a single society. Nietzsche himself suggests that master and slave morality "at times . . . occur directly along side each other—even in the same human being, within a *single* soul" (Nietzsche 1966, 260). Our own society seems to be a mixed one.

Finally, we might use the typology to look at moral change. The first thing we would learn is that a moral revolution need not result in replacement of one set of principles by another, or in the reinterpretation of principles held under the old paradigm. It might result in a morality of a new type. This parallels the way a political revolution might result, not in the replacement of one form of government by another, but in an anarchistic society.

The second thing we would learn is that the moral revolutionary is behaving morally, but under a different type of morality from that which the traditional view recognizes. I mentioned in section II that the women's revolution workers had to *change the way they were as women* in bringing about their revolution. I do not want to claim that all—or even that any—of these women became "persons of conscience." But it is *that* sort of morality that best captures the moral behavior of each of them, as revolutionaries.

Each of the serious workers in this revolution had to overcome herself in the sense of morally disciplining herself. But she also had to create herself as an individual like only to herself. That she later met others like her is irrelevant. The Southern aristocrat who was Sarah Grimke, the overworked farm girl who was Lucy Stone, the slave mother of thirteen who became Sojourner Truth, all had to be overcome. Each woman had to create herself anew, in a process of self-overcoming, which took no models (there were none to take) and which continued as long as she was a revolutionary. Today we have example after example of young black people who have gone through this self-overcoming, and many others of us have gone through it in a more modest way.

Nietzsche's morality of the person of conscience captures the morality of individual revolutionaries far better than the traditional view does. It offers a beginning for understanding how moral revolutions take place. As we saw in section III, it is necessary to change the world, to create new facts and a new paradigm, in bringing about the revolution. The process of self-overcoming explains some of this, and it indicates that the creation of values begins with the creation of the individual revolutionary as a new type of human being.

But this is individual morality. It is not the aim of the moral revolutionary to become the "sovereign individual" when this brings with it the *isolation* of uniqueness. And given Nietzsche's attitude toward revolutions of the people, we would not expect his favorite moral type to fit revolutionaries too well.

Revolutionaries cannot create themselves in isolation as sovereign individuals. They must begin to create themselves as the first of their kind. This creation, this self-overcoming, continues throughout the revolutionary process. But it is part of the task of a revolutionary of the people to help *them* to overcome themselves, to help each create him- or herself as a new kind of individual. In this process, the new paradigm comes into being—that is, the new values are created.

## V

Art is worth *more* than the truth.

—Nietzsche, *The Will to Power*

Given all of this, we can begin to see the difference between the moral revolutionary and the moral reformer. Both activities involve a struggle against the conservative forces in power. But the moral revolutionary is like the scientific revolutionary in struggling to overthrow some part of the present structure. In doing this, one must overcome oneself in the process of the revolution. One must work to help one's people overcome themselves. And this is a necessary process to the end that a new kind of human being may be brought into being, and thus a new paradigm and new values as well—for a moral revolution essentially involves creation of a new human being. It was one of Nietzsche's insights that moralities determine *kinds* of persons.

The reformer, on the other hand, is doing "normal morality." Like scientists doing normal science, reformers operate within the present paradigm. They find contradictions in held principles, or contradictions between principle and application of principle, acting to eliminate suffering or injustice (as injustice is understood under the prevailing paradigm). They make those demands that the minority group represented wants *now*.[13] And this is necessary so that the principles of their paradigm are consistent and so that practice follows principle. Reform essentially involves the *preservation* of values.

The behavior of moral reformers seems to be explicable under the traditional view on morality—after all, they are doing "normal morality." But because the behavior of moral revolutionaries is not explicable under the traditional view, all moral change is seen as reform. This may explain why so many contemporary Anglo-American philosophers find virtue in the reformer but not in the revolutionary.

Moral revolutionaries may sometimes *feel* they want to relieve suffering and injustice. But it is creation, and not the relief of suffering and injustice, that must serve as their foundation. And there are reasons for this.

Workers in the women's revolution might have *felt* that injustice was being done, but according to the notion of justice within their paradigm, it was not. They may have *felt* that women were suffering under a sexist society, but the vast majority of nineteenth-century women *did not feel* they were suffering from sexism. It is difficult to make a case that one is struggling to relieve suffering when the "sufferers" themselves deny the suffering.

It is of the reformer that we might say: "Either his reforms will be acceptable to the people, or they will not: if they are acceptable, the people have in principle the power to implement them, and it will be a question not of overthrowing the system but of making it function; if they are not, he has no business to impose them" (Caws 1972, 98).

Revolutionaries will not (generally, cannot) impose their demands. But they cease to be revolutionaries if the demands are only those that are acceptable to the people at the time. That is not a way to creation of values, to creation of a new human being.

I have spoken of "normal morality" and "moral revolution." But the condition that is normal to human life is not a state of stasis but a state of revolution. Stasis is less painful, more easy to rationalize, more sure, more safe. It encourages us to believe we can rest, because we have the truth. But if we think in term of Nietzschean epistemology, or in terms of Kuhnian paradigms, we see that in science and morality, it is a continued state of revolution that expresses our humanity best. Nietzsche says, in *Thus Spake Zarathustra,*

> And life itself confided this secret to me: "Behold," it said, "I am *that which must always overcome itself.* Indeed, you call it a will to procreate or a drive to an end, to something higher, farther, more manifold: but all this is one . . . whatever I create and however much I love it— soon I must oppose it and my love. (1968a, 2:12)

## Notes

1. I found an unpublished paper by Simmie Freeman Turner, "Nietzsche on Truth," very helpful in understanding the relative merits of Arthur Danto's and Walter Kaufmann's interpretations of Nietzsche's epistemology. Her paper contains many quotations from Nietzsche's works, some of which I have used in the chapter (see Flexner 1971).

2. The relevant "objective" position is discussed at length in Scheffler 1967. Scheffler displays a very deep misunderstanding of the Kuhn-Feyerabend position in this book—one that is similar to the misunderstanding of the Nietzschean epistemology and ethics shown by superficial readers.

3. I say that these laws are "allegedly" derivable because they are alleged to be so by some philosophers holding the traditional view. Paul Feyerabend criticizes this view and argues that they are not so derivable in Feyerabend 1962.

4. I must put in a caveat here. In this chapter, I am emphasizing the *creative* aspect of science and morality as an antidote to certain traditional views. Nietzsche did the same. This leads to an overemphasis on the contribution of interpretation, which comes out clearly in the quotation from Nietzsche 1966 (22). "Nature's conformity to law" does not exist only because of an interpretation (but it does not exist because of some metaphysically real and unique structure of reality either, and that is the point). I think much of the dispute over what Nietzsche meant by "the truth" is due to the fact that we ourselves do not have an adequate view of the truth in light of which to take his hints. Simmie Freeman Turner argues in "Nietzsche on Truth" (1978) that Nietzsche indeed holds a perspectivist view, which Danto attributes to him, but that he also uses the word *truth* in a common-sense way. Turner says this use can be accounted for by talking about the truth in one perspective as compared to another.

5. In our own day, the whole Freudian view on neurosis has operated to support Frelinghuysen's moral principle.

6. There is also a means-end argument included by the senator. It involves the evaluative claim that maintenance of the home is good, and the factual claim that granting the women's demands will lead to the destruction of the home. It is a long-lived argument and was used by Illinois House Majority Leader Henry Hyde, who opposed ratification of the Equal Rights Amendment on the grounds that it constitutes "an attack on the home and motherhood" (*Chicago Sun Times*, May 19, 1972). Frelinghuysen and Hyde are correct.

7. Grimke's sociological and psychological analyses in the *Letters* (1972) are remarkable. See her remarks on the "butterflies of fashionable world" in the Old South (43–44). Many people, including Nietzsche, have criticized these "butterflies," but Grimke's analysis could have been written in the mid-twentieth century. Her criticism is very positive and gets at the roots of the difficulty.

8. Rule utilitarianism (under which rules are justified by the consequences of adopting them, and acts justified by the rules) and pure act-utilitarianism (under which acts are justified by the goodness resulting) will not do as principles under which the revolutionary can justify him- or herself. The understanding of the rules and the understanding of "goodness" (except where this is happiness or pleasure) are thoroughly paradigm-dependent.

9. See n. 4.

10. This difference in analogies constitutes one of the core differences between the conservative and the revolutionary. The basic vision of the revolutionary springs from seeing the family structure in light of the master-servant analogy. It is the beginnings of their new way of seeing the world. In this regard, we might notice the importance of analogies in science on the one hand, and the use of analogies by Nietzsche on the other (his use of master and slave as analogies in setting out types of moralities is one striking example). Overemphasis on principles leads to overlooking the importance of analogies.

11. This structural interdependence was explicitly brought out by many conservatives. Consider a remark made by Senator Williams of Oregon shortly after the Civil War: "When God married our first parents in the garden according to that ordinance they were made 'bone of one bone and flesh of one flesh' and the whole theory of government and society proceeds upon the assumption that their interests are one" (Flexner 1971, 148). Revolutionaries tended to ignore this interdependence, although it is stressed by Engels in "Origin of the Family, Private Property, and the State" (1884). That work was too late for our revolutionaries to use, and even if it had not been, it was far too politically radical.

12. I speak of "noble morality" rather than "master morality" for reasons given below.

13. See Michael Walzer's remark in Walzer 1970: "I should think the immediate goals

of the activists must be set by the general consciousness of the oppressed group rather than by their own ideology. The effects can only be judged by those who will feel them. 'Helping' someone usually means doing something for him that he regards or seems likely to regard (*given his present state of mind*) as helpful" (my emphasis). The women's revolution never would have come about if its "activists" had followed this advice. That fact that these remarks have only to do with reform is also evident in the title of the article: "The Obligations of Oppressed Minorities." I think one of Nietzsche's major contributions to the understanding of change lies in his insight that change need not take place only to relieve oppression. In fact, the claim that a change is necessary to relieve oppression is very often merely a rationalization to explain and justify the natural and creative drive that is essential to human beings. The people are themselves oppressed when their consciousness is raised, that is, when they begin to look at things from the perspective of a budding new paradigm.

# 3

## Moral Revolution
### (1977)

## I. INTRODUCTION

Has a covert bias been introduced into our world view by the near exclusion of women from the domain of intellectual pursuits?

Philosophers and scientists both have argued long and hard that it is a virtue of science that the sex, race, ethnic background, or creed of the investigator is irrelevant to scientific results, provided only that scientific method is practiced correctly. They have taken that to be one consequence of the *objectivity* of science, and some have even felt that the remedy for bias is to become *more* scientific. Although philosophers and scientists generally conclude that there is no bias, the question somehow keeps arising. One reason it cannot be laid to rest is that detecting bias is itself a philosophic or scientific enterprise, and the methods used in the detection may themselves be questioned as to bias. In fact, the major question concerns how to define what bias amounts to.

Sometimes bias in intellectual work has been said to be the result of doing "bad science," or "bad philosophy." In principle, the work is biased because of the biases of the investigators using the theory. Let me give an example from Judith Jarvis Thomson's paper, "A Defense of Abortion" (1971), which I'll consider in some detail in section II below. In this paper, she says that most philosophical discussions of abortion have taken the point of view of a third party (lawgiver, abortionist, interested onlooker) and not the point of view of the pregnant woman. She argues that the moral decision from the point of view of the pregnant woman is quite dif-

Reprinted, with changes, from Julia A. Sherman and Evelyn Torton Beck, eds., *The Prism of Sex* (Madison: University of Wisconsin Press, 1979), 189–227, by permission of the author. Copyright 1979 by Kathryn Pyne Addelson.

ferent and that we can't generalize from the third-party point of view to hers. For example, considerations of self-defense may enter for the pregnant woman when they don't enter for an outsider. This criticism Judith Thomson raises shows bias in the *application* of the philosophical theory she is working with. It doesn't correct the philosophical theory itself. Her criticism shows that other papers on abortion have been biased *in the use of the theory*. The bias would be corrected by reforming the way the theory is applied.

Some criticisms of bias in the use of a theory show that fairly basic assumptions of the theory may need to be corrected to do "good science" with it. Let's take an example from sociology. Arlene Daniels reports on a paper by Joan Acker:

> [Joan Acker] points out that stratification literature—whether written by functionalists, Marxists, or others—contains assumptions about the social position of women that are quite inadequate. The first assumption is that the family is the unit in the stratification system. From this view, a number of other assumptions are derived, such as that the social position of a family is determined by the male head of household or that the status of females living in families is determined by the males to whom they are attached. But these assumptions do not accurately reflect the actual state of relationships for large segments of the population. There are many females and female heads of households who are not attached to males. Why should such persons be ignored or placed in some residual category indicating their irrelevance to any major analysis of the stratification system? No male stratification theorists have previously questioned the usefulness of a world view that excludes the conditions of so much of the population from consideration. But it has been convenient to assume that females have no relevant role in stratification processes independent of their ties to men. (Daniels 1975)

In this passage, Arlene Daniels isn't suggesting that the functionalist or Marxist theories have to be thrown out because they are sexist. She is saying that they contain inadequate assumptions about the social position of women, and that those assumptions need to be corrected by reforming the theory.

There is a more radical kind of bias that may infect a theory, a kind that can't be corrected by reforming the application of the theory or a few of its assumptions. To reform this kind of bias, we need a scientific revolution in which the old theory is scrapped and a new theory introduced. Let me give another example from sociology. In *Another Voice*, Lyn Lofland reviews urban sociology.

> Women in that portion of the literature of urban sociology here under review are mostly and simply, just there. They are part of the locale or neighborhood or area—described like other important aspects of the setting such as income, ecology, or demography—but largely irrelevant to the analytic *action*. . . . To the degree that urban researchers have taken seriously (and of course many have not) the Blumerian injunction to "look upon human group life as chiefly a vast interpretative process in which people, singly and collectively, *guide themselves* by *defining* the objects, events and situations they encounter," they have done so primarily for the male participants in the human group life. The female participants are "just there." (Lofland 1975 citing Blumer 1969)

Lyn Lofland feels a radical change in urban sociology is necessary to correct this bias and that no mere reform will do. She says: "The problems which lead to the portrayal of women as 'only there' are among the central conceptual, focal, and methodological difficulties of urban sociology itself" (Lofland 1975, 162). She suggests that to remedy this bias, completely new models, concepts, and variables would have to be developed out of studies that gave proper investigation to women; the resulting theory, she feels, would very likely differ in a radical way from the one currently used by many urban sociologists. Such a radical change in theory is a *scientific revolution*.

Since the publication of the first edition of Thomas Kuhn's *Structure of Scientific Revolutions* in 1962, a good deal of research has been done on scientific revolutions (see Kuhn 1970). Charles Darwin's evolutionary theory constituted a scientific revolution of very great magnitude, since it brought with it a revolution in patterns of thinking in philosophy of science and many other sciences in addition to biology. Lavoisier's revolution, which transformed alchemy to chemistry, was important but of smaller magnitude. The Copernican revolution in astronomy and the Newtonian in physics were also far-reaching.

The bias that Lyn Lofland found in urban sociology has ancient roots. In this chapter, as a philosopher, I will be investigating a bias of the third sort in contemporary American moral philosophy. A main bias in moral philosophy for two millennia has been the bias that Lyn Lofland points out in urban sociology: the moral-social world has been taken to be the world as men know it. A meaningful life (or a "good life") has been a life seen from the perspective of males and open only to males—and in fact, only to higher-class white adult males, so that the bias is classist and racist and ageist as well as sexist. I believe a moral, social, and philosophical revolution is necessary to change it.


# II. A DEFENSE OF ABORTION

In September 1971 the first issue of *Philosophy and Public Affairs* was published. It was a very different kind of journal from the philosophy journals existing then. Its purpose was to highlight the philosophical dimension in issues of public concern and to encourage "philosophically inclined writers from various disciplines . . . [to] bring their distinctive methods to bear on problems that concern everyone." The journal had an effect on the direction of work in philosophy.

In the first issue of *Philosophy and Public Affairs*, there was a paper by Judith Jarvis Thomson titled "A Defense of Abortion." In the paper, Judith Thomson considers whether or not abortion is ever morally justifiable, concluding that it sometimes is. In the years since this paper was published, it has become one of the classic works used when the abortion problem is considered in philosophy courses and in medicine and ethics courses. It is an example of excellent work in its tradition—which I'll call the "Judith Thomson tradition," even though its roots lie in the seventeenth century, and even though some philosophers in the tradition today disagree with some of Judith Thomson's analyses.


*Analyzing Arguments*

There is a particular pattern of analysis, a particular method, which philosophers in Judith Thomson's tradition use, and there is a particular pattern of thinking, which they take to be *moral reasoning*. *Moral reasoning* constitutes a technical category within this philosophic tradition, but it is really supposed to capture the kind of thinking people would do in moral matters if they were thinking properly. Let me go over the Judith Thomson paper to show the method and to indicate what moral reasoning is supposed to be.

In the introduction to an anthology in which Judith Thomson's abortion paper is reprinted, editor Joel Feinberg says: "Abortion raises subtle problems for private conscience, public policy, and constitutional law. Most of these problems are essentially philosophical, requiring a degree of clarity about basic concepts that is seldom achieved in legislative debates and letters to the newspaper."[1] As the analytic philosopher sees it, matters of private conscience have to do with a *moral agent* doing whatever *moral reasoning* is necessary to decide whether a *moral act* (or kind of moral act) is *morally justifiable*. Moral reasoning may show that an act is morally unjustifiable as well, of course. One way of showing that an act is justifiable is by finding a *moral principle* that covers it. One moral principle that Judith Thomson considers is "Every person has a right to life." Often, though, the matter is much more complicated, and the moral reasoning requires a *moral argument*.

Philosophers in this tradition spend a great deal of time analyzing arguments. It is a main part of their method. In the process of examining arguments, the philosopher clarifies and develops concepts, and often establishes the basis for a new position. Superficially, the widely used tactic of examining arguments makes this philosophy seem destructive and merely critical. But this is misleading. Razing buildings in a city would look merely destructive unless you realized that the buildings were unsafe for people to live in and that, perhaps, the neighborhood people wanted to build a park on the site.

Here is the line of argument Judith Thomson criticizes:

A. The fetus is a *person* from the moment of conception.
B. Every person has a *right to life*.
∴C. The fetus has a *right to life*.
D. The mother has a *right* to decide what will happen in and to her body.
E. A person's *right to life* is stronger and more stringent than the mother's *right* to decide what happens in and to her own body and so outweighs it.
∴F. The fetus may not be killed.

Since aborting the birth amounts (in nearly all cases) to killing the fetus, the conclusion of interest is:

∴G. Abortion is impermissible.

Using the word *mother* here reflects a bias—not Judith Thomson's bias, since she is just citing an argument that some "right-to-lifers" give. A pregnant woman is not a mother, nor is a woman giving birth a mother, except in the barest of biological senses. In the context of this argument, using *mother* constitutes an emotional and moral bias, and it begs the question. So I'll use the term *pregnant woman*.

The method of examining arguments is an exact science in philosophy, and there are various questions to ask in doing the examination. For example, a foremost question to ask is whether the argument is *valid*. That amounts to asking whether the conclusion follows by the laws of logic from the premises. In the argument I set out above, which Judith Thomson will be examining, C is a conclusion from premises A and B. Conclusions may also be premises, and C is in fact a premise in the argument that has F as a conclusion. So a question that Judith Thomson raises is whether the argument having A, B, C, D, and E as premises, and F as conclusion is valid.

In fact, that argument is not valid. Like nearly all arguments given in real life, it is *enthymematic*—that is, it has many suppressed premises not set out explicitly in the argument. If our arguments in real life weren't enthymematic, we would all die of boredom because the premises that have to be made explicit include enormous numbers of trivial premises that everyone would agree to and which everyone realized are presupposed. Sometimes, however, the suppressed premises are not at all obvious, and they may include unacknowledged prejudices and presuppositions that would be rejected if they were brought to light. For example, Judith Thomson's criticism of many arguments, about abortion which I mentioned in the introduction to this paper—that they assume that the pregnant woman's moral decision is on a par with the decision of any other moral agent—is a criticism that reveals an unacknowledged prejudice and presupposition. There are other suppressed premises, or "gaps," in the argument from A to E to conclusion F, which Judith Thomson reveals in the course of her paper.

*Using Hypothetical Cases*

One tactic that Judith Thomson used, and one that is a staple in her tradition, is that of introducing hypothetical cases. Philosophers in this tradition suppose that moral agents understand the arguments they are using, although that understanding may need clarification; and they suppose that moral agents grasp the concepts involved in the arguments. The philosopher (so they say) merely clarifies the thinking and the concepts that the moral agent already grasps. The philosopher adds nothing new. In fact, adding something new would not be doing philosophy, they claim. It would be doing substantive morality, or moral persuasion. Sometimes philosophers talk of this in terms of clarifying the *meaning of the moral terms.* In that phrasing, it may seem even more obvious that the philosopher is merely dealing with what the moral agents already understand, and clarifying it.

Let me give the main hypothetical case that Judith Thomson uses in her paper:

> Let me ask you to imagine this. You wake up in the morning and find yourself in bed with an unconscious violinist. A famous violinist. He has been found to have a fatal kidney ailment, and the Society of Music Lovers has canvassed all the available medical records and found that you alone have the right blood type to help. They have therefore kidnapped you, and last night the violinist's circulatory system was plugged into yours, so that your kidneys can be used to extract poisons from his blood as well as your own. The director of the hospital now tells you, "Look, we're sorry the Society of Music Lovers did this to you—we would never have permitted it if we had known." But still, they did it, and the violinist now is plugged into you. To unplug you would be to kill him. But never mind, it's only for nine months. By then he will have recovered from his ailment, and can safely be unplugged from you. (48–49)

Judith Thomson takes this hypothetical case to have obvious analogies to the abortion case, analogies she will use in examining the antiabortion argument. I'll trace the outline of her discussion.

The conclusion of the antiabortion argument is:

F. Abortion is impermissible.

Does this mean that the abortion is impermissible absolutely, under any and all circumstances? Or does it mean that it is impermissible under normal circumstances, but that there are extraordinary circumstances in which it might be permissible? To work that out, Judith Thomson begins clarifying premise E.

E. A person's right to life is stronger and more stringent than the mother's right to decide what happens in and to her own body and outweighs it.

But, she asks, what if the pregnant woman will die if the fetus is not aborted? In that case, we have the pregnant woman's right to life balanced against the fetal right to life. Judith Thomson insists that in order for the valid conclusion to be that abortion is absolutely impermissible, two important, suppressed premises have to be made explicit. They are:

E(1) Performing an abortion would be *directly killing* the fetus and doing nothing will merely be *letting* the mother *die*.

E(2) Directly killing an innocent person is always and absolutely impermissible.

Judith Thomson now tests premise E(2) by bringing in the hypothetical violinist example. Suppose your kidneys will break down under the strain of purifying the violinist's blood and your own? If someone walks in and unplugs the violinist from you, he will be directly killing the violinist, which is impermissible, by E(2). But, she asks, what if you turn around and unplug *yourself* from the violinist. Is that impermissible? A low murmur rises from all the comfortable nooks in which people are reading Judith Thomson's paper. "Surely not," goes the murmur. "Surely unplugging *yourself* is not impermissible." The moral principle embodied in E(2), that directly killing an innocent person is absolutely impermissible, is overridden by a principle of self-defense (or perhaps qualified by a principle of self-defense). We can see this clearly in the violinist example. But the abortion case also falls under E(2). So if it is not impermissible for you to unplug yourself from the violinist in the hypothetical case, then it is not impermissible for the pregnant woman to abort the fetus.

In the course of her discussion of the pregnant woman's decision to abort, Judith Thomson criticized other writings on abortion for having what amounts to a sexist bias (though she does not use that term):

> The main focus of attention in writings on abortion has been on what a third party may or may not do in answer to a request from a woman for an abortion. . . . So, the question asked is what a third party may do, and what the mother may do is decided, almost as an afterthought, from what it is concluded that the third party may do. But it seems to me that to treat the matter in this way is to refuse to grant to the mother that very status of person which is so firmly insisted on for the fetus. (52)

This is a prime example of a woman working within the methods of a particular tradition in philosophy and correcting a bias that has its roots in sexism.

*Clarifying Concepts*

So far, we see that abortion is not *absolutely* impermissible. In some cases, the pregnant woman may abort herself—or at least her decision to do so may be morally justifiable. Now Judith Thomson goes on to argue that the pregnant woman's right to life and the fetus's right to life are not on a par. She does this by using an analogy. The pregnant woman and the child, she says, aren't simply like "two tenants in a small house which has, by unfortunate mistake, been rented to both. The mother *owns* the house" (53). She goes on to clarify this with another hypothetical example: "If Jones has found and fastened on a certain coat which he needs to keep him from freezing, but which Smith also needs to keep him from freezing, then it is not impartiality that says, 'I cannot choose between you' when Smith owns the coat. Women have said again and again, 'This body is *my* body!'" (53). At this point, some readers may raise their eyebrows and ask what owning a house or coat has to do with the right to life. Many philosophers, including Judith Thomson, would say that property rights are the very model we work with in discussing rights, that our picture of what rights are, and our understanding of what they are, is gained by focusing on property rights.[2] The reader should pay heed also to the fact that Judith Thomson analyzes the pregnant woman's relation to her body by analogy with the legal relation of property ownership (as distinct from the legal relation of tenancy). She then uses this clarification in terms of property relations to help clarify the question of whether abortion is impermissible.

At this point, the murmur rising from the comfortable nooks may show ripples of shock. "Does this mean *I* have an obligation to seize the coat from Jones so that Smith won't freeze to death?" (Or, by analogy, to seize the woman's body back from the fetus by helping her with an abortion?) Judith Thomson saves us from such actions. We *decide* that it is right that Smith have the coat (or that the woman have her body), but we need not ourselves be the agent who does the confiscating. We must grant, she says, that a person has a right to refuse to confiscate that coat: "But then what should be said is . . . 'I will not *act*,' leaving it open that somebody else can or should and, in particular, that anyone in a position of authority with the job of securing people's rights, both can and should" (54).

Judith Thomson's process of clarifying concepts here has been to show their links with other concepts in the broad conceptual scheme that we moral agents allegedly work within. This network includes the concept of *property* and also the concept of the *law*, which is presupposed in the concepts of property and tenancy (those being legalistic concepts). She also links the concept of rights to the concept of a *legitimate authority* who has the *responsibility* for seeing that rights are secured. We will see later that these linkages are important. But at the moment, the concept of the right to life needs further clarification—a clarification that involves bringing in the additional moral concept of *justice*.

## The Right to Life

Investigating the concept of a right to life is part of clarifying premises B and E of the antiabortion argument:

B. Every person has a *right to life*.
E. A person's *right to life* is stronger and more stringent than the mother's *right to decide* what happens in and to her own body and so outweighs it.

Judith Thomson investigates the concept of the right to life in stages. First she asks, "Does having a right to life mean that you have the right to be given the bare minimum you need to continue life?" This is a specific application of the general question of whether having a right to something means that a person has the right to the means to that something, and is one of the very general clarifications of rights that she will make. Looking at the violinist example again, she concludes that although the violinist has a right to life, and he may need to use my kidneys as his means to keep on living, he has no right to their use. What is important here is that Judith Thomson has distinguished between having the right to something and having the right to the means to that something. She claims it is a feature of all rights and something with which any adequate account of rights must deal (56).

If the right to life doesn't necessarily involve the right to the means essential to life, what does it involve? Judith Thomson finally concludes that the right to life must simply be the right not to be killed *unjustly*. She then clarifies the concept of justice she is using by a hypothetical example, once again leaning on the concept of property rights (60).

Suppose two brothers are given a single box of chocolates for Christmas, that is, it is their joint possession. Suppose further that the big brother grabs the box, won't let the little brother have any of the chocolates, and instead eats them all himself. We would all surely agree, she says, that the big brother is treating the little one unjustly, because the little brother has been given a right to half of them (56). She goes on with the example. Suppose the older brother had been given the chocolates for his very own, and he ate them all himself, refusing to give the little brother even a single one. He wouldn't be treating the little boy unjustly unless he had somehow given him a right to some of the chocolates. The big boy might be greedy, stingy, callous, and mean. But he would not be unjust.[3]

There are many different concept of justice, and some of them certainly bear a resemblance to this one, which Judith Thomson claims is one we moral agents use. But according to her concept of justice, one may have a right to something by owning it, or by having been given a right to it (by its rightful owner or perhaps by God or by whatever gives natural rights). To act unjustly, then, seems to mean not letting someone have or use something that person has a right to. Having a right to life comes down to not being deprived of life unjustly.

The question of whether abortion is permissible in a given case, then, seems to turn on whether the woman has given the fetus a right to use her body. Once the area of explicit legal contract and long-standing custom is left behind, it becomes very difficult to decide under what conditions someone has given someone else a right to use something. In trying to clarify this in the abortion case, Judith Thomson brings in some of her most memorable hypothetical examples, about people seeds that float in through the living room windows and root themselves in the carpets. But the upshot is that there are cases of pregnancy in which the woman has not given the fetus a right to use her body and in which the fetus may be aborted without killing it unjustly. And so there are cases in which abortion is not impermissible.

## Matters of Public Policy

I have discussed work in the Judith Thomson tradition so far as matters of private conscience go. But Joel Feinberg also said that the abortion issue raised questions for public policy and constitutional law, so it would seem that the tradition deals with moral aspects of those things too. I won't take up the question of constitutional law, but it is important to say some things about the way the tradition handles the moral aspects of matters of public policy.[4]

In Judith Thomson's discussion of rights, a person makes his or her decision of private conscience against a background environment that is fixed so far as the distinction of rights goes. Some rights everyone has, like the right to life. Other rights not everyone has, particularly rights to property or rights to some of the means necessary to exercise rights that everyone has. The result is that not everyone can exercise even the rights that everyone has. This background distribution may be changed by actions based on individual conscience; for example, the pregnant woman may decide that she ought to give the fetus a right to use her body. In the main, however, the distribution is changed by public policy; for example, the legislature or the courts may decide that public funds must be used to pay for the abortions of indigent women.

Interestingly enough, philosophers in this tradition clarify questions of public policy in the same way that they clarify questions of private conscience. The only difference they see is that in private conscience, individuals without special status are making decisions about their personal lives; and in public policy, individuals who are acting in certain offices (congressmen, circuit court justices, heads of public health divisions) are making policy decisions, which will have effects on the public at large. These philosophers suppose that the process of moral reasoning is the same in both cases. In the public case, each individual supposedly clarifies his or her conscience and then votes. In cases of legislation or in board decisions this is exactly what happens. Executive decisions may be construed as decisions of one-member groups. In this view, public policy is made by aggregates of individuals, each of whom reasons his or her way through the moral arguments and then votes.

This should serve as enough of a discussion of work in the Judith Thomson tradition to give the reader a feel for the style and to set out enough of the method, categories, and concepts so that I may later argue for bias in the tradition. I'll now turn to an altogether different sort of discussion of abortion.

## III. JANE

In 1969 most state laws prohibited abortion unless the life of the pregnant woman was threatened.[5] A few states had reformed their abortion laws to allow abortion by doctors in hospitals in cases of threat to the health of the woman, threat of fetal deformity, or rape.[6] In the mid-1960s, the estimated death rate for abortions performed in hospitals was 3 deaths per 100,000 abortions; the rate for illegal abortions was guessed to be about ten times that—30 deaths per 100,000 abortions was a rough estimate and almost certainly conservative (see Cates and Rochat 1976). For minority and poorer women, it was certainly very much higher.

The women's liberation movement was in its infancy in 1969. In that year, a group of Chicago women who had been active in radical politics formed an organization called Jane. Over the next year and a half, Jane evolved from an abortion counseling and referral service to a service in which abortions were actually performed by the Jane members themselves. By 1973 when they closed the service, over 12,000 abortions had been performed under Jane's auspices. The medical record equaled that of abortions done under legal, licensed conditions by physicians in hospitals. The service charged on a sliding scale; eventually all abortions were cheaper than the going rate, and some women paid nothing. Jane served many poor women, black women, and very young women who could not have had an abortion otherwise.

My discussion of Jane is based on one newspaper series and an interview with one member. Perhaps not all Jane members will agree with this member's interpretation, but that is not the point here because I'm not doing a sociological study. I am investigating patterns of moral thinking and acting that the Judith Thomson tradition makes invisible. The fact that one person's thinking and action are concealed is enough to show bias. Pauline B. Bart has done a broader-based study.[7]

*What Jane Did*

This is the way Jane operated, as reported in the June 1973 Hyde Park–Kenwood *Voices* article on the organization: "Jane was the pseudonym we chose to represent the service. A phone was opened in her name and an answering service secured, later replaced by a tape recorder. Jane kept all records and served as control-central." "Jane" was not a particular woman but the code name for whichever counselor was taking calls and coordinating activities on a given day.

For four years, Jane kept the same phone number. . . . At first she received only eight to ten calls a week. A year later she was receiving well more than 100 calls a week.

All phoned-in messages were returned the same day: "Hello, Marcia. This is Jane from women's liberation returning your call. We can't talk freely over the phone, but I want you to know that we can help you."

Then Jane would refer the name to a counselor, who would meet personally with the woman and talk with her at length about available alternatives.

The counselor would also help the woman arrange finances and, whenever possible, collect a $25 donation for the service loan fund. The counseling session was also a screening process for detecting conflicts and potential legal threats.[8]

Jane worked with several male abortionists. One of these was "Dr. C." Dr. C worked alone with his nurse in motel rooms until the day an abortion was interrupted by a pounding on the door and a man's voice shouting, "Come on out of there, baby killer!" After a wild chase between buildings and down alleys, Dr. C escaped the irate husband. When he caught his breath, he decided that it might be better to quit working in motels.

Jane members then began renting apartments for Dr. C and his nurse to work in. Jane describes the first day they used a rented apartment: "Seven women were done that day, in a setting where they could relax and talk with other women in a similar predicament. And when the first woman walked out of the bedroom, feeling fine and no longer pregnant, the other six were noticeably relieved. They asked her questions and got firsthand answers."[9] Another advantage of the new arrangement was that Jane counselors were with a woman during the abortion, giving her psychological and moral support and explaining to her what was going on. Still another was that the counselors gradually began assisting Dr. C in the abortion itself, and he began training them in the abortion procedures.

After a few months of operation, members of Jane had begun inducing miscarriages for women more than twelve weeks pregnant.[10] During this time, Dr. C was teaching the women of Jane more and more about the process of doing direct abortions. Finally, some counselors were doing the entire direct abortion themselves, under Dr. C's eye. In the midst of all this, they learned that Dr. C was no doctor at all, but just a man who had become an expert in performing abortions. Later, they broke off the relationship with Dr. C and began doing all of their own abortions. For good or ill, this meant that they had a sudden abundance of funds, since the abortion fee went to Jane instead of to Dr. C. In the eyes of the law, they became full-fledged abortionists: "We could no longer hide behind the label of 'counselor' or expect 'Dr. C' to act as a buffer, with his know-how and ready cash for dealing with a bust."[11] Jane members were arrested only once, although they were harassed by the police.[12]

The change in the abortion service meant that Jane members had to accept the full consequences of what they were doing—even if it resulted in illness, personal tragedy, or death—and they had to bear this without the protection that a doctor's professionalism provides.[13] They worked under these conditions until April 1, 1973. Then, two months after the United States Supreme Court passed its opinion on the constitutionality of restrictive abortion laws, Jane officially closed.


## What Jane Meant

In describing what Jane did, I selected data to a certain purpose. It was a selection different in many respects from the selection someone in Judith Thomson's tradition would have made. I did not, however, use any special technical concepts or categories from some philosophical theory. In this section, I will use Jane as a basis for discussing a moral theory, which competes with theories of the Judith Thomson tradition, in order to reveal value implications of bias in that tradition.

Jane was an abortion clinic, and the women of Jane were working out moral and political beliefs and activities, not constructing a theory. I want to try to give a fragment of a theory that is able to capture their thinking and their work. The theory should be taken as *hypothesis* about what Jane meant, subject to correction through further investigation of Jane and groups like Jane, and through seeing what comes of acting on the theory. I believe the theory is based on anarchist, or anarchist-feminist principles, but I won't discuss that. Instead I will call the tradition out of which the theory arises the Jane tradition, to contrast with the Judith Thomson tradition.

In March 1977 I interviewed one of the founders of Jane. She said that the women who founded the organization had been active in civil rights or antiwar work in the late 1960s. They wanted to begin work in the newly born women's liberation movement. But how should they begin? What should they do? Someone suggested abortion as an issue. It was a difficult decision, and they struggled over it for months. Deciding on an issue required an analysis of a network of larger issues, and of the place of the abortion issue in that network. According to the woman I interviewed, the question was one of a woman's opportunities for life choices: "It was a question of free choice about reproduction, free choice about life style, because the old roles of women weren't viable any more. In frontier times, childbearing was valuable and important. So was housework. But that role is gone. The old ways are gone. We felt nothing *could* come in to replace them unless women could make a choice about childbearing. That seemed necessary for any other choice." These alternatives had to be *created* within our social system. The members of Jane hoped that other groups within the women's movement would work on other alternatives—

offering alternative living arrangements, working on ways that women could become economically independent, and so on—while Jane members tried to offer the alternative of choosing not to have the child by aborting. That is, they thought in terms of a division of labor among women working to change the society so that women would have real alternatives for meaningful lives.

As I mentioned in the introduction to this chapter, the concept of a *meaningful life* (more often called "a good life") has traditionally been a central concept in moral philosophy. The pattern of thinking Jane members use requires a holistic analysis of the society in terms of the resources it actually offers for women to have meaningful lives, plus an analysis of how to change the society so that it can offer such resources. I'll take this up in more detail in section IV.

In offering the alternative of abortion, Jane was offering a service that was badly needed. The alternative was open to all kinds of women—rich and poor, older and young, white and nonwhite, but it was a service most desperately needed by the poorer, younger, and minority women. One author says:

> In a comparison of blacks and whites, both for premarital and marital conceptions, we find that whites have higher percentages ending in induced abortions at the lower educational levels, while at the higher educational levels there is little or no difference between blacks and whites . . . the data point to the greater reliance upon abortion on the part of whites over blacks and on the part of the more affluent or more educated over the less affluent and less educated. [14]

When they did turn to illegal abortion methods, poorer and nonwhite women came out far worse. Nationally in 1968 the black death rate from abortion was six times that of the white death rate. In New York in the early 1960s, 42 percent of the pregnancy-related deaths resulted from illegal abortions; and of those women who died, half were black and 44 percent were Puerto Rican. Only 6 percent were white. [15]

More affluent women were also able to pay the high fees that all good, illegal abortionists charged. [16] Jane overcame this by calculating fees on a sliding scale according to income. Some women paid nothing.

Jane's purpose, however, was not simply to provide a service for women, however valuable that service might be. The Jane group could not provide abortions to all Chicago women who needed them. More than that, Jane members knew that when abortion was legalized, their service would have to disappear. Jane's purpose was to show women a much broader alternative than simply not having a baby, to show that by acting together, women can change society so that all women can have an opportunity to choose a meaningful life. They tried to show this in different ways. One way was through sliding scale for fees. Counselors explained to a woman paying $300 that she was helping to pay the cost for a woman who could pay only $5. She was, in a small way, helping to undercut the unfairness of a society that would allow her an abortion but not the poorer woman.

Jane itself was the most dramatic demonstration of an alternative for women acting together. Jane members were themselves future or past candidates for abortion, and in the present, they were doing something dangerous, exhausting, and illegal for the sake of changing society for all women. Jane showed that women could take change into their own hands. By coming to Jane for their abortions, other women were also acting for this change. They were trusting women to do things that traditionally were done by men in their society, and legally done only by doctors (overwhelmingly male) within the rigid, hierarchically ordered medical profession. This was a leap of trust.

In the structure of their service, Jane members were trying to build an alternative kind of medical structure as well.[17]

> We—the counselors—we learned the medical mystiques are just bullshit. That was a great up for us. Do you know, you're required to have a license as a nurse just to give a shot. Nurses can't even give an intravenous on their own. That takes a different kind of license. We would just explain to our workers how you had to fill the syringe, and how to be certain there was no air in it, and why that was important, and so on. We'd spend a lot of time explaining it. Then we would say to the patient, "Well this is the first time that Sue is giving anyone a shot. Maybe you can help her, and be patient with her." The patient was part of what was happening too. Part of the whole team.
>
> Sometimes in the middle of an abortion, we would switch positions to show that everyone in the service could do things, to show that the woman who was counseling could give a shot, and the one who was giving a shot could counsel too. We did it to make people see that they could do it too. They have the power to learn to counsel and give a shot. They have the power to change things and build alternatives.

We here come to the central analysis within the Jane tradition, as it is expressed in Jane's practice. The analysis operates in a very general way to criticize our society and to offer direction to move toward change. Let me state it first in terms of the social structure of the institution of medicine in the United States today.

In the United States medical people operate within a hierarchical system of dominance and subordination. Those higher in the hierarchy have power that those lower do not have—and the power to order those lower ones around is the least of it. One key aspect of that power is what Howard Becker calls "the right to define the nature of reality." He uses the notion of a "hierarchy of credibility": "In any system of ranked groups, participants take it as given that members of the highest group have the right to define the way things really are" (Becker 1977). I would argue that this "right of definition" means not only that the word of the higher has heavier weight than that of the lower (teacher over student, doctor over intern or aide) but that the very categories and concepts that are used, the "official" descriptions of reality, are descriptions from the point of view of the dominant persons in the hierarchy. What counts as knowledge itself is defined in terms of that viewpoint, and the definition further legitimates the power of the dominant person.

The power of those in dominant positions in the hierarchy is *legitimate authority*. This contrasts with the *natural authority* of a person who, regardless of position, happens to have a great deal of knowledge, experience, or wisdom about a subject. A doctor's authority is legitimated by the criteria, standards, and institutions that control access to his place in the hierarchy. These criteria and requirements for training on the one hand are aimed at insuring that those with legitimate authority in the hierarchy also have the natural authority required to do the jobs they are doing. Although we all know there are incompetent doctors, these criteria do operate to screen out incompetence as *defined from the top of the hierarchy*. Do they insure that those at the top have natural authority? I think not, and that is because *legitimate authority* carries with it a definition of what counts as knowledge: the definition from the top of the hierarchy, the "official" point of view.

This outlook on knowledge is sometimes called "objective" or "the scientific outlook" of experts. In fact, it is absolutist, and when the definition of reality is given solely in terms of the tradition of the dominant in a dominant-subordinate structure, the outlook is, in fact, biased.

In part, Jane members were operating from the viewpoint of a subordinate group in our society: women. They were using this viewpoint to try to create new social structures that were not based on dominance and subordination and in which authority was natural authority—knowledge that suits the situation to the best degree that we know at the moment. When the woman I interviewed said that the members of Jane tried to show other women that they "have the power to learn to counsel and give a shot" and that they "have the power to change things and build alternatives," she was talking not only about the natural authority of knowledge but what we might call natural *moral* power, or *moral* authority.

In structuring the abortion service as they did, the members of Jane were developing an alternative to hierarchy, but they were also overcoming the vices of dependency and feelings of ignorance and impotence by showing women that they did have the power to learn and do things themselves. The Jane organization itself was built on nonauthoritarian, nonhierarchical principles, and Jane members tried to run it as a collective.

> We tried to make it as nonauthoritarian as we could. We had rotating chairs. There wasn't a high value placed on one kind of work and a low value on another. Every position was so important to what we were doing, and it was treated as equally important, to the highest degree possible. This meant every one of us could do what she was best at. You didn't have people competing to do what was important, or feeling what they were doing wasn't valuable.

In April of 1973 the women of Jane asked themselves, "What next?" Whether abortion had been a good issue to move on or not, there was no place for an illegal abortion service now that abortions were legal. Some of the women went on to found a "well woman clinic," the Emma Goldman Clinic. They hoped to run the clinic on the nonauthoritarian, nonhierarchical model used by Jane.[18] The clinic was organized around the concept of self-help, in which the "patients" are trained too in the kind of medical knowledge they need to understand and care for their own bodies for a large range of normal functions and slight disorders.

## IV. BIAS IN THE WORLD VIEW

In my discussion here, both the Judith Thomson tradition and the Jane tradition were dealing with the problem of abortion. Neither would take it to be *the* problem. Abortion is a subsidiary problem chosen because of its connection with more central concerns. For Judith Thomson, it is a question of rights—we might even say a question of equal rights.[19] But it cannot be described that way for the Jane tradition without begging questions.

Within the Jane tradition the problem was taken to be one of meaningful lives for women, or of free choice among genuine alternatives for meaningful lives. Some phrasing of the general problem in these terms seems appropriate to both traditions. Let me quote Betty Friedan, an activist who stands within traditions associated with Judith Thomson's:

> It is my thesis that the core of the problem for women today is not sexual but a problem of identity—a stunting or evasion of growth that is perpetuated by the feminine mystique. It is my thesis that as the Victorian culture did not permit women to accept or gratify their basic sexual needs, our culture does not permit women to accept or gratify their basic need to grow and fulfill their potentialities as human beings, a need which is not solely defined by their sexual roles.[20]

The statement of purpose of the liberal feminist National Organization for Women (NOW) also concerns opportunities for a meaningful life and moral development as a human being: NOW pledges to "take action to bring women into full participation in the mainstream of American society now, exercising all the privileges and responsibilities thereof, in truly equal partnership with men."[21] This makes it appear that for both traditions, the problem may be stated as one of equality, particularly equality so far as it relates to the moral questions of being a full human being and of having a meaningful (or good) life. I believe that this is a central concern of those within the Judith Thomson tradition. But it may be that the problem cannot be resolved under that tradition or its associated world view.

*Concealing Data*

In section III, I presented the moral activity of the organization Jane under one tradition. If we look at the Jane organization under the Judith Thomson tradition, we get a different selection of data. Here is a quotation from the newspaper article:

> From the beginning, we discussed the moral implications of abortion from all angles. We listened to right-to-lifers, Catholic clergy, population-control freaks and women's liberationists.
> We heard legislators and lobbyists and political commentators arguing fine points of "fetal viability." When does a fetus become a person? When it can survive outside the womb (after six months)?

When it begins to move (after four months)? Or from the moment of conception?

Many opponents of abortion called it "murder." We argued the logical counterarguments: If a fetus is a person, then why aren't abortionists and women who have abortions charged with murder?

Or, if the fetus has the rights of a person, then does the woman who carries it become subject to its rights? What happens when the rights of the woman and those of the fetus come into conflict?

All philosophical and legalistic positions lost relevance when we began doing and viewing abortions . . . we knew that we were grappling with matters of life and death and no philosophical arguments could alter that belief.[22]

Judith Thomson, or someone from her tradition, would have been a great help to the Jane women in these early discussions on abortion. On the other hand, these early discussions had no clear relevance to the central moral activity the women of Jane were engaging in—*by their own judgment.* The terms in which they saw the problem were different. Their perception and their moral activity constitute data that are important to solving the problem of equality, but the Judith Thomson tradition not only ignores those data: It makes them invisible. Let's look at some of the mechanisms by which the data are concealed.

One way a tradition conceals data is through the concepts and categories it uses. The Judith Thomson tradition would focus on the Jane discussions of rights. It would ignore the discussions of hierarchy, dominance, and subordination; and perhaps some within the tradition would not take these as morally relevant discussions at all. Any theory must use concepts. Through their very use, some data are selected and some ignored. Yet the question of whether the concepts properly capture the data, or of whether they are *appropriate,* is a central, critical question about the adequacy of any tradition.

In a similar way, the categories a tradition uses to organize data reveal some and conceal others. For example, the Judith Thomson tradition uses the categories of moral agent and of groups of moral agents as aggregates. The tradition also uses a division of moral phenomena into questions of individual conscience and those of public policy, where the latter is a matter of *official* public policy, made by those with legitimate authority. I don't want to argue that the tradition *rules out* other sorts of moral phenomena. But using those categories, it cannot capture the sort of moral phenomena Jane members took to be central: people in a subordinate position acting to create a set of social relations that are not structured by dominance and subordination, through the subordinates' coming to know their own power (as opposed to legitimate authority) through acting in collectives (not aggregates).

But am I being fair to the Judith Thomson tradition? After all, people within it don't claim to cover *all* moral phenomena. Few theories claim to cover everything within their purview, and even within chemistry there are divisions into organic and inorganic. Might not there be divisions within the field of moral phenomena so that another part of the tradition might deal with Jane's moral activity and thus reveal it?

Perhaps any new moral tradition we develop will have to have something to do with the concept of rights (and associated concepts), and deal in some way with groups as aggregates and with public policy as officially handed down. But that new tradition could not be the Judith Thomson tradition, for a revolutionary change in the methodology of her tradition is necessary to uncover data like Jane's.

The Judith Thomson tradition supposes that there exists a set of moral concepts embedded in moral principles that "we" all know and understand. In her paper, Judith Thomson herself is clarifying concepts "we" grasp by the standard method of the tradition: the use of hypothetical cases. This method presupposes a very mentalistic view of concepts and word meanings—mentalistic in the way philosophical empiricists are mentalistic in their views on meanings as "ideas." The concepts exist in the speaker's understanding. If someone understands the concept, he or she knows whether it applies in any given case.[23] Considering hypothetical cases (in this view) points out cases the speaker might have overlooked; but once they are brought to his or her attention, the speaker allegedly knows whether the concepts apply or not, and so his or her explicit understanding of the concept is clarified. Similarly, one's explicit understanding of "our" moral principles is supposed to be clarified by considering hypothetical cases.

The most obvious thing to say about this method is that although bringing up hypothetical cases may clarify our understanding of concepts and principles, everyone knows that the selection of hypothetical cases also biases understanding. This bias may be (unintentionally) systematic. For example, Judith Thomson gives a case where Jones faces a frosty death because Smith owns the coat. Why not, instead, use a case where men, women, and children face poor diets, poor housing, and loss of dignity because the owner of a mill decides to move it out of one region into another having cheaper labor and lower tax rates? Philosophers may say the second example is too complicated, but the selection is not a trivial matter of simplicity. The coat example ignores an essential distinction in kinds of property ownership, which the mill example reveals.

The method rules out empirical investigation to see what sorts of hypothetical cases might capture what is morally important to persons in a variety of circumstances in the United States. There seems to be no way whatsoever to insure that a fair consideration of hypothetical cases is made to reduce the bias. One cannot develop a sampling procedure for hypothetical cases.

Worst of all, the method rules out empirical investigation to discover whether the moral concepts and principles the philosophers are dealing with are really the moral concepts that people use in the United States. It rules out empirical investigation to discover whether those concepts and those moral principles are relevant to the lives of people in different walks of life, investigation to discover whether they are relevant to solving those people's problems of human dignity and a meaningful life *as those people perceive* those problems.

The method itself has the mere appearance of being plausible only for ancient systems of concepts that are well worked out. It has not even the appearance of plausibility for a case like Jane's, in which people are in the process of creating new concepts through creating new social forms. The fundamental theory of meaning, of understanding, and of concept formation on which the method is based is not only inadequate: It is false.

All of this means that to encompass the Jane data, a revolutionary change is necessary in the methodology of the Judith Thomson tradition. Without it, the data remain concealed.

The data being concealed concern human moral activity and the possibilities of changing society. This constitutes a direct and very important value consequence. The Judith Thomson tradition dominates philosophy departments in the prestigious American universities, and even teachers in nonprestigious colleges are trained within it. This means the students are taught to see moral activity within that tradition. Activity requiring patterns of thinking and concepts and categories like Jane's is made invisible to them.

## Official Points of View

From its beginnings, the tradition Judith Thomson works within has been centrally concerned with equality. People in this tradition have particularly been concerned that all human beings be equal under the moral law and under the positive law of the state. Equality before the moral or positive law means that the same laws and principles apply to all. Whether or not this is enlightened depends on which laws and principles one chooses and the society in which they apply.

The question of equality that those in the Jane tradition raise is one that takes dominant-subordinate structures in the society as *creators* of inequality. Their solution to the problem of equality is the use of the perception and power of the subordinate to eliminate dominant-subordinate structures through the creation of new social forms that do not have that structure. Those in the Judith Thomson tradition do not raise questions of dominance and subordination except in the moral, legal, and political spheres, where they are seen in terms of moral, legal, and political equality. Particularly, they do not raise the question of whether equality before the moral or positive law may not be rendered empty because of the dominant-subordinate structures in the economic or social (e.g., family) spheres.

It appears that there is a bias in our world view. It is a bias that allows moral problems to be defined from the top of various hierarchies of authority in such a way that the existence of the authority is concealed, and so the existence of alternative definitions that might challenge that authority and radically change our social organization is also concealed. But having acknowledged that, we must return to the question I asked at the beginning of the chapter.

## V. THE INTELLECTUAL PURSUITS

In this chapter I believe I uncovered a bias that requires a revolutionary change in ethics to remedy. But in the process of considering two approaches to the moral problem of abortion, it has become clear that there are serious questions to ask about the question with which I began the chapter: "Has a covert bias been introduced into our world view by the near exclusion of women from the domain of intellectual pursuits?" If we ask about a bias in "our" world view, mustn't we ask who that "we" refers to? In fact, doesn't the question presuppose that "our" world view is constructed by people in the "intellectual pursuits"? That is, doesn't it presuppose a hierarchy of authority in which people in some occupations (academic humanists and scientists, professional writers, etc.) define a world view for everyone else? If so, then there is something further that the Jane case shows.

Judith Jarvis Thomson is a woman working in an established intellectual pursuit, and at the time she wrote her paper, she took a stand that amounted to criticizing certain ethical arguments for sex bias. She took her stand as an authority, she criticized other authorities, and her paper has been widely used by still other authorities who are certified to teach ethics classes. I have criticized her work in this chapter, but I too write as an authority. This leads us to a certain conundrum—if I may call it that.

The women of Jane were certainly challenging the way men in important positions are certified to define the way we do things and, in fact, their authority to define "our" world view and say how things "really are." But some of the Jane members, at least, were not saying that we should remedy the problem by having women in important positions define the way we do things. They were saying that we should change the way we do things so that we do not have some important people giving the official world view for everyone else. That change cannot be accomplished merely by hiring more women to work in the intellectual pursuits. It requires changing the intellectual pursuits themselves. If Jane shows that we need a revolutionary change from the old moral theory, it is a change in the status of the authorities as well as a change in what has been taken to be moral theory. Unless we strive to find ways to do that, we violate the central moral and scientific injunction for respecting other human beings: "Look upon human group life as chiefly a vast interpretive process in which people, singly and collectively *guide themselves by defining* the objects, events and situations they encounter" (Blumer 1969, 132).

## Notes

1. Feinberg 1973, 1. All subsequent quotations from Judith Thomson's essay are from this edition.

2. John Locke's work forms an important foundation to this tradition.

3. Both the Marxists and the Freudians among us will raise their eyebrows at the use of this hypothetical case to explain the concept of justice. Plato would turn over in his grave.

4. Some repercussions for constitutional law are discussed in Sarvis and Rodman 1974, 159.

5. For their help in this part of the essay, I thank Howard Becker for his assistance with references on abortion and Shawn Pyne for her zeal and imagination in searching the library. I am much indebted to Shawn Pyne for very helpful conversations and to her unpublished paper "Alternatives to the Health System" (1977).

6. For a discussion of abortion laws, see Sarvis and Rodman 1974. An excellent and more detailed discussion is given by Kristin Booth Glen in Glen 1978. Glen traces the political implications of the fact that the decision turned on the right of physicians to make medical decisions, not on the rights of women. The Supreme Court declared state laws restricting abortion unconstitutional on January 22, 1973.

7. Bart 1980, based on interviews with forty-two members of the Jane collective. I did not know of this study in time to incorporate it into my discussion in this section. I am grateful to Pauline Bart for reading this chapter and suggesting two places where my informant's perceptions differed from the majority perception so that I might delete them.

8. Jane, "The Most Remarkable Abortion Story Ever Told," Hyde Park–Kenwood *Voices*, June 1973, 2–3.

9. Ibid.

10. At this time, most abortionists refused to handle women more than twelve weeks pregnant (Lee 1969, 6, 161, 169–70).

11. Jane, "Most Remarkable Abortion Story," pt. 6, Hyde Park-Kenwood *Voices*, November 1973, 3.

12. The arrest was in the third year of the service. It appears to have been a renegade action by a few policemen, not a planned political arrest.

13. Jane members had to take on other duties too. Each week during its peak, the service used fifty ampules of ergotrate, ten bottles of xylocaine, a hundred disposable syringes, and six hundred tablets each of tetracycline and ergotrate. For a while, Dr. C's nurse had obtained the drugs. Eventually, Jane members had to devise ways of getting illegal supplies.

14. Lee 1969, 161. In New York in the early 1960s, 93 percent of legal, therapeutic abortions were performed on white, private patients. During that period in the United States as a whole, the rate of legal abortions per 1,000 live births was 3.17 for private patients and 0.87 for clinic patients (those entering the hospital without a private physician). In Georgia in 1970, twenty-four times as many legal abortions were performed on unmarried white women as on unmarried black women. Sarvis and Rodman 1974, 159.

15. Lee 1969, 169–70.

16. Information about illegal abortionists is spread through informal networks of acquaintances. More affluent women have more access to information about illegal abortionists of quality because they have acquaintances (some of them physicians) who have this information. Jane overcame this by publishing the telephone number of the service in underground newspapers and otherwise publicly spreading word about the service, through brochures, the Chicago Women's Liberation Union, and so on. See Lee 1969 for extensive discussions on this.

17. I spoke with two women who worked with Jane, although only one interview is used in this chapter. Both said that patients waited in the *living room*. They never called it the waiting room—although professionals using a house or apartment as an office, for example, psychotherapists, call the living room the waiting room. Both said that abortions were done in the *bedroom*. They never used the term *operating room* or anything similar. This was part of the attempt to demystify medicine. Some other abortionists made great efforts to cloak themselves in medical mystique—Dr. C is an example, since he called himself "Doctor" when he was not. For a description of one service that smothered the patient in medical mystique (and for a glaring contrast with Jane), see Ball 1967.

18. From what I had learned from other sources, it seemed to me that Emma Goldman had been less successful as a nonauthoritarian, nonhierarchical collective activity offering first-quality service. I asked Jane about this. She said that because the abortion service was illegal, it was free of many authoritarian and hierarchical pressures from the medical profession. Because Emma Goldman was a legal clinic, it had to accommodate itself to the medical profession—by maintaining relations with physicians, for example, who would let the clinic use their licenses. This introduced factors of authority because of the licensing procedure, and with it, hierarchy. For a discussion of self-help, see Boston Women's Health Book Collective 1976, 361–68.

19. For example, her interpreting "This body is *my* body" on analogy with rights involved in property ownership parallels the great initial step toward equality made by John Locke when he interpreted a man's relation to his body and labor power on analogy with rights involved in property ownership.

20. Friedan 1974, 69, 270. The work originally published in 1963 was a major force in initiating the "second wave" in feminism.

21. Ibid., 270. Betty Friedan was one of the founders of NOW. Liberal feminists share important parts of a world view with those in the Judith Thomson tradition. They are much more radical than the philosophers, however, in part because they are feminists, in part because they are activists.

22. Jane, "Most Remarkable Abortion Story," pt. 6.

23. Unless the concept is vague, in which case no one knows whether it applies in certain cases until some sort of definitional decision is made on whether it applies.

# 4

## The Man of Professional Wisdom
(1980)

## I. COGNITIVE AUTHORITY AND THE GROWTH OF KNOWLEDGE

Most of us are introduced to scientific knowledge by our schoolteachers, in classrooms and laboratories, using textbooks and lab manuals as guides. As beginners, we believe that the goal of science is "the growth of knowledge through new scientific discoveries" (Cole, 1979, 6n). We believe that the methods of science are the most rational that human kind has devised for investigating the world and that (practiced properly) they yield objective knowledge. It seems to us that because there is only one reality, there can be only one real truth and that science describes those facts. Our teachers and our texts affirm this authority of scientific specialists.

The authority of specialists in science is not per se an authority to command obedience from some group of people, or to make decisions on either public policy or private investment. Specialists have, rather, an epistemological or cognitive authority: We take their understanding of factual matters and the nature of the world within their sphere of expertise as knowledge, or as the definitive understanding. I don't mean that we suppose scientific specialists to be infallible. Quite the contrary. We believe scientific methods are rational because we believe that they require, and get, criticism of a most far-reaching sort. Science is supposed to be distinguished from religion, metaphysics, and superstition *because* its methods require criticism, test, falsifiability.

Our word "science" is ambiguous. Is it a body of knowledge, a method, or an activity? Until recently many Anglo-American philoso-

Reprinted, with changes, from Sandra Harding and Merrill B. Hintikka, eds., *Discovering Reality* (Boston: D. Reidel, 1983), 165–86, by permission of the author. Copyright 1983 by Kathryn Pyne Addelson.

phers of science ignored science as an activity and applied themselves to analyzing the structure of the body of knowledge, which they conceived narrowly as consisting of theories, laws, and statements of prediction. To a lesser degree, they spoke of "scientific method," conceived narrowly as a set of abstract canons. With such an emphasis, it is easy to assume that it is theory and method that give science its authority. It is easy to assume that researchers' cognitive authority derives from their use of an authoritative method, and that they are justified in exercising authority only within the narrow range of understanding contained in the theories and laws within their purview. Everyone knew, of course, that "scientific method" had been developed within a historical situation; but commitment to abstract canons led philosophers to put aside questions of how particular methods were developed, came to dominate, and (perhaps) were later criticized and rejected.[1] Everyone believed that it is an essential characteristic of scientific knowledge that it *grows*, and that new theories are suggested, tested, criticized, and developed. But the narrow focus on knowledge as theories and laws, and the emphasis on analyzing their abstract structure or the logical form of scientific explanation, led philosophers to neglect asking how one theory was historically chosen for development and test rather than another.[2] Most important, philosophers did not ask about the social arrangements through which methods and theories came to dominate or to wither away. Although the "rationality of science" is supposed to lie in the fact that scientific understanding is the most open to criticism of *all* understanding, a crucial area for criticism was ruled out of consideration: the social arrangements through which scientific understanding is developed and through which cognitive authority of the specialist is exercised.

Within the past twenty years, many scientists, historians, and philosophers have begun to move away from the abstract and absolutist conceptions of theory and method. The work that has reached the widest audience is Thomas Kuhn's *The Structure of Scientific Revolutions* (1970). Two major changes in analytic emphasis show in his work. First, Kuhn focuses on science as an activity. Second, given this focus, he construes the content of scientific understanding to include not only theories and laws but also metaphysical commitments, exemplars, puzzles, anomalies, and various other features. Altering the focus to activity does lead one to ask some questions about rise and fall of methods and theories, and so Kuhn could make his famous distinction between the growth of knowledge in normal science and its growth in revolutionary science. However, he makes only the most limited inquiry into social arrangements in the practice of science. And, although he says that under revolutionary science proponents of the old and the new paradigms may engage in a power struggle, he does not explicitly consider cognitive authority.[3] Yet the power struggle in a period of revolutionary change is over which community of scientists will legitimately exercise cognitive authority—whose practices will define the normal science of the specialty and whose understanding will define the nature of the world that falls within their purview. To take cognitive authority seriously, one must ask seriously after its exercise, as embodied in social arrangements inside and outside science.

Within the activity of science in the United States today, researchers exercise cognitive authority in various ways.[4] One major way is within the specialties themselves. In accord with the norm of the "autonomy of science," researchers develop hypotheses and theories, discover laws, define problems and solutions, criticize and falsify beliefs, make scientific revolutions. They have the authority to do that on matters in their professional specialty: microbiologists have authority on questions of viruses and demographers, on questions of population changes, though within a specialty some have more power to exercise cognitive authority than others. Researchers have authority to revise the history of ideas in their field, so that each new text portrays the specialty as progressing by developing and preserving kernels of truth and rooting out error and superstition, up to the knowledge of the present.

Researchers also exercise cognitive authority outside their professions, for scientific specialists have an authority to define the true nature of the living and nonliving world around us. We are taught their scientific understanding in school. Public and private officials accept it to use in solving political, social, military, and manufacturing problems. The external authority follows the lines of the internal authority. Experts are hired and their texts adopted according to their credentials as specialists in the division of authority-by-specialty within science. But because, within specialties, some people have more power than others, many people never have a text adopted and most never serve as expert advisors.

If we admit Kuhn's claim that metaphysical commitments are an integral part of scientific activity, then we see that scientific authority to define the nature of the world is not limited to the laws and theories printed in boldface sentences in our textbooks. Metaphysical commitments are beliefs about the nature of the living and nonliving things of our world and about their relations with us and with each other. In teaching us their scientific specialties, researchers simultaneously teach us these broader understandings. Speaking of Nobel Prize winners in physics from the time of Roentgen to Yukawa, Nicholas Rescher says, "The revolution wrought by these men in our understanding of nature was so massive that their names became household words throughout the scientifically literate world" (Rescher 1978, 27). The Darwinian revolution, even more thoroughgoing, changed the metaphysics of a world designed by God in which all creatures were ordered in a great chain of being, to a world of natural selection. These scientific breakthroughs were not simply changes in laws, hypotheses, and theories. They were changes in scientists' understanding of the categories of reality, changes in the questions they asked, the problems they worked with, the solutions they found acceptable. After the revolution, the changed understanding defined "normal science."

I will use the notion of cognitive authority to argue that making scientific activity more rational requires that criticizing and testing social arrangements in science be as much a part of scientific method as criticizing and testing theories and experiments. In doing this, I will talk a little more about how cognitive authority is exercised within professional specialties (section II). To make my case, I assume (with Kuhn) that metaphysical commitments are an essential part of scientific understanding, and that greater rationality in science requires criticizing such commitments. I give a number of examples in section III. Section IV considers whether social arrangements within the sciences limit criticism of scientific understanding. I suggest that prestige hierarchies, power within and without the scientific professions, and the social positions of researchers themselves affect which group can exercise cognitive authority. Thus these features of social arrangements play a major role in determining which metaphysical commitments come to dominate, thus what counts as a legitimate scientific problem and solution. In the end, they affect how we all understand the nature of our world and our selves.

## II. COGNITIVE AUTHORITY, AUTONOMY, AND CERTIFIED KNOWLEDGE

Philosophy of science texts, as well as the *New York Times*, talk of "science" and "scientific knowledge" as if there were one unified activity and one stock of information. But, as we all know, there are many scientific specialties, each with its own Ph.D. program. Members of each specialty or subspecialty certify and criticize their own opinions in their own journals and at their own professional meetings. Each specialist shows excellence by climbing the prestige ladder of the specialty.

Only some of the many people who work within a research specialty have epistemological authority within it. Barbara Reskin remarks, "The roles of both student and technician are characterized by lower status and by a technical division of labor that allocates scientific creativity and decision making to scientists and laboratory work to those assigned the role of technician or student" (Reskin 1978, 20).[5] The role division justifies assigning credit to the chief investigator, but its most important effect is on communication. Technicians and students work on the chief investigator's problems in ways he or she considers appropriate.[6] They rarely communicate with other researchers through conferences or journal articles or by chatting over the WATS line. They are not among the significant communicators of the specialty.

Researchers who *are* significant communicators set categories for classifying their subjects of study, and they define the meaning of what is taking place. With the aid of physicists, chemists define what chemical substance and interaction are. Microbiologists categorize viruses and molecules and explain the significance of electron microscopes. These are different from the understandings we all have of the physical and chemical parts of our world *as we live in it*. We choose honey by taste, smell, and color, not by chemical composition, and we meet viruses in interactions we know as flus and colds.[7]

Scientific understandings appear in hypotheses, laws, and theories, but they presuppose metaphysics and methodology. Thomas Kuhn mentions the importance of metaphysics, using physical science in the seventeenth century as an example:

> [Among the] still not unchanging characteristics of science are the . . . quasi-metaphysical commitments that historical study so regularly displays. After about 1630, for example, and particularly after the appearance of Descartes' immensely influential scientific writings, most physical scientists assumed that the universe was composed of microscopic corpuscles and that all natural phenomena could be explained in terms of corpuscular shape, size, motion, and interaction. That nest of commitments proved to be both metaphysical and methodological. As methodological, it told them what ultimate laws and fundamental explanations must be like: laws must specify corpuscular motion and interaction, and explanation must reduce any given natural phenomenon to corpuscular action under laws. More important still, the corpuscular conception of the universe told scientists what many of their research problems should be. (Kuhn 1970, 41)

The seventeenth-century scientists also made metaphysical assumptions that most contemporary scientists share. They assumed that because there is *one* reality, there can be only one correct understanding of it. That metaphysical assumption, disguised as a point of logic, took root in Western thought more than two millennia ago, when Parmenides said that being and thinking are the same; that which exists and that which can be thought are the same. From that maxim, he concluded that the reality that is the object of knowledge, and not mere opinion, is one and unchanging. Differ though they might about the nature of reality, both Plato and Aristotle shared the metaphysical assumption that the object of scientific knowledge is the one, essential, intelligible structure of the one reality. Contemporary scientists share an analogous metaphysical assumption when they presuppose that reality is known through universal laws and predictions, which give the correct description of the world. All admit, of course, that in its present state, scientific knowledge is partial, suffering from inaccuracies, and so on. But, they say, this incompleteness and error is what is to be corrected by the scientific method. In principle the scientific enterprise is based on the metaphysical premises that because there is one reality, there must be one, correctly described truth. This premise is the foundation of the cognitive authority of scientific specialists. The specialist offers the correct understanding of reality while the lay person struggles in the relativity of mere opinion.

In some specialties researchers deal with living subjects, which may have their own understanding of what is going on. But the researchers' understanding is scientifically definitive. Donna Haraway reports on the 1938 field studies of rhesus monkeys done by Clarence Ray Carpenter, an outstanding scientist in his day (Haraway 1978, 30). The studies were designed to answer questions about dominance and social order. Researchers observed an "undisturbed" group for a week as a control, then removed the "alpha male" (the dominant male in terms of priority access to food and sex). Carpenter found that without the alpha male, the group's territory was restricted relative to other groups and intragroup conflict and fights increased. As the next two males in order of dominance were removed, social chaos seemed to result. Upon returning the males, researchers observed that social order was restored.

"Alpha male" is obviously a technical term. But understanding primate subjects in terms of dominance and competition is Carpenter's definition of the situation, not the rhesus monkeys'—and not the understanding of their former keepers or the man in the street either, for Carpenter was making scientific discoveries. Underlying Carpenter's definition of the primate interactions is a metaphysics. Haraway puts the understanding this way:[8]

True social order must rest on a balance of dominance, interpreted as the foundation of cooperation. Competitive aggression became the chief form that organized other forms of social integration. Far from competition and cooperation being mutual opposites, the former is the precondition of the latter—on physiological grounds. If the most active (dominant) regions, the organization centers, of an organism are removed, other gradient systems compete to reestablish organic order: a period of fights and fluidity ensues. (Haraway 1978, 33)

The metaphysics clearly enters into questions asked—from "Which male is dominant?" to "What happens to social order when the dominant males are removed?"

If we look at scientific research this way, then theories and explanations can be taken as *the conventional understandings among significant communicators in a scientific specialty of the interactions of researchers with the subjects of the field of study, and of the interactions of those subjects among themselves and with their environments* (whether natural, social, or laboratory).[9]

The conventional understandings are published in journals and presented at conferences, and the significant communicators of the specialty criticize and alter the understandings, correct hypotheses, expand theories and explanations—as part of the process of certifying the knowledge. Some of the understandings are shown to be false in the process. Others emerge as pretty certainly true. Eventually, conventional understandings are ritualized in college texts. To use other language: "The community's paradigms [are] revealed in its textbooks, lectures, and laboratory exercises. By studying them and by practicing with them, the members of the corresponding community learn their trade" (Kuhn 1970, 43).

Through the textbooks and lectures, and through advice to government and industry, the conventional understandings are passed on to the rest of us as part of the exercise of the specialist's external authority.

## III. METAPHYSICAL COMMITMENTS AND THE GROWTH OF SCIENTIFIC KNOWLEDGE

Within a specialty, certified knowledge consists, at any given time, of the conventional understandings of researchers not only about the subjects and instruments of their field of study but about metaphysics, methodology, and the nature of science itself. Scientific discovery and the extension of certified knowledge may therefore sometimes arise from a change in understandings of metaphysics, methodology, and the appropriate questions to ask rather than changes in theories, methods, or instruments. The example of functionalist metaphysics in some of the life sciences and social sciences indicates how knowledge has grown as a result of such changes as widespread sharing of a metaphysics across disciplines. Clarence Ray Carpenter's work is an example. Concurrent with the sharing of a metaphysics, there may be differences in the understanding of that metaphysics. These differences seem important to the criticism that leads to scientific advance; my example here is Robert K. Merton's theory of deviance.

Finally, although a metaphysics may be shared across disciplines, a single discipline may contain quite different and competing metaphysical commitments. The interactionist theory of deviance in sociology illustrates this and shows how a difference in a metaphysics may lead to a difference in scientific questions asked. The interactionist example also indicates that the scientific questions asked may not merely define factual problems, they may also define *social problems*. This raises serious questions about the epistemological authority we grant to research specialists and leads to the analysis of power and cognitive authority in section IV.

In our own day, advance of knowledge in the life sciences has included a change in metaphysics. The historian of science Donna Haraway says, "Between World War I and the present, biology has been transformed from a science centered on the organism, understood in functionalist terms, to a science studying automated technological devices, understood in terms of cybernetic systems" (Haraway 1979, 207). Haraway does not talk about metaphysical changes. But the change she mentions involves a move to a new metaphysics, one based not on the organism and a physiological paradigm but on "the analysis of information and energy in statistical assemblages," a "communication revolution." "A communication revolution means a retheorizing of natural objects as technological devices properly understood in terms of mechanism of production, transfer, and storage of information. . . . Nature is structured as a series of interlocking cybernetic systems, which are theorized as communications problems" (Haraway 1979, 222–23). Individual specialties that share a metaphysics change on a widespread basis when there is a metaphysical change of this sort, and scientific knowledge grows by leaps and bounds. For example, the "communication revolution" made possible the revolutionary discoveries in genetics after the Second World War. Those discoveries in turn gave plausibility and prestige to the communications metaphysics. This is one way in which metaphysics spreads.

Clarence Ray Carpenter worked under the earlier metaphysics (based on the organism) in his rhesus monkey studies I mentioned above. He conceived social space to be like the organic space of a developing organism, and he shared functionalist metaphysical presuppositions, which were current. Haraway remarks, "Functionalism has been developed on a foundation of organismic metaphors, in which diverse physiological parts of subsystems are coordinated into a harmonious, hierarchical whole" (Haraway 1978, 40). Carpenter himself was important in the cross-disciplinary spread of metaphysics. Haraway says that, theoretically, Carpenter "tied the interpretations of the laboratory discipline of comparative psychology and sex physiology to evolutionary and ecological field biology centered on the concepts of population and community" (Haraway 1978, 30).

Functionalism (in various forms) was also the metaphysics of some of the most progressive work done in sociology and anthropology during Carpenter's time, and even today it underlies some respected work in those fields. Sociologist Robert K. Merton was a significant communicator in sociology. In an essay written in 1949, he remarks on the widespread use of the "functional approach": "The central orientation of functionalism— expressed in the practice of interpreting data by establishing their consequences for larger structures in which they are implicated—has been found in virtually all the sciences of man—biology and physiology, psychology, economics, and law, anthropology and sociology" (Merton 1949, 47). In this essay, Merton reviews literature in the social sciences and he clarifies the notion of function—relying on the use of the concept in other fields: "Stemming in part from the native mathematical sense of the term [the sociological] usage is more often explicitly adopted from the biological sciences, where the term function is understood to refer to the 'vital or organic processes considered in the respects in which they contribute to the maintenance of the organism'" (Merton 1949, 23). Merton insists that he is only borrowing a *methodological framework* from the biological sciences. In fact, the framework carries with it a metaphysics—as the change in life sciences reported by Haraway shows. This widespread use of metaphysics confirms its truth, through the internal authority of specialists.[10] It changes dominant world views in a society through the external authority of specialists.

Although a generally functionalist metaphysics was widely shared between the two world wars, it is more accurate to speak of *varieties* of functionalism. Some of the varieties arose (or were clarified) through metaphysical criticism of earlier varieties.[11] I'll use one of Robert K. Merton's criticisms as an example.

In "Social Structure and Anomie" (originally published before World War II), Merton developed a theory of deviance in which he criticized an earlier, widely held metaphysics:

> A decade ago, and all the more so before then, one could speak of a marked tendency in psychological and sociological theory to attribute the faulty operation of social structures to failures of social control over man's imperious biological drives. The imagery of the relations between man and society implied by this doctrine is as clear as it is questionable. In the beginning, there are man's biological impulses which see full expression. And then, there is the social order, essentially an apparatus for the management of impulses. . . . Nonconformity with the demands of a social structure is thus assumed to be anchored in original nature. It is the biologically rooted impulses which from time to time break through social control. And by implication, conformity is the result of a utilitarian calculus or of unreasoned conditioning. (Merton 1949, 125)

Haraway calls this "management of impulses" perspective the "body politic" view, and she indicates that Clarence Ray Carpenter (and many others) held it (Haraway 1978). So, for that matter, did Freud and Aristotle.[12] In criticizing this metaphysics, Merton advanced knowledge in a way that was both scientifically enlightened and morally humane.

As a functionalist, Merton does suppose that deviance indicates faulty operation of the social structure. His metaphysics assumes social structures and functions exist in a way that makes them suitable for use in scientific explanation. But social structures are not understood as functioning to restrain biological impulses. Using monetary success goals in American culture as his example, he considers how people in different social positions adapt to those goals. He notes that rates of some kinds of deviance are much higher in the underclasses then in the upper classes. Rather than saying that some members of the underclasses are driven by ungoverned impulses, he suggests they are responding normally to problematic social conditions they face. They accept the goal of monetary success but have little opportunity to achieve it through legitimate, institutionally approved means. So some choose innovative means to reach the goal—perhaps becoming criminally deviant as bank robbers. Others, unable to take the strain, may retreat and become "psychotics, autists, pariahs, outcasts, vagrants, vagabonds, tramps, chronic drunkards, and drug addicts."[13] But it is not due to "ungoverned impulses." Rather, the cause is that "some social structures exert a definite pressure on certain persons in the society to engage in nonconformist rather than conformist conduct" (Merton 1949, 125).

Conformist conduct, in Merton's view, is conduct within an institution that serves a positive function in the society. It's not simply that being a banker is approved, and being a bank robber is disapproved. Banking is an institution that contributes to the stability of our society. Bank robbing undermines stability, running a danger of destroying the vital processes necessary to maintenance of our social organism. In this regard, Merton says,

> Insofar as one of the most general functions of social structure is to provide a basis for predictability and regularity of social behavior, it becomes increasingly limited in effectiveness as these elements of the social structure become dissociated. At the extreme, predictability is minimized and what may be properly called anomie or cultural chaos supervenes. (Merton 1949, 149)

Scientific knowledge grew by Merton's criticism of one variety of functionalism. This "pluralism" of metaphysics seems as important as the sharing of metaphysics. For example, within sociology, functionalists compete with the tradition called interactionism, whose adherents assume that human society must be explained in terms of acting units, which themselves have interpretations of the world. Interactionist Herbert Blumer criticizes functionalist metaphysics in this way:

> Sociological thought rarely recognizes or treats human societies as composed of individuals who have selves. Instead, they [sic] assume human beings to be merely organisms, with some kind of organization, responding to forces that play upon them. Generally, though not exclusively, these forces are lodged in the make-up of the society as in the case of "social system."

> Some conceptions, in treating societies or human groups as "social systems" regard group action as an expression of a system, either in a state of balance or seeking to achieve balance. Or group action is conceived as an expression of the "functions" of a society or a group. . . . These typical conceptions ignore or blot out a view of group life or of group action as consisting of the collective or concerted actions

of individuals seeking to meet their life situations. (Blumer 1967, 143–44)

The interactionist theory of deviance, quite different from Merton's functionalist theory, offers a good case in which to see how a different metaphysics influences the questions asked.

In 1963 Howard Becker's *Outsiders* was published, marking the emergence of what was misleadingly called the "labeling" theory of deviance. In an interview about the development of the theory, Becker said, "The theory, and it really was a pretty rudimentary theory, wasn't designed to explain why people robbed banks but rather how robbing banks came to have the quality of being deviant" (Debro 1970, 167). Merton looked for the *cause* of deviant behavior (as did the "management of impulses" functionalists he criticized) and found the cause in "social structures exerting a definite pressure on some people." Becker asks about deviant behavior as behavior under *ban*, and so he asks about who does the banning, how the ban is maintained, and what effect the ban has on the activity itself.[14] On the basis of interactionist metaphysics, he doesn't assume that deviance is something there for the natural scientific eye to discern. Whether something is deviant or normal in a society is a question of perspective and power within the society. Although bank robbers and marijuana smokers may be considered deviant by "the population at large," that is, in the dominant opinion, the deviants themselves have their own perspective on the matter, and within their perspective, most are not much interested in looking for the alleged *causes* of their activities so that they can be cured.

The interactionist criticism brings out an important connection between metaphysics, scientific questions, and social problems.[15] Bank robbing, pot smoking, and homosexuality are social problems in the eyes of certain segments of our population, not others. Becker and other sociologists in the interactionist tradition have argued that social problems do not exist for the neutral scientific eye to discern any more than deviance does. Something is a social problem or not depending on one's social position and perspective. It is often a political question—as is the question of what function a social institution serves. In fact, "the function of a group or organization [is sometimes] decided in political conflict, not 'given in the nature of the organization" (Becker 1973, 7).

The examples I've given in this section indicate that metaphysical commitments have been important to scientific criticism and the growth of knowledge. In some cases at least, they may enter into the definition of a social problem and its solution.

Functionalist metaphysics was widely accepted in the natural sciences before World War II when Merton formulated his anomie. Functionalist sociologists offered a theory of society that was coherent with then current understandings in biology. This is not simply a case of a "pseudoscience" (sociology) putting on the trappings of a "real science" (biology), for any biological specialty dealing with social organisms requires a theory of society and social behavior.[16] Rather, the sociological case shows that metaphysical understandings in the natural sciences help define the human world in which social problems are categorized and dealt with. In the Merton example, labeling theorist criticism indicates that the cognitive authority of science supported one set of political positions over another by that definition of the human world. This happened not by abuse of authority but by the normal procedures in the normal social arrangements of science. The time has now come to ask more explicitly how those social arrangements influence scientific criticism and the growth of knowledge.

## IV. COGNITIVE AUTHORITY AND POWER

In section II, I suggested that the conventional understandings of significant communicators in science are the definitive understandings of the nature of the world within their spheres of expertise. In section III, I suggested that metaphysical commitments are important to the growth of knowledge. In those sections, I spoke as though any researcher with the appropriate certificates of training could serve as a significant communicator, and the reader might think that if one group exercised greater cognitive authority it was on meritocratic or purely rational grounds: Their theories and commitments have been shown to withstand test and criticism better than those of their competitors. I believe it is a valuable feature of the scientific enterprise that rational criticism is a factor in determining which group exercises cognitive authority. However, social arrangements are factors as well, and to the degree that we refuse to acknowledge that fact, we limit criticism and cause scientific work to be less rational than it might be. In this section, I will indicate some social factors that may be relevant, and then I will close with an example of how scientific understanding has been improved by recent criticisms that did take social arrangements into account.

First, let me take up questions of prestige. The sciences differ in prestige, physics having more than economics, and both having more than educational psychology. Specialties in a science, too, differ in prestige, experimental having more than clinical psychology, for example. Prestige differences affect researchers' judgments on which metaphysical and methodological commitments are to be preferred. Carolyn Wood Sherif remarks on the "prestige hierarchy" in psychology in the 1950s:

> Each of the fields and specialties in psychology sought to improve its status by adopting (as well and as closely as stomachs permitted) the perspectives, theories, and methodologies as high on the hierarchy as possible. The way to "respectability" in this scheme has been the appearance of rigor and scientific inquiry, bolstered by highly restricted notions of what science is about. (Sherif 1979, 98)

Many philosophers of science have not only taken prestige hierarchies to be irrelevant to scientific rationality, they have accepted the hierarchies themselves and in doing so have shared and justified "highly restricted notions of what science is about." This failing was blatant in the work of logical positivists and their followers, for they constructed their analysis of scientific method to accord with an idealization of what goes on in physics, and they discussed the "unity of science" in a way that gave physics star status.[17]

Within specialties, researchers differ in prestige, so that some have access to positions of power while others do not. Some teach in prestigious institutions and train the next generations of successful researchers. Researchers judge excellence in terms of their own understanding of their field, of which problems are important, of which methods are best suited to solving them. Researchers in positions of power can spread their understandings and their metaphysical commitments. Consider the primatology example in section III.

Because Robert Yerkes held influential positions, he was able to give an important backing to Clarence Ray Carpenter's career, helping Carpenter to compete successfully for the positions and funding needed to do his research. Haraway says of Carpenter, "From his education, funding, and social environment, there was little reason for Carpenter to reject the basic assumptions that identified reproduction and dominance based on sex with the fundamental organizing principles of a body politic" (Haraway 1978, 30). Yerkes shared the "body politic" metaphysics. In helping Carpenter, he was helping to spread his own metaphysical commitments.

The question is not whether top scientists in most fields produce some very good work but rather the more important question of whether other good work, even work critical of the top scientists, is not taken seriously because its proponents are not members of the same powerful networks and so cannot exercise the same cognitive authority. The question is made particularly difficult because, by disregarding or downgrading competing research, the "top scientists" cut off the resources necessary for their competition to develop really good work. In most fields it is next to impossible to do research without free time, aid from research assistants, secretaries, craftsmen, custodians, and in many cases, access to equipment.

Some very influential philosophers of science have insisted that criticism is an essential part of scientific method, and that criticism requires that there be competing scientific theories. (See Popper 1965; Feyerabend 1970.) Accepting that as an abstract canon, one might philosophically point out that Yerkes should have encouraged more competition and (if one became particularly moralistic) that he should have been more careful about showing favoritism and bias. But is would be a mistake to describe Yerkes as showing favoritism and bias. As a matter of fact, he did much to set the practice of researchers investigating unpopular subjects and reaching unpopular results in the interests of scientific freedom and research in "pure science." But he made his judgments according to his own understanding of scientific research. Any researcher must do that. Researchers are also the judges of which competing theories it makes sense to pursue or to encourage others to pursue. If this seems to result in bias, the way to correct it is not by blaming individual researchers for showing favoritism because they depart from some mythical set of abstract canons. They way to begin to correct it is to broaden rational criticism in science by requiring that both philosophers of science and scientists understand how prestige and power are factors in the way cognitive authority is exercised.

So far I have talked about influences on the exercises of cognitive authority with the scientific professions. Many people have observed that there are outside influences on scientific research—funding, for example. Given legally dominant understandings of capitalism in the United States, many people consider it proper for private business to fund research on problems that need solving for reasons of economic competition and expansion. Most of us considered it appropriate that public agencies in a democracy should fund research to help solve social problems of the moment (as do private philanthropic foundations for the most part). If we think of science as a stock of knowledge embodied in theories, then the problem of funding does not seem to be a problem having to do with rationality and criticism in science. Instead it may appear to be a question of political or other outside interference with the autonomy of the researchers, at worst preventing them from setting their own problems to investigate.[18] If we use the notion of cognitive authority, however, we may see that the question of funding indeed has to do with scientific rationality and with the content of our scientific understanding of the world.

Metaphysical commitments of a science tell scientists what many of their research problems should be (Kuhn 1970, 41). As we saw from the Merton-Becker example, a difference in metaphysics may bring a difference in *what the problem is taken to be.* In that case, it was a difference between explaining why people rob banks and explaining how robbing banks comes to have the quality of being deviant (Debro 1970, 167). Because problems investigated by a tradition are related to the metaphysical and methodological commitments of its researchers, some understandings of nature will have a better chance for support than others.[19] Those researchers will have a better opportunity to exercise cognitive authority and to help others of their metaphysical persuasion rise in the ranks. They will write the texts and serve as advisors and use their external authority to popularize their metaphysical outlook. So funding influences the content of science at a given historical moment, and it influences the way we all come to understand the world.

The influence goes beyond the question of which of a number of competing traditions are to be rewarded. Arlene Daniels traces some of the ramifications in discussing Allan Schnaiberg's remarks on obstacles to environmental research.

> Schnaiberg shows us how unpopular socioenvironmental research is within establishment contexts. The science industries won't pay for it, the research foundations won't sanction it. Rewards in the academic market place depend on quick payoffs; accordingly, independent researchers there cannot wait for results that require large expenditures of time in unfunded research. (Daniels 1979, 38–39)

This means not only that some existing metaphysical and methodological traditions will flourish while others are passed over. It means that potentially fruitful metaphysics and methods will not get a chance for development at all, because social arrangements in the scientific professions and the influence of funding work against it.

So far, I've suggested that social arrangements within the scientific professions, and between those professions and the larger society, involve factors relevant to the exercise of cognitive authority in the sciences and thus to the content of scientific understanding. Are the professional and social life experiences of researchers also relevant to their metaphysical commitments? This is an extremely interesting question because of the quite general assumption in the United States that there is a privileged definition of reality that scientists capture, a main assumption underlying the authority we give them. Feminists in nearly every scientific field have questioned that assumption.[20] I questioned it from an interactionist perspective in discussing Merton, above. Let me give two suggestive examples here.

The anthropologist Edwin Ardener suggests that because of their social experience, men and women conceptualize their societies and communities differently (Ardener 1975a, 1975b). In most societies, men more frequently engage in political activities and public discourse and have the definitional problem of bounding their own society or community off from others. Models suited to the usual women's experience aren't the object of public discourse, so when circumstances call for it, women will use men's models, not their own.

Ethnographers tend to report the male models for three reasons, according to Ardener. They are more accessible to the researcher. Male models are the officially accepted ones in the ethnographer's home society. And they accord with the metaphysical and theoretical outlook of functionalism which, in the past, many ethnographers have held. Milton reports Ardener's claim this way: "Ethnographers, especially those who have adopted a functionalist approach, tend to be attracted to the bounded models of society, with which they are presented mainly by men and occasionally by women. These models accord well with functionalist theory and so tend to be presented as *the* models of society" (Milton 1979, 48).

We need not accept Ardener's claims as gospel truth to realize that we *cannot* accept without test the empirical assumption that a specialist's social experience has no significant effect on his or her scientific understanding of the world.

Nor can we accept, without test, the empirical hypothesis that the long training and isolating, professional experience of scientific specialists has no significant effect on their scientific understanding. The sociologist Vilhelm Aubert says,

> Members of society have, through their own planning and their own subsequent observations, verifications, and falsifications, built up a cognitive structure bearing some resemblances to a scientific theory. . . . But . . . social man behaves only in some, albeit important, areas in this purposive way. Any attempt, therefore, to stretch the predictability criterion beyond these areas—their limits are largely

unknown—may result in a misrepresentation of the nature of human behavior. This danger is greatly increased by origin of most social scientists in cultures which heavily stress a utilitarian outlook, and by their belonging even to the subcultures within these, which are the main bearers of this ethos. A sociology produced by fishermen from northern Norway or by Andalusian peasants might have been fundamentally different. The leading social scientists are people with tenure and right of pension. (Aubert 1965, 135)

The leading physicists, biologists, and philosophers of science are also people with tenure and right of pension. They live in societies marked by dominance of group over group. As specialists, they compete for positions at the top of their professional hierarchies that allow them to exercise cognitive authority more widely. Out of such cultural understandings and social orderings, it is no wonder that we get an emphasis on predictive law and an insistence that the currently popular theories of a specialty represent the one, true, authoritative description of the world. It is no wonder that our specialists continually present us with metaphysical descriptions of the world in terms of hierarchy, dominance, and competition. The wonder is that we get any development of our understanding at all.

But we do. Scientific understanding does seem to grow (in however ungainly a fashion), and our knowledge does seem to "advance" (however crabwise).

In our own century, scientific knowledge has often seemed to grow at the expense of wisdom. However, the corrective is not to dismiss science as hopelessly biased and wrongheaded and return to some kind of folk wisdom. We can't get along without science anymore. The corrective seems rather to ferret out all the irrationalities we can find in scientific activity and to expand our understanding of science and scientific rationality. To do this, we should acknowledge metaphysical commitments as part of the content of scientific understanding and thus open them to scrutiny and criticism by specialist and nonspecialist alike. Feminist criticism offers a very instructive example here. In the past twenty years, political feminists have given lay criticisms of much of our scientific metaphysics. Other feminists have gained specialist training and brought the lay criticisms to bear on technical theories within their fields.[21] This was possible because sexism is a political issue at the moment, and funding, journals, and other resources are available for this sort of research and criticism. I am suggesting that we should institutionalize this form of criticism and make it an explicit part of "scientific method." We should also try using the notion of cognitive authority and expanding the range of the criteria of scientific rationality and criticism so that it includes social arrangements within the scientific professions.

If we expand the range of criticism, I believe that philosophers of science and scientists as well will find themselves advocating change in our social system. This would not result in a sudden illegitimate politicization of science or an opening of the floodgates of irrationality. Quite the contrary. Because they have cognitive authority, our scientists already *are* politicized. It is the *unexamined* exercise of cognitive authority within our present social arrangements that is most to be feared. Illegitimate politicization and rampant irrationality find their most fruitful soil when our activities are mystified and protected from criticism.

## Notes

*Acknowledgments:* Research for this paper was supported in part by a grant from the National Endowment for the Humanities and by the Mellon Foundation grant to the Smith College project on Women and Social Change. I am very grateful for criticism or advice I received from Howard Becker, Donna Haraway, Arlene Daniels, Sandra Harding, Vicky Spelman, Helen Longino, Kay Warren, Noretta Koertge, Arnold Feldman, and members of two seminars I taught in the Northwestern University sociology department, fall 1980. I have previously published work under the name Kathryn Pyne Parsons.

1. Instead, philosophers criticized one another's versions of the abstract canons. Positivist Rudolf Carnap was particularly painstaking at criticizing his own and other positivists' analyses of the structure of scientific theories. See, for example, Carnap 1956. Karl Popper also devoted time and energy to criticizing the positivists. See, for example, Popper 1965.

2. At the beginning of the "new wave" in philosophy of science, N. R. Hanson did ask after the choosing of new theories, but he did so by discussing the logic of discovery and the ways in which theories that groups of scientists develop are constrained by their patterns of conceptual organization rather than by asking after constraints in the social arrangements within which scientific understanding is developed and criticized. See Hanson 1958.

3. It is there implicitly, however, particularly in his wonderful discussion of science texts.

4. Whether or not a group has authority regarding something depends on social arrangements in the society in which they form a group, thus my restriction to "the United States today." I should make more severe restrictions because there are subgroups in the USA, which don't grant "scientists" much authority. We do it through our public and major private educational systems, however.

5. One doesn't usually think of artisans as part of science, but one physicist said of his university's craftsmen, "The gadgets they produce for us are just crucial. The reason the work the department does is internationally competitive with major research centers all over the world is in part due to the capabilities of the people in the machine shop. Some of the research simply could not be done without them." *Contact*, August 1980, 8 (University of Massachusetts, Amherst, publication).

6. Within the hierarchical social relations of the research group, the chief inves-

tigator has authority to command obedience from technicians, students, secretaries, and the like. I am not concerned with that kind of authority in this chapter.

7. My remark about honey may still be true, but because of changes in the food industry consequent to the "growth of scientific knowledge," we are learning to choose foods by applying the chemist's categories to lists of ingredients on packages at the supermarket.

8. Haraway does not explicitly talk about metaphysics in her paper, and in fact she may use the term in a more limited way than I do (personal communication, 1979).

9. In fields like history or archeology, researchers themselves interact with non-living material not with the (formerly living) subjects of study, but their theories and explanations represent the researchers' conventional understandings of those subjects.

10. Merton himself says, "The prevalence of the functional outlook is in itself no warrant for its scientific value, but it does suggest that cumulative experience has forced this orientation upon the disciplined observers of man as biological organism, psychological actor, members of society and bearer of culture" (Merton 1949, 47). A whole metaphysic and theory of science underlies that remark, as the reader may see by comparing my remarks and those of other authors in section IV of this chapter. For example, Merton hints that scientific observation and laboratory and field experience "forces" the outlook, while some authors I report on in section IV suggest that social experience in the professions and the specialists' society are major influences.

11. Haraway 1978 also indicates that other researchers in the life sciences later criticized the metaphysics, from the standpoint of other varieties of functionalism.

12. See Elizabeth V. Spelman's chapter in Harding and Hintikka (1983) for an illuminating discussion of the view as Aristotle held it.

13. Merton 1949, 142. Merton's theory of deviance is broader and more complex than I am representing it here. I am selecting features for a dual purpose: to show the criticism of the "uncontrolled impulse" view and to contrast with the interactionist theory I give below.

14. Becker himself does not speak of behavior under *ban*. That conceptualization is David Matza's (1969).

15. See Spector and Kitsuse (1977) for a discussion of social problems.

16. Philip Green discusses this issue in criticizing sociobiologists' theories in Green (1981).

17. Some philosophers of science have insisted that the methods of the physical sciences are not suitable for historical sciences—see, for example, the whole *Verstehen* controversy (Collingwood 1946) as a classic source. For social sciences generally, see Winch (1958).

18. George H. Daniels suggests that the rise of the ideal of pure scientific research in the late-nineteenth century led to conflicts with democratic assumptions in "The Pure-Science Ideal and Democratic Culture," *Science* 156 (1967): 1699–1705. My discussion here displays the other side of the conflict.

19. I am not claiming here that stating a problem in a certain way ensures that you'll have a certain metaphysics, or even determines it in some unidirectional way. My point is about the ranges of theories and traditions available at a historical moment and which of them will receive encouragement and support.

20. See, for example, the essays in Millman and Kanter (1975), Sherman and Beck (1979), and Harding and Hintikka (1983).

21. Feminist criticism may seem more obviously politicized than, say, Yerkes's or Merton's or Becker's criticisms discussed above, but I think that is because feminists themselves insist on the political connections.

# 5

## *Moral Passages*
(1985)

If we want to know about women and moral theory, in a way that is not simply concerned with technical academic constructions, we have to be concerned with the question, What is morality? One of the deans of philosophical ethics in the United States, William Frankena, once said that answering that question was the philosopher's work in ethics.

> Contemporary moral philosophy may . . . be represented as primarily an attempt to understand what morality is, meaning by "morality" not the quality of conduct which is opposed to immorality but what Butler so nicely refers to as "the moral institution of life." The current endeavor is not to promote certain moral goals or principles, or to clarify only such words as "right" and "ought," but rather to grasp the nature of morality itself, as compared with law, religion or science. In this endeavor both Continental and English-speaking philosophers are engaged, though to different degrees, in different ways, and with different equipment. (Frankena 1963, 1–2)

There is a certain ambiguity to the phrase, "the moral institution of life." There are, on the one hand, the philosophers' definitions and analyses of the moral institution. There is, on the other hand, the living human life that constitutes "the moral institution." Frankena and other philosophers write as if separating morality from law, religion, or science were a conceptual, not a political and social (and perhaps even moral) matter. As if one could understand the moral institution of life without being thoroughly

---

Reprinted, with changes, from Eva Feder Kittay and Diana T. Meyers, eds., *Women and Moral Theory* (Totowa, N.J.: Rowman and Littlefield, 1987), 87–110, by permission of the author. Copyright 1987 by Kathryn Pyne Addelson.

enmeshed in helping to create or legitimate that institution. As if one had no need to see whether one's analysis respected the living human life.

In this essay, I offer a different approach to understanding the moral institution of life by asking how morality itself emerges out of people's interactions. My approach is based on work in the sociological tradition called symbolic interactionism that allows us to find out about the place of authorities, like Frankena, in legitimating certain definitions of morality. In the end, it allows us to question fundamental models of moral explanation and action that have been widely assumed by traditional analysts as well as many of their feminist critics. Under these models, the analyst "grasps the nature of morality itself" by defining or uncovering categories of moral explanation—whether that explanation is in terms of principles justifying acts, or of characters or responsibility, or of some end like happiness or the good life. The analysts then assume that these general moral categories are (or ought to be) used by individuals in making their moral choices or in explaining their own and others' moral activities and lives. Sometimes the analysts offer the categories as ones to be autonomously chosen, sometimes they claim to be describing the categories people in fact use. The approach I take indicates that moral explanation (and the categories of explanation) are constructed in social interactions, and that when we examine those interactions, we find that systematic social and political relations are created and maintained in the process of the construction. The consequence is that we cannot properly understand problems of women and moral theory if we use the usual approaches. I'll begin making my case by considering the moral problem of abortion.

The "classical" philosophical analysis of the moral problem of abortion is to treat it as a conflict of rights: the fetal right to life in conflict with the woman's right to decide what happens in and to her own body (see, for example, articles in Pearsall 1986). If one decides that fetuses are not persons, morally speaking, then abortion becomes a practical decision, not a moral one (see Smetana 1982; Sumner 1981).

The "classical" analysis distinguishes two contexts in which the moral problem of abortion may arise: the primary context is the "personal" one in which people make their choices and justify actual abortions of fetuses. The secondary context is that of justifying public policy on abortion, understood as policy for regulating activities in the primary context (Sumner 1981).

Although there are still many philosophers who take a conflict of rights approach, changes and challenges in philosophical ethics itself—as well as the politics of abortion—have brought criticism (Hauerwas and

MacIntyre 1983; Pearsall 1986). Two of the most interesting criticisms have been raised by Stanley Hauerwas and Beverly Harrison.

Hauerwas has argued strongly that "Christians" opposing abortion cannot properly represent *their* positions in the terms in which philosophers have set the moral problem of abortion. He says,

> When the issue is limited to the determination of when human life does or does not begin, we cannot prevail, given the moral presuppositions of our culture. Put more forcefully, where the debate is limited to the issue of when human life begins, it has already been uncritically shaped by the political considerations of our culture. The "moral" has already been determined by the "political"—something we fail to notice in the measure that we simply presume the moral presuppositions of our culture to be valid. (Hauerwas 1980, 327)

Hauerwas insists that Christian respect for life is a statement not about life but about God. Life is not ours to take. Furthermore, our place here on earth is to take part in the unfolding of the great Christian drama. Having children is one of the important ways we take part in God's great adventure (Hauerwas 1980; Hauerwas and MacIntyre 1983).

The "classic" philosophical analysis separates theories of the good (which concern morally good lives, among other things) from theories about obligation, rights, and what is morally right or wrong. Hauerwas's argument is that the "classic" analysis of abortion as a conflict of rights in fact *presupposes* a definition of the good life, one that is at odds with the Christian one he accepts. Hauerwas himself offers a very interesting alternative moral theory in terms of narratives; but what is important for my purposes here is that there is a difference not only in ideas of what constitutes a good life but also in what constitutes a moral problem. Taking part in the unfolding of the great Christian drama means (among other things) that sex and marriage and the *having* of children are moral matters that cannot be separated from the moral problem of abortion. The conflict of rights analysis rules them out, sometimes implicitly, sometimes explicitly.

Beverly Harrison takes a feminist standpoint. She says that the conflict of rights analysis does not take women seriously as moral agents (Harrison 1983). One major reason is that the "classic" philosophical approach takes abortion as a "discrete deed" to be decided on in abstraction from the circumstances in which women make their procreative choices. In doing this, the analysis presupposes the existing social order—something Hauerwas describes as a "conservative thrust" (Hauerwas 1977, 19). Harrison insists that women must work to change the circumstances in which they make reproductive choices so that all children may be cared for. Women must make social changes so that they will be able to choose to have children, not merely not to have them. On the one hand, Harrison is taking seriously the situations in which individual women make their procreative choices. She is saying that procreation must be considered as part of the good life of women, children, and the community as a whole. On the other hand, she is saying that the moral problem of abortion cannot be gerrymandered out of the larger question of procreation. Women do not simply decide to abort or not to abort. Harrison is saying that we should see women's moral choice as making, at every moment, the choice to go on with the pregnancy, and after it, at every moment, to rear the child. That is what procreative choice is about.[2]

Harrison is not the only feminist who has said that the standard analysis in terms of a conflict of rights will not do for women. Philosopher Caroline Whitbeck argued for a new moral theory on those grounds (Whitbeck 1983).

> One of the striking things about the philosophical debate on the ethics of abortion is how few women enter it. I believe that the relatively small number of women who enter the discussion is a result, as well as a cause, of the way in which the subject is demarcated, and the way in which it is conceptualized. Given the way in which the issue is presently framed, it is difficult for many women to find any position for which they wish to argue. I shall argue, first, that abortion is actually a fragment of several other moral issues surrounding pregnancy and childbirth so that the moral situation can be adequately understood only if this larger context is considered, and second, that the choice of the terms in which the analysis is generally carried out is mistaken. In particular, I shall argue that neglect of matters that cannot be adequately expressed in terms of "rights" and the employment of an atomistic model of people (a model that represents moral relationships as incidental to being a person) confuses many moral issues, but especially those concerning pregnancy, childbirth, and infant care. (Whitbeck 1983, 247)

Whitbeck argues that philosophers and other experts have neglected interpretations of the human condition from women's perspective.

Whitbeck explicitly offers an alternative ethics of responsibility. Harrison's discussion also seems to point toward an ethics of responsibility—

one in which women take responsibility for the circumstances within which they make procreative choices. Both accept a rights analysis, but modified, and put in its proper place. This is also Carol Gilligan's strategy, although she bases her position on claims that she has empirically uncovered the new moral voice of responsibility and care.

Gilligan's work took off from anomalies she discerned in Lawrence Kohlberg's widely used theory of moral development. Kohlberg incorporated a technical, philosophical ethics (of the rights and obligations sort) into a basically Piagetian model of moral development.

Carol Gilligan was concerned that the style of moral explanation Kohlberg favored and the scoring method he used did not do justice (so to speak) to the moral thinking of women students and women subjects. In her now well-known abortion study (Gilligan 1977), she dropped the hypothetical-dilemma approach and interviewed women about their own abortion experiences, recorded their explanations, then developed both moral categories and a scoring manual out of the interview material. She claims that her subjects think in terms of care and responsibility rather than justice and obligation, and a "psychologic logic of relationships" rather than the abstract logic suited to deriving decisions from principles or to solving hypothetical dilemmas.[3] Both women and men use the care-responsibility orientation, but women tend to use it more. Both men and women use the justice-obligation orientation, but men tend to use it more. In this study, she speaks of a gestalt switch—the same relationships seen from two different orientations.

Although Gilligan's analysis does not accommodate Hauerwas's objections, it does seem to give an empirical grounding to the feminist approaches offered by Harrison and Whitbeck. It does, that is, if we suppose that accommodating moral explanations reported by individual women can alter accounts of the moral institution of life so that gender bias is overcome and women are taken seriously. But to suppose that is to give the game away. The reason is not that women might be forgetful or self-deceptive in their reports, or that there is a white, middle-class bias, and that other women might explain things differently (though both of those factors are present). The reason is that the women's very explanations have been constructed as a part of a process of interaction, which itself brings into existence gender, age, class, and race relations. The explanations that Gilligan uncovers cannot give us a fair and nonsexist account of the moral institution of life because those explanations themselves are products of processes by which gender, age, class, race, and other systematic, social-political relations are created and maintained. It is that process that must be examined if we are even to begin to understand the moral institution of life. As C. Wright Mills once said, the explanations people offer are themselves in need of explanation (Mills 1963).

I will argue these claims on the basis of sociological field studies. But serious objections can also be made (in a negative way) in terms of shortcomings of the general models, which are presupposed. Two main objections are to the accounts of individual decision, choice, or action and to the accounts of how individual moral explanation is social.

So far as the individual goes, both the classic analysis and many of the revisionist ones are voluntaristic, in the sense that the person comes to the situation with a grasp of moral explanations and uses them as "guides" to action. In the paradigm case of explicit moral reasoning, one weighs principles, then makes the moral decision. Or one ponders responsibilities and relationships, then chooses. In "nonparadigm cases" the thinking need not be explicit, and on other voluntarist accounts, one merely reads the situation and acts out of virtue or habit. There would not be a major objection to such voluntarism if we had some explanation of how it works, materially, in the moral institution of life. As I will say in the conclusion to this chapter, we have none.[4]

Nearly all of the accounts, from "classical" to feminist, also presuppose that moral explanation by individuals is social in this sense: There are categories, principles, narratives, paradigm cases, language games, or other devices that are (or ought to be) shared among some group of people (or all humanity); individual members explain their moral activities in those group terms. In this light, Gilligan corrected Kohlberg's overgeneralization of the rights-obligations ethics by showing that there are two different kinds of moral explanations used by members of humanity. But this is a sociologically mistaken view of the relationship of individual to "group culture." It is also a mistaken view of the relationship of individual to the moral institution of life. Let me begin by offering a more appropriate sociological account.

The sociological tradition I shall rely upon is called symbolic interactionism. The tradition began its development early in the century, at the University of Chicago; its practitioners now are widely dispersed. My own work has been with Howard Becker, and theoretically, I rely particularly on writings by his teachers, Herbert Blumer and Everett Hughes.[5] The tradition is marked by using methods of participant observation to do small group studies.

One basic premise, which Blumer articulates well, is that any human social world consists of the actions and experiences of the people who make it up. Furthermore, the nature of both the social and the natural environment, and the objects composing them, is set by the meanings they have for those people (Blumer 1969, 11, 35). This sort of claim has become common enough in recent years, but it would be a mistake to make a leap to saying that the meanings are given in terms of the group rules or language games (as Winch and other Wittgensteinians do), or that they are given in terms of institutionalized norms that are interiorized through socialization (as even social constructionalists like Berger and Luckmann do) (Winch 1958; Berger and Luckmann 1967). The interactionist approach is to study actual processes of interaction by which the meanings are constructed: It is the social process in group life that creates and upholds the rules, not the rules that create and uphold group life (Blumer 1969, 19). These social processes are studied by participant observation of small groups. They include processes that will aid in understanding the moral institution of life.

To investigate the processes involved in moral explanation, we need a perspicuous working notion. I will use the notion of a moral passage. As I use it, it is derivative on the notion of a career, which is widely used in interactionist studies.[6]

A career covers both an individual's movement through an activity (in biographical terms) and the general pattern followed by any person going through "that sort of thing." The pattern is displayed in the movements from one *step* to another—so that a career is a pattern of steps. Howard Becker explains the steps in terms of career contingencies—continuing in the career is contingent on moving to the next in the series of steps (Becker 1973, 24). The steps are uncovered by field investigation, and they need not match the steps subjects take to be definitive. Nor do they explain psychological or moral differences among the people who finish the career and those who do not. The steps are contingencies in the sense that what people who make the passage have in common is that they pass through those steps.

To study abortion, we might begin by doing field studies of some women's passages through abortion—as Mary K. Zimmerman did (Zimmerman 1977). However, to make proper sense of Harrison's, Whitbeck's, and Hauerwas's observations, those abortion passages would have to be placed in a larger network of passages suitable for field studies. That large network would accommodate Harrisons's wide-ranging "procreative choice" and Whitbeck's "larger context," as well as Hauerwas's concern with sex, marriage, and the *having* of children. What we need is a schema that can serve as a hypothesis or theoretical guide for other, related field studies, or a schema that would (when empirically filled out) give us a pattern of social options that exist or that can be created, of which the passage through abortion is one. But how is such a schema to be constructed?

In this chapter, I will use work by sociologist Prudence Rains to shed light on the moral institution of life. Rains herself did several field studies in the late 1960s, which she reported and discussed in her book, *Becoming an Unwed Mother*. They included studies of mainly white and middle-class young women at a home for unwed mothers and of black, mainly poor teenagers at a day school for unwed mothers. Rains opens the book with this statement:

> Becoming an unwed mother is the outcome of a particular sequence of events that begins with forays into intimacy and sexuality, results in pregnancy, and terminates in the birth of an illegitimate child. Many girls do not have sexual relations before marriage. Many who do, do not get pregnant. And most girls who get pregnant while unmarried do not end up as unwed mothers. Girls who become unwed mothers, in this sense, share a common career that consists of the steps by which they came to be unwed mothers rather than brides, the clients of abortionists, contraceptively prepared lovers, or virtuous young ladies. (Rains 1971, 1)

Rains studied one line of passage in this network of passages in the seas of young womanhood: becoming an unwed mother. Field-workers must limit themselves. But her understanding of the place of unwed motherhood in a larger network of passages gives us a way to make a schema of social options.

Figure 5.1 represents Rains's remarks. Rains herself names the common starting point, "the situation of moral jeopardy." The starting point is important and problematic.

The schema in Figure 1 represents patterns of moral passages in the late 1960s, when Rains did her studies. There are branching paths to abortion because restrictive abortion laws made abortion illicit in all but a few circumstances (or places). The figure operates as a guide to further empirical study. It is not a decision-making tree, nor does it define social options. But it does offer a theoretical aid to Harrison's and Whitbeck's discussions. Both women insist that we take women's circumstances seriously. Figure 5.1, as a guide to empirical study, offers a systematic way to discover what "women's circumstances" amount to in given times and places. In analogous ways, I believe, this sort of schema offers a necessary aid to any

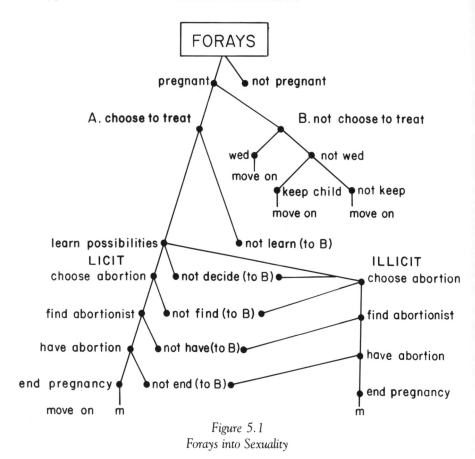

Figure 5.1
Forays into Sexuality

responsibility ethics, and to Hauerwas's account of "God's great adventure" as well.

The figure allows me to make a methodological distinction that is important. The terms "pregnant," "abortion," and "unwed motherhood,"
and others appear on the chart. Now Rains's subjects were involved in
pregnancy, and some thought about abortion and other possible passages.
The young women (and those around them) used the words "pregnancy"
and "abortion" as *folk terms*. Folk terms are used by people in organizing
their social interactions, and they carry with them assumptions about
what activities are involved, what cast of characters is important, what
courses might be followed. They offer guides as to what to expect.

The notion of a moral passage is a construct to be used by the scholarly investigator, not the "folk" who are being studied. The scholarly investigators use what Herbert Blumer calls *sensitizing concepts*. Blumer contrasts sensitizing concepts with definitive concepts—the sort with which philosophers usually concern themselves. Definitive concepts refer to a class of objects, and they carry with them criteria or "benchmarks" by which one can tell whether something belongs to the class or not. Sensitizing concepts are not designed to offer such criteria but to offer guidance in approaching empirical instances.

Blumer goes on to say that even if definitive concepts were possible to construct in sociology, they would not be proper for sociologists to use in describing the human social world. Definitive concepts give what is common to the instances. With sensitizing concepts, "we seem forced to reach what is common by accepting and using what is distinctive to the given empirical instance" (Blumer 1969, 152). This, he says, is due not to the immaturity of the discipline of sociology but to the nature of the empirical world that is its object of study.

In a certain way, Blumer takes meaning to be use—not use by the subject population but use by the sensitized researcher. He says that by taking concepts as sensitizing, his line of approach

> seeks to improve concepts by naturalistic research, that is, by direct study of our natural social world wherein empirical instances are accepted in their concrete and distinctive form. It depends on faithful reportorial depiction of the instances and on analytical probing into their character. As such its procedure is markedly different from that employed in the effort to develop definitive concepts. Its success depends on patient, careful and imaginative life study, not on quick shortcuts or technical instruments. While its progress may be slow and tedious, it has the virtue of remaining in close and continuing relations with the natural social world. (Blumer 1969, 152)

This is a statement of sociological theory as well as of sociological field method.

In my theoretical reconstruction of Rains's work, I would say that as a field researcher, she herself uses "unwed mother" and "pregnant" as sensitizing concepts—though she does not speak in these terms, nor does she distinguish her use from her subjects' use of those terms. However, her studies show how the meanings of "pregnant" and "unwed mother" come to be constructed as folk terms among her subjects, and so it is theoretically necessary to take her to be using sensitizing concepts. In this light, I should remind readers that *who* gets pregnant is more a social than a biological question. (See Luker 1975; Harrison 1983.)

~

To write *Becoming an Unwed Mother*, Prudence Rains did three field studies. Two were the extended studies that form the core of the book. These are the study at "Hawthorne House," the home run by social workers for mostly white, middle-class young women; and the study at "The Project," a day school for pregnant, black, young women. In addition to these two, Rains briefly studied a traditional maternity home, which she called "Kelman Place." The restrictions on her data gathering there were severe because of secrecy requirements at the home, and she ultimately used the study only to contrast traditional homes with the situations at Hawthorne House and the Project.[7]

Rains's view is that illicit pregnancy is "the incidental product of the way sexual activity is *normally* organized among unmarried girls in this society (Rains 1971, 4). She names the common situation out of which unwed mothers begin their careers, "The Situation of Moral Jeopardy" (see Figure 5.1). Somehow, in passing from childhood to womanhood, a girl must learn how to become the kind of woman she would be.[8] The learning takes place on many fronts, but girls (and boys) must come to change their early, childish ways to ways suitable to the adult world—and given our society, that means finding a place in a heterosexual world, though not necessarily as a heterosexual. In the process, the girl begins (with others) to construct her place as a woman in the adult world—a construction that includes her understanding of both self and world, as well as other people's understanding of her. These things are not simple opinions or beliefs, for they exist in interactions, in the activities and doings that make up her life. Rains says that a central moral experience for the young women she studied is the ambivalence they feel when they find themselves acting in ways they only recently, as children, had disapproved.

Rains says, "The central feature of these girls' moral careers as unwed mothers is the experience of coming to realign themselves with the conventional, respectable world; the central theme of this book has to do with the ways in which the maternity homes sponsor and organize this experience of moral realignment" (Rains 1971, 34).

Becoming pregnant was a blatant way of going public about things customarily hidden in the journey from childhood to adulthood (and hidden in adulthood as well). For the young men involved, it was usually relatively easy to restrict the range of the publicity. For a young woman, it required major, institutionalized methods to deal with the publicity. And it had to be dealt with because of what would be jeopardized by going public in an unrestricted way. The passages of Rains's unwed mothers show how managing the publicity was essential not only to the girls' futures but to the social organization of morality as well.

## KELMAN PLACE

Rains quotes a remark by a spokesperson for a Florence Crittenden home that indicates the policy of traditional homes like Kelman Place. "These are your loving, trusting girls in here. Your other girl who is probably doing the same thing doesn't get caught because she is too smart. . . . What is needed is more understanding on the part of the parents and the general public. I don't mean condoning. I mean understanding . . . that this kind of thing can happen and these girls do need help" (quoted in the St. Petersburg, Florida, *Times*, May 17, 1968; Rains 1971, 48). This "philosophy" was shared by staff at Kelman Place. One staff member put it this way, "I talk a lot with the girls. In general, with the whole group, I would say they know what they have done is not condoned by society and never will be—never. I do not condemn a girl for making one mistake. I just hope they learn a lesson" (Rains 1971, 49). These remarks capture the major features of a classic sort of moral explanation. We do not condemn a person of good character who has made a mistake, who will learn from the mistake, and who is determined not to make the mistake again.

In the context, the explanation carries an old-fashioned image of a nice girl led astray, whose mistake is punishment enough in itself. This sort of explanation presupposes that reputation, self-respect, and respectability are risked by getting pregnant out of wedlock. It is not the simple getting pregnant that is the problem. It is the woman herself—her character or the motive one derives from traits of her character. Illicit pregnancy is a visible mark of character that somehow must be dealt with.

At both Kelman Place and Hawthorne House, the young women's explanations of their own pregnancies came to be in harmony with this venerable story. Rains quotes her field notes from Hawthorne House: "Louise asked during group meeting, 'Can you remember what you thought of unwed mothers in places like this before? I mean, think of what we thought, before we came here, about unwed mothers and maternity homes.' Peg said, 'That's right. Whenever I thought of places like this, I always thought, "Well, I'm not that type of girl."'" Everyone looked agreeing to this" (Rains 1971, 43–44). Rains says, "Girls enter maternity homes expecting to confront the concrete proof of what they have become and encounter instead a reminder of what they "really" are, what they presumably have been all along" (Rains 1971, 54).

There is, however, a certain ominous tone in the staff member's remark, "I do not condemn a girl for making one mistake. I just hope they learn a lesson." The remark raises the awful specter that the event may happen again if the girl doesn't learn from it. This specter was raised at each of the three locations Rains studied, but it was dealt with differently at each of them. But interestingly enough, the young women at each of the locations begin with the same explanation: There were two kinds of girls—respectable and "that kind" (see Figure 5.2). They then modified the explanation so that the "nice girl" category might contain a loop covering the passage through unwed motherhood, after which the girl returns to respectability if she learns her lesson. It was a loop they believed could only be taken once, otherwise the chart would have been the passage of "that type of girl" (see Figure 5.3).

At Kelman Place, the young women's self-respect and reputation were rescued by this explanation. I do not mean that the verbal explanation rescued them by magically changing people's opinions. Kelman Place had the material wherewithal to let the young women "move on" back to their normal lives with their reputations saved by concealing their mistakes—

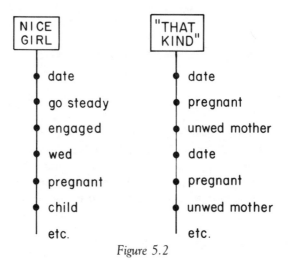

Figure 5.2

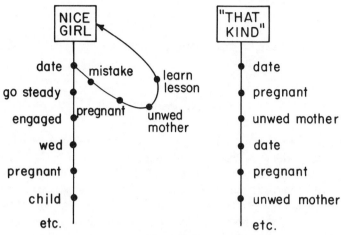

Figure 5.3

and in fact, Kelman Place was part of the *institutionalized* means in the society for that kind of moral rescue.

An important part of the Kelman Place rescue turned on the ways in which a young woman's public interaction was altered. During her stay at a traditional home, secrecy was preserved as much as possible, so that the young woman might reenter respectable society without her mistake "ruining" her. Her passage was hidden by her physically leaving her usual public locations of home, school, and so on. It was also hidden by cover stories.[9]

Which authorities had to be dealt with varied with the young woman's previous life. For women in school they included principals and counselors, truant officers, and police; for women in college, they included the deans, teachers, and registrars. For all of the young women, they included physicians, lawyers, adoption agency and birth registry officials, as well as the maternity-home staff, whose stance was one of stern but benign rescue. Because of the way the rescue was institutionalized, the outside authorities involved were either kept in ignorance or were parties to the conspiracy. This was part of the standard operating procedure of maternity homes. The Kelman Place staff's judgment on character was accepted, and the category of "nice girl who made a mistake" was socially real, not a matter of opinion. The young women could accept authorities at face value because they could simply and unconsciously count on their protection in this hidden salvage operation. The institutional salvage included dealing with the public remainder of the "mistake"—the child—because nearly all of the girls gave their babies up for adoption. The entire operation confirmed the fact that the girl's past was really that of a nice girl who had made a mistake, by creating the possibility for her to be a respectable young woman in the future.

## HAWTHORNE HOUSE

In entering Hawthorne House, the young women changed their public interactions in the same way that the Kelman Place women did, for both homes had the same institutional status and connections. Hawthorne House staff dealt with authorities such as judges, lawyers, hospital personnel, and adoption-agency staff generally by the same institutional means used at the traditional homes. However, Hawthorne House was operated by professional social workers whose disciplinary training was aimed at bringing people to face emotional and psychological realities and the truth about their motives.

The social workers regarded becoming an unwed mother as having its cause in a prior, unhealthy psychological state. Their task was to help the young women uncover and correct that state so that it would not continue to operate in the future, with the risk of repeated illicit pregnancy. When one father expressed reservations about "the girls" returning to dating, a staff member said, "We expect girls will resume their heterosexual relationships in the manner of dating, but we feel that if they have learned something during their stay here, they can communicate better with their parents and they don't need to act out in inappropriate ways" (Rains 1971, 98).

Rains says that the social workers were concerned that the young women accept responsibility for their behavior, as well as acknowledge the seriousness of the consequences. For the girls to accept the traditional explanation that they were trusting young women who had made a mistake counted as denial. Understanding the emotional roots of their actions was necessary to avoid another illicit pregnancy. This amounts to a straightforward criticism of the traditional maternity homes. The criticism shows that the responsibility the social workers wanted was not responsibility for being a respectable woman in the traditional sense—and this marks a deep difference from the Kelman Place approach.

In criticizing traditional maternity-home practices of extreme secrecy and protection, one staff member said,

After all, girls come here because they acted irresponsibly to start with, particularly now that ways to prevent getting pregnant are so common. And I don't think we should encourage that kind of thing. A lot of what we try to do is based on this philosophy that girls should be encouraged to accept responsibility for themselves, and to take responsibility. (Rains 1971, 63)

This is not the traditional moral view that having sex in itself is either irresponsible or promiscuous. In fact, it appears to be a liberated view that takes young women seriously as moral agents who autonomously choose their moral principles and who make their own lives.

From Rains's report, all the Hawthorne House women seem to accept the benign, helpful posture of the social workers, and they accepted the intrusion of these authorities into areas that are customarily hidden and private. This does not mean that they all accepted the psychotherapeutic explanation. One young woman said,

My social worker is always trying to convince me. . . . I keep telling her that it doesn't seem to me to be true, and she'll agree, but there's always the implied idea that there was an emotional reason. It's insinuated all the time, in every question. I just keep wondering where the explanation came from to begin with. I mean I wonder what girl they knew well enough to arrive at this idea, this explanation. (Rains 1971, 92)

But another girl responded,

I know I felt that way when I came, but I feel now that if you don't know why you're here, you'll end up here again. (Rains 1971, 92)

The first girl questions the social worker's redefinition of the past, and the second accepts it. On the social worker picture, the first girl will return to the fog of denial (see Figure 5.4).

The adequacy of psychotherapeutic explanation does not turn on there *always* being a hidden explanation for illicit pregnancy, of course, for there may be many classes of exceptions. However, what *is* essential to the viewpoint is the contrast between the inner truth and ordinary, everyday ways of explaining things. The professional social worker's job is to unveil the truth that is hidden under the illusions of "nice girl" and "that kind of

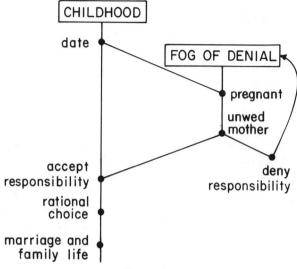

*Figure 5.4*

girl." The body of knowledge that the professional learns through her training penetrates to the underlying realities. Everyone *can* come to know those kinds of truths, but with the expert's help. This is different from the Kelman Place staff's reliance on "what everyone knows," but like the Kelman Place explanation, it overlooks the effect of the arrangements for maintaining secrecy about the young woman's future.

## THE PROJECT

The black teenagers of the Project dealt with the public reality in ways quite different from those used by the mainly white, middle-class women of the maternity homes—in part because of differences in their options and in their relationships with authorities. The Project teenagers' passages were public in two ways that those of the maternity-home women were not. They were public in the sense that the teenagers continued to live at home, so the pregnancy was widely known and questions of respectability and responsibility had to be handled in school, on the street, and in the kitchen. They were also public in the sense that public officials and public records defined an *official* reputation for the young women.

At the time Rains did her study, "The Project" was funded as a pilot school for pregnant teens, located in a black ghetto of a large Midwestern city—handling a maximum of about thirty-five teenagers (roughly four-teen-year-olds) at a time.[10] The Project staff included two teachers (one black, one white), a white psychiatric nurse, and a black social worker. The social worker had standard, professional views on how group discussions should be handled, what sorts of problems should be discussed, and what the discussion should accomplish—views much like those of the social workers at Hawthorne House. She tried to encourage the girls to express themselves, and she hoped to help the girls develop abstract skills to help them take responsibility for the course of their lives. Accordingly, her style in running the meetings was one of "moral neutrality," encouraging the girls to speak of their feelings. Rains says that the style "was simultaneously unbelievable, unbelieved, misunderstood, and unacceptable to the Project girls" (Rains 1971, 132). Rains quotes one of the young women: "Dorene said, 'I mean why do social workers want to ask you all kinds of personal questions, but you can never ask them back?'" (Rains 1971, 133). They saw asking questions as implying a right to know—and they believed that the social worker had no right to know some of the things she asked. This seemed to be both because she was an adult and because she was in a position of official authority.

The Project clients' experience with authorities was very different from that of the young women at the maternity homes. They had developed a warranted disbelief in moral neutrality and questions asked "for their own good." Here is part of a transcript of one of Rains's interviews:

> The truant officer asked me all sorts of questions—had I been picked up for curfew, had I ever been in jail, the boy's name, where I lived, did I work after school. He say he didn't know if they would let me stay in school or throw me out. [How did you feel?] He just be screaming at you like you was some slut dog. (Rains 1971, 134)

One of the young women said about official questioners, "They keep records."

The records the truant and probation officers kept were accessible records. They made up a public reputation that allowed authorities to meddle in the girl's future life. Was she an incorrigible and fit for reform school? Was she a fit mother? Were her claims that she was raped or assaulted to be given credence? Was an employer to be wary of offering her a job? Even social workers kept records, and the privacy that the middle-class people believed in was much less plausible in an agency that, for all of its humanitarian concerns, was part of a public effort to deal with the social problems of being poor and black, young and pregnant. In the mid-1960s, neither being middle-class and white, nor being an illicitly pregnant refined girl constituted a social problem.

In the Project girls' circumstances, there was no chance of rescue by redefining the past psychotherapeutically. The teenagers *did* consider themselves girls who had made a mistake, however.

Salvaging one's reputation did not have the same meaning for the black teenagers of the Project because reputation in the black community did not offer the same protection that it did for the middle-class women. Since the pregnancies of black women were not kept secret, the "mistake" view didn't function to preserve future options by salvaging their past reputations, but it did serve to say that they were not condemned to carry out the common fate they saw around them, of women on welfare, struggling to support their children, with or without a husband. Rains said, "An illegitimate pregnancy jeopardized more than moral respectability for these girls; it lessened their changes for continuing in school and possibly attaining a better way of life. Marriage was seen by many Project girls and their parents as more of an obstacle than a solution to this other type of respectability. As one girl put it:

> Some of these girls just don't think ahead. They think they'll get married and leave school and they don't think that maybe their husband won't stay around and then where will they be when they can't do anything. Some of them don't even graduate from grammar school. What kind of mother could you be not even out of grammar school? If your kid has work from school, you can't even help him, maybe can't even read. At least that's one thing I've learned. When I got pregnant, my mother talked to me. She told me that everybody's ship is going to come in sometime, but that you had to be there when it came 'cause you can only get it once. She said I was only part way up the gangplank. I think it is foolish to get married with so much ahead of you. (Rains 1971, 39–40)

Going to the Project school was not simply an illusion of this other type of respectability. It was *in fact* continuing on the path to respectable adult life by continuing in *school*. At fourteen, school was a major step toward a respectable life.

Nearly all of the black young women kept their babies. The social workers regarded it as their responsibility to point out the possibility of adoption or foster-home placement. But girls and their mothers often regarded the suggestion as a moral affront. Here are May's remarks: "She talked to my mother first—asked her did she want me to give the baby up for adoption. My mother say, 'No, May be a nice mother. Yes, she love that child and she feel about it like it was hers. She was mad about it at first.'" These feelings show in differences in the ways children were raised.

For most of the middle-class young women, "moving on" was publicly moving back to the original position of "respectable young woman." The passage was a loop. For the young black women of the project, moving on was moving from "pregnant girl" to "girl with a baby." It was this transformation that, in the end, stifled public comment. From Rains's quotations, it appears that the Project girls gained strength from their *own* love and pride in the baby ("I love my baby enough that I don't care what they say" [Rains 1971, 169]). But also, they gained from other people's love of babies—their interest focused on baby rather than girl ("They just like babies"). Rains describes the situation:

> The Project girls shared a way of life in which motherly responsibilities were usually diffused among a number of persons. The Project girls themselves had been involved in caring for their younger brothers and sisters and were themselves cared for by a variety of aunts, stepfathers and stepmothers, mothers—persons who for reasons of blood relationship or sense of kinship took interest in them. The Project girls' babies thus did not so much enter the world to an exclusive relation to a single mother, as to a web of persons with a variety of interests and concerns in their welfare. (Rains 1971, 171)

There is much to be learned from Rains's cases. I will begin with some further explanation as to why relying on women's own accounts, as Gilligan does, is not sufficient for understanding the moral institution of life, or for correcting bias in analysis. I'll go on to insist that academics ask serious questions about their authority and responsibility, and conclude with a mention of some positive contributions from my own approach.

We should note that the young women of Kelman Place and Hawthorne House certainly regarded getting pregnant as a moral matter that required explanation. But their explanations changed over time, through the process of the young woman's interactions with others—her intimates, neighbors, the other pregnant young women she met, and particularly, through her interaction with authorities. The young women reported the explanations and changes as belonging to themselves and to their own perceptions (see remarks quoted above in the sections on Kelman Place and Hawthorne House). Yet these explanations were socially constructed, with the help of upstanding members of the general community at Kelman Place, and with the guidance of social workers at Hawthorne House. They were constructed differently in different social locations—differently in the maternity homes than at the Project, and with different effect. Let me discuss the social workers, because their model is in many ways the philosopher's model in ethics.

The authority that the social workers exercised was a professional authority that had been politically won during the 1920s, in the course of the struggle to have the occupation designated a profession. Theirs was a chapter in the great movement of professionalization that began in the United States after the Civil War, a movement that transformed our democracy. Professionalization produced new and powerful authorities who worked at defining health and disease, law and justice, nature and the good life—authorities that came to include not only doctors and lawyers but physicists, botanists, psychologists, and, of course, philosophers (See above, Chapter 4; Addelson 1985). The professional authorities eventually replaced the clergymen and the "educated laymen of good character" as advisors to the nation. The social workers' debunking of the "nice girl" explanation has a place in the secularization of "the moral institution of life" that was concurrent with the professionalization process in the United States (Boller 1981; Haskell 1977). Nonetheless, they retained the basic religious model of explaining human activity: explanation in terms of preconditions of the activity, preconditions that exist somehow within the individual. They differed in the classifications of preconditions, using technical categories of their profession: Preconditions may be irrational, as when a person is acting out, but with the social workers' help the emotional preconditions may be dealt with, and then the young woman may make free and reasonable choices. That is where the philosophers come in.

I am not here disputing the truth of psychotherapeutic explanations. I am saying that truth does not come in a bottle with a label on it that says, TRUTH. What we call "truth" is based on the authority of someone or other. Some truths are based on "what everyone knows" ("everyone" here referring to some particular selection of people). Some truths may be based on first-hand experience. But in professionalized fields, the confirmation or falsification of truths is handled by professionals. What is relevant here is the authority the social workers had in constructing the explanations of the young women's pasts—explanations accepted by the young women at Hawthorne House and rejected by the young women at the Project (though despite this rejection, the social worker's explanation carried the day in the official records).

The rational action the social workers postulated as the fruit of overcoming denial is, in fact, the model of moral activity that many philosophers presuppose as the way that moral reasoning or moral explanation relates to moral activity. Preconditions exist in the explicit reasoning process that the agent goes through, although people also act out of preconditions of habit, unexpressed motive, good character, and so on. Even unarticulated preconditions can be retroactively captured in explanations. This is quite a realist view, for it presupposes that the preconditions of the act are objectively there to be uncovered later, by the person herself or by an outside judge. It requires, for the paradigm cases at least, that one's moral reasoning actually be applied in a situation so as to bring about one's action.

Unfortunately, there exists no adequate explanation of how moral reasoning is applied by a rational agent in an actual situation. Philosophers do not usually raise the question. Psychologists have not even hypothesized such a model, much less discovered the actual mechanisms (see note 4). But even if there *were* such a model hypothesized, we would have to ask, "On whose authority do we use this model in explaining our activities? By what social means is that authority exercised? And what consequences does its use have? All of these questions have answers in Rains's studies, and we see that consequences differ by class and race. These questions have answers, even when Rains's subjects come to report the explanations as their own.

Gilligan doesn't use the "precondition" model in an obvious way. Her interest lies more in tracing the women's changing explanations and their relationship to changing conceptions of self. Her approach may be analogous to that of multitudes of social scientists who investigate folk explanations while remaining agnostic as to whether they pick out existing objects or acts—phlogiston and witches are time-worn examples. It is a peculiar sort of bracketing (to use the phenomenologist's term). Gilligan herself developed the "responsibilities-care" orientation by seeing that the Kohlberg scheme imposed gender dominance. She saw that moral reasoning was being socially constructed in the Kohlberg "laboratory" and classroom. But in developing her new "orientation," she did not relinquish the supposition that group members individually apply the concepts she defines in understanding their own moral activities (or in understanding what other group members do). In assuming this, she removes the moral institution of life from the social and political institutions of life. She ignores the processes by which explanations come to be socially constructed. It is within those processes that systematic relations of gender, age, class, and race come into existence and come to be preserved.

With their analyses of the moral institution of life, philosophers contribute to the processes and the preservation of systematic gender, age, class, and race divisions. Their authority to publish and teach their opinions is a professional authority; it was politically won and it is politically maintained (see Boller 1981; Haskell 1977). Philosophers cannot simply assume that "academic freedom" allows them to teach and publish whatever definitions of the moral institution their graduate schools supported. Academic freedom is a political instrument, and it should not be used unless academics make explicit their moral, social, and political responsibilities. At a minimum, that requires knowing the implications of our work, and it requires asking by what authority we define the moral institution of life.

The dominant philosophic definitions of the moral institution analyze abortion as a conflict of rights. Academic feminists (including Gilligan) rightly complain that this silences women. Other academics complain that it silences Christians. By the results of Kohlberg's tests, it silences nonwhites, members of lower classes, and citizens of Third World nations—to say nothing of the clients of our prisons, mental institutions, and elementary schools. Some citizens complain about secular humanism, values clarification courses, and about the ethics hidden in sex-education courses and family-planning services. The ethical theories that support the definition of abortion as a conflict of rights are implicated in all these things. It is within these sorts of contexts that philosophers must ask about their own authority and responsibility. Members of all professions must do so, and the questions cannot be answered in narrow professional terms.[11] Feminist academics must ask as well, and their questions of authority and responsibility are as tangled as those of mainstream academics.

I believe that the first implication of being responsible in analyzing "the moral institution of life" is that philosophers must vacate their armchairs, and developmental psychologists must vacate their "laboratories." Those who cannot give up the falsified models and abstract, elitist thinking should face the fact that the cloak of professional authority has come to resemble the emperor's new clothes. They might act honestly by quitting academia and earning their pay as workers for interest-group organizations or industry (which would offer interesting market tests for theory validity). Those who elect to remain academics would have to vacate their armchairs and develop proper empirical and political sensitivities and go humbly to look the moral institution of life in the eyes. Humbly and

naked, without the academic robes that have hidden our parts in the construction of moral explanations—hidden them from ourselves if from no
others.

But I want to end this chapter on a joyous note about what we begin
to see if we pay heed to what is hidden and the means by which it is hidden. My discussion of Rains's cases makes it evident that the moral institution of life cannot be understood by looking at moral explanations and
ignoring silences and secrets (see Rich 1979). The moral superiority of the
respectable higher classes owes less to money than to the wealth of secrecy
they control and use to cover their moral mistakes. The secrecy required is
an official one, as well as a private, family one. The advantage of this
wealth is evident when we see the consequences of lacking it—for example, in the publicity the young Project women faced, both in their
neighborhoods and in the official records. Their experiences went on
record, not in their own terms, but in the terms of the professionals.

These things we can learn from Rains's studies. But the general approach that I am suggesting offers us systematic ways of understanding
many things feminists and others have pointed out. For example, when we
take "abortion" as a folk term, we can trace its construction with Ruth
Hubbard, Barbara Ehrenreich, and Deirdre English, and many others who
have spoken of physicians' authority in medicalizing the definitions of our
life experiences.

By taking the passage through abortion as one among a network of
passages, we begin to have a way of representing some of the most fruitful
criticisms of the standard analysis of the moral problem of abortion as a
conflict of rights. The network of passages gives us a way to represent
Hauerwas's Christian concerns. It gives us a way to represent Harrison's
and Whitbeck's feminist concerns, and it shows that they are right in saying that the conflict of rights' analysis tears abortion out of the context of
women's lives. In fact, the moral-passages approach shows how the conflict
of rights' analysis tears abortion out of the context of women's, children's,
and men's lives—for although we may not make our passages as equals, we
do make them together.

## Notes

*Acknowledgments:* I am grateful for suggestions given by my commentators, the editors
of *Women and Moral Theory,* and students at SUNY Stony Brook. I owe particular thanks to
Howard Becker, Merideth Michaels, and Phil Temko. Prudence Rains was kind enough to

read the original version of the essay. I am grateful to Libby Potter and Caroline Whitbeck for intellectual aid and comfort.

1. For the most part, questions of sex have been ignored by secular, academic moral theorists. Susan Teft Nicholson did raise the issue of sex—though only to dismiss it—in her book *Abortion and the Roman Catholic Church* (Knoxville: Religious Ethics, 1978). She found a two-fold basis for Roman Catholic opposition: abortion as a sin of sex, and abortion as a sin of killing. Kurt Baier says in his introduction to the book, that Nicholson "doesn't probe" the argument on sex "because it rests on a moral premise, the tying of sexual activity to reproduction, which is not now . . . an element in the common moral convictions of our society" (xvii). But this is a curious remark, because we could just as well say that Nicholson *divides* sex and procreation, and then sees the religious ethic as joining them out of a "conviction" that is prohibited in a "secular society." Baier's appeal to "common moral convictions" is, in fact, an attempt to justify a particular "secular" authoritative definition of abortion. The moral problem of abortion becomes a question of fetal life.

2. Many thanks to Merideth Michaels for helping me to state Harrison's position in this perspicuous way.

3. Later work by Gilligan and others shows that the care orientation also exists in presentation of dilemmas (see Gilligan 1984a)

4. For a psychologist's case that we have none, see Blasi 1980. See also papers in *Ethics* 92, no. 3 (April 1982). Mills 1963 and Aubert 1965 are provocative, but Blumer (1969) offers my theoretical basis. Hauerwas's analysis in terms of narratives is an attempt to overcome what I would call a "free will" analysis of the moral institution. I am not saying we do not have free will. (Nor is Hauerwas.) I am saying there is no psychological or sociological model for either free or unfree will, that is, that the notion should be jettisoned, and our decisions and choices must be otherwise analyzed. That would required jettisoning most of philosophical ethics.

5. I also owe more than I can say to Arlene Kaplan Daniels.

6. The concept of a career came initially from the sociology of occupations, particularly as it was developed by Everett Hughes and his students. It very quickly came to have a broader use, referring to patterns of changes over time, which were common to members of a variety of social categories, not merely occupational ones. For example, Howard Becker described the career of a marijuana user; Prudence Rains described the career of an unwed mother; Erving Goffman described the career of a mental patient.

Goffman takes a different emphasis from Becker, though the notion of a career is in many ways similar. In his essay "The Moral Career of the Mental Patient," Erving Goffman puts forth reasons why the notion is valuable. "One value of the concept of career is its two-sidedness. One side is linked to internal matters held dearly and closely, such as the image of self and felt identity; the other side concerns official position, jural relations, and style of life, and is part of a publicly accessible institutional complex. The concept of career, then, allows one to move back and forth between the personal and the public, between the self and its significant society, without having to rely overly for data upon what the person says he thinks he imagines himself to be" (Goffman 1961, 127). Goffman calls his essay, "an exercise in the institutional approach to the self."

7. A fourth source of information was a small pilot study of contraceptive use among sexually experienced college women, which Rains used to supplement the published literature in giving the setting, or the origin point, from which unwed mothers begin their careers.

8. This situation must be placed within systematic social themes. Rains does not do so.

9. Cover stories were used to explain a young woman's absence from home ground and to explain her pregnancy in the new public life—for example, wearing a wedding ring and calling herself "Mrs." saved embarrassment at temporary jobs, or while out shopping. Within the maternity home, secrecy was maintained by not using last names, by using letter drops, and by various other means.

10. It was jointly sponsored by the city's boards of mental health and education. The services offered under the Project included a day school for the girls, prenatal care (at public clinics), and counseling. Initially, the school was limited to black girls in elementary school. The girls were from low-income backgrounds, and many had records of truancy. When Rains did the major part of her study, most of them were about fourteen—many of them old for their grade because they had been "held back."

11. John Ladd has done very interesting work on professional responsibility, and philosophers would benefit from taking some of the advice he offers to engineers. See, for example, his "Philosophical Remarks on Professional Responsibility in Organizations" (Applied Philosphy vol. I, no. 2 (Fall 1982). Both Ladd and Whitbeck are offering *moralities*, and at the moment, I find some version of their responsibility ethics to be useful to me as a member of a profession speaking to members of my own and other professions, that is, as a folk morality in which my own place is clearly one of the folk. I do not mean that I can ever cease being one of the folk—that is the myth of disinterest and objectivity that shrouds professional authority. There is a difference in authority, social position, and political meaning when I talk as a worker to workers about our common moral concerns and when I speak as a professional out of the social location of academia. I have very serious reservations about taking my academic task to be to formulate an ethics or a metaethics. My discussion of moral passages is meant to be an aid to uncovering the moral institution of life, not a definition of it.

# 6

## Why Philosophers Should Become Sociologists (and Vice Versa)
### (1988)

Today, philosophy and sociology are in ferment—new concepts and theories, new methods, even newly opened fields of research. The ferment is the consequence of many historical changes, but intellectually, within the disciplines, it owes a great deal to the collapse of what has been dubbed "the enlightenment orientation." That orientation came to dominance in sociology and philosophy departments in the United States after World War II, though it has often been read back into history, particularly to the origins of modern science and liberal democratic theory (see MacIntyre 1984).[1]

Under the enlightenment orientation, objective knowledge is the goal of sociology and philosophy—one world, one truth, a unity of science and a unity of morality or all mankind.[2] It is the foundation of a liberal, secular humanism. This metaphysics and epistemology justified the methods philosophers and sociologists used within their disciplines, and it justified their authority as educators and policy advisors. The justification is familiar to sociologists.

> An enlightenment orientation toward social science has been a major presupposition of conventional sociology. The hope has been that public policy could be made to rest on a body of politically neutral theory and fact, validated by scientific method and beyond the disputes of moral and political sides. (Gusfield 1984, 48)

Philosophers rely on conceptual or linguistic methods to provide theories and analyses that are also supposed to be neutral among moral and political sides. The enlightenment orientation justifies scholars' authority as researchers and as educators and policy advisors. It sets philosophers and sociologists as professional experts, not as partisans.

Even in its heyday, the enlightenment orientation was never without its serious critics. By the mid-1960s, the criticisms were widespread and widely known in the United States—in history, sociology, philosophy, and even some of the natural sciences. Thomas Kuhn described scientific progress in terms that had more to do with science training and politics than with enlightenment rationality. [3]

In philosophy W. V. Quine made seemingly parochial arguments against the analytic-synthetic distinction. But one consequence of the arguments is that there are no neutral, theory-independent, observable facts. Observation (Quine said) is polluted by scientific language and theory, and by the language and conceptual scheme of the society at large (Quine 1963, 1969). These arguments have generally been accepted about natural and social science. They affect the philosopher's use of conceptual analysis as well. If observation is inseparable from concept, then concept is inseparable from observation. Scientists have no neutral observational data, and philosophers have no neutral conceptual data—both methods fail when the analytic-synthetic distinction collapses.

In the philosophy of the social sciences, Peter Winch (1972) pressed his earlier distinction between scientist's rules and native's rules. Cultural relativism was extended to fact and science, not simply value and morality. The question became, How are we to study a human world in which meaning and morality, science and truth are all in the process of construction?

In philosophy, there is ferment as scholars work out methods and metaphysics for studying such worlds, but so far, the efforts amount to work of the "transition," as Richard Rorty (1979) calls it, not the new philosophy itself. In contrast, in sociology the collapse of the enlightenment orientation can be seen as a triumph of symbolic interactionism. [4] In this chapter, I will argue that in their research, philosophers should move out of the "transition" by adopting the methods and metaphysics of the symbolic interactionists. That move would resolve the internal problems that philosophers are struggling with within their discipline. That is why (and how) philosophers should become sociologists. It doesn't solve the "external" problems that philosophers and sociologists alike face as educators and policy advisors—Joseph Gusfield's worry. That requires some philosophical work—and so the phrase "(and vice versa)" in the title of this chapter.

Because of our social locations as researchers, educators, and policy advisors, we have, as a matter of fact, institutional warrant for making and dispersing knowledge. The enlightenment orientation, with its ideal of objectivity and the unity of mankind, gives a metaphysical and epistemological basis for that warrant, not a political and institutional one: If we develop our methods properly, we will discover neutral fact and make neutral theory. On the enlightenment approach, the methods and metaphysics that we develop internally justify the authority that we exercise externally.[5] The social, political, and moral questions about our cognitive authority in the society become moot.

Some of the critics of the enlightenment orientation have taken our authority seriously. Feminist Dorothy Smith speaks of the ruling apparatus—"that familiar complex of management, government administration, professions, and intelligentsia, as well as the textually mediated discourses that coordinate and interpenetrate it" (1987, 109). Smith says that sociology is part of the ruling apparatus, and, of course, philosophy is as well. That is another way of talking about our authority as scholars. But we should not understand Smith as saying that as part of the ruling apparatus, we mechanically and ineluctably manufacture oppression. As a feminist scholar, Smith works at producing a sociology for women, presumably as a work of liberation. What ought a sociology for sociologists to be, scientifically and morally, given that sociology is part of what Smith calls the ruling apparatus? A similar question must be asked about a philosophy for philosophers. These are social, political, and moral questions about our cognitive authority in society, questions that become moot under the enlightenment orientation.[6]

As scholarly authorities, symbolic interactionists have been in a curious position. Internally, they use a metaphysics and method that is contrary to the enlightenment orientation, and they have often criticized sociologists using that orientation.[7] But externally, it is the dominant enlightenment orientation that justifies their authority as educators and policy advisors—as part of the ruling apparatus. In its popular (rather than scholarly) form, the orientation justified developing the academic professions and disciplines. If we are explicit about changing our methods and metaphysics to those of symbolic interactionism, then we have to be explicit about the social, political, and moral questions about our authority.

The postenlightenment question is, How are we to study a human world in which meaning and morality, science and truth are all in the process of construction? We must give a double answer, one that takes account of method and metaphysics within the disciplines and our authority outside them. Both philosophers and sociologists have to make the double answer together. Here is my own beginning on the answer.

On the enlightenment orientation, the world is a world of facts and objects in which truth is discovered. My own understanding of the metaphysics of symbolic interactionism is this: Truth is not discovered, it is enacted. Enacting truth requires authority of one sort or another. The folk, whose activities both philosophers and sociologists are concerned with, enact truth in various ways, and both philosophers and sociologists must be able to explain how. Symbolic interactionists have ways of explaining how. But in doing research on those folk, scholars also enact truth. The question of how they do so is in part a question internal to their disciplines, as a question of method and evidence. But it is also, in part, a question of the social organization of knowledge in the United States today. In both cases, it concerns our scholarly authority and our moral responsibility. It concerns our authority as scholars living in the folk society. The question of a sociology for sociologists (or a philosophy for philosophers) is a question of how to be morally, politically, and scientifically responsible in our place within the "ruling apparatus."

I will proceed to expand my remarks by making links between philosophy and sociology. I will draw my cases from ethics and the study of morality, in part because morality is central to sociological work—even as philosophers benefit from knowing the empirical work, sociologists benefit from a more precise understanding of moral theories. And, of course, morality is also central to solving our own scholarly problem of passing beyond the enlightenment orientation.

But first, a look at the state of philosophy today.

## SOME PROBLEMS OF PHILOSOPHY

The profession of philosophy has been in a state of flux for the past fifteen years. The *New York Times* playfully represents the flux as a dispute between analytic philosophers and "philosophers for pluralism" and has fun talking about philosophers doing battle (see, for example, December 20, 1987, front page). The internecine squabble is an outward sign of transformations within analytic philosophy that have already taken place—transformations that came out of a crisis in analytic philosophy. The crisis shows in the titles of books of the recent past—*Beyond Objectivism and Relativism* (Bernstein 1983); *Revisions* (Hauerwas and MacIntyre 1983); *Post Analytic Philosophy* (Rajchman and West 1985); *After Philosophy* (Baynes, Bohman, and McCarthy 1987); and *After Virtue* (MacIntyre 1984). Some of the best sellers are books dismantling the analytic tradition, books of the transition—as Richard Rorty (1979) says of his *Philoso-*

*phy and the Mirror of Nature.* Rorty has remarked, "The notion of 'logical analysis' turned upon itself and committed slow suicide" (1982, 227).[8]

Analytic philosophy came to dominance in the United States after World War II. In its more technical quarters, it was rooted in the scientific revolutions of the earlier twentieth century—not only in physics, but the great advances in logic, formal languages, and metamathematics based on work by Gottlob Frege, Bertrand Russell, Alfred Tarski, Kurt Gödel, and others. In its less technical quarters, including ethics, it relied on the premise that the conceptual (or linguistic) is separable from the empirical (or factual).[9] This is a version of the analytic-synthetic distinction, and it relies on analyses within the enlightenment orientation. The philosophical method is conceptual or linguistic analysis.

Use of the analytic method is widespread, and it dominates the understanding of philosophical research and teaching. In sheer numbers, most analytic philosophers continue with their old methods of conceptual analysis. In "basic research" they construct moral theories or new moral vocabularies. In applied philosophy (a counterpart of policy work in sociology), they analyze moral concepts and arguments that they feel are relevant to social problems (abortion, animal rights, environmental issues are examples), or institutional settings (informed consent, issues in professional ethics), or to everyday life (promising, sex, drugs, love, racism, pornography). The grand effort in the discipline is still on reasoning, and one of the expanding areas for jobs in philosophy is that of "critical thinking." One quite typical introductory text published in 1988 tells students that philosophy trains us in "the critical and rational examination of the most fundamental assumptions that underlie our lives" (Velasquez and Barry 1988, 4). An introductory text in applied ethics defines four goals of the philosophical study of morality: clarification of moral ideas and issues, comprehensive vision of ideas and insights, critical assessment of moral claims, and moral guidance (Martin 1989).

In her 1985 paper reviewing current, workaday, philosophical research, "Standards in Philosophy," analytic philosopher Ruth Macklin cited some "paradigmatic characteristics of the Philosophical enterprise."[10]

A. Defining terms and analyzing concepts.
B. Attending to the logic of arguments, detecting fallacies, and uncovering assumptions.
C. Analyzing and interpreting other writings—within or without philosophy.
D. Constructing hypothetical arguments for or against positions (whether or not one accepts the underlying assumptions or the conclusions of the arguments).

E. Offering sustained normative arguments in favor of a substantive position held by thinkers outside philosophy (Macklin 1985, 276).

This is a succinct statement of the traditional conceptual method.

No one would argue that muddy thinking is preferable to clear thinking. But these definitions of philosophical work preserve the separation of
concept and fact as well as the image of human society as an aggregate of
individuals doing mental gymnastics on the way to separate value choices
and decisions. That is the enlightenment orientation in ethics, as it shows
in a liberal, secular humanism.

What of the "postanalytic philosophers" (as we might call them) who
are making a new philosophy out of the collapse of the enlightenment orientation?[11] In ethics there is a focus on character, community, narrative,
care, trust, and the like. However, the main emphasis is still on language
and ideas. At times, "conversation" is a term that substitutes for method.
Richard Rorty says that philosophy becomes "a voice in the conversation
of mankind" (1979).[12] In the source reader for the television series "Ethics
in America," Lisa Newton speaks of "the conversation about ethics,"
which "intensifies and dies out as the civilizations around it provide or
deny" what is needed for systematic, extended thought (1988, 3). The
prime difficulty here is that "conversation of mankind" is a metaphor
when we need to know literally who is making the meaning of ethics, how
they do it, what authority they exercise in doing it, and what are the outcomes of their doing it. In Dorothy Smith's language, what does this "conversation" amount to in the work of the ruling apparatus? These are not
questions extrinsic to the doing of philosophy, they are questions that are
constitutive of the philosophical task.

The conversational method has not been the only one proposed, of
course. And, other critics certainly have argued that philosophy should be
given up in favor of some science or other. Quine came to that conclusion
from his own criticism of the analytic tradition. His point was that we cannot separate meaning of terms from their references in the world. We cannot peel the concepts off the facts. The consequence is that we cannot
distinguish the task of philosophy from that of science. Quine concluded
that epistemology (the study of our knowledge of the world) should be
done not by philosophers but by neurophysiologists. The neurophysiologists, of course, cannot get ourside our conceptual scheme to give us neutral theories about the objective facts. There are no neutral facts, says
Quine, only a world conceptualized; the best we can do is go with the best
science of the day (Quine 1963, 1969).

Neurophysiology will not do as the best science of the day because the
human world is a world of meaning, and for scientific and moral reasons,

we must respect that. Symbolic interactionism offers appropriate methods for studying a world of meaning. Symbolic interactionism offers an appropriate metaphysics of human nature and human group life (which neurophysiology does not and cannot).

A criticism of the enlightenment orientation must give us a way to move beyond the transition to a new philosophy and sociology. In the next section, I'll discuss the "rules and norms" view of morality that attends the enlightenment orientation in order to give an interactionist criticism that leads to a new understanding of human nature and society. In the following section, I'll discuss postanalytic ethics of narrative and character to show how interactionist sociologists can work with philosophers in making a more adequate ethics. In the last section, I will return to the fundamental question of how our method and metaphysics can allow us to do responsible sociology and philosophy, even within the ruling apparatus.

## MORAL THEORY: PRINCIPLES AND RULES

In *The Idea of a Social Science*, Peter Winch claimed that "the analysis of meaningful behaviour must allot a central role to the notion of a rule; that all behaviour which is meaningful (therefore all specifically human behaviour) is ipso facto rule governed" (1958, 51–52). Not everyone agrees with Winch—Quine talked about neurophysiology replacing epistemology; behavioral psychologists and population geneticists formulate their own theories. Not everyone who agrees with Winch's remark means the same thing by it. But the view that meaningful behavior involves rules has been compelling for many people. The ethics of principles and rules is one important mainstream interpretation of it.

*The Encyclopedia of Philosophy* was published in 1968. The philosopher writing the entry "Rules" gave a general statement of the approach in ethics. He describes rules as "prescribed guides for conduct," which are essential to any practice or institution "such as a game"—and he gives the standard philosophic examples of baseball, bridge, and informal children's games. He continues:

> Morality is a rule-governed activity that guides conduct and molds and alters actions and attitudes. . . .
> Moral rules are precepts that ought to be followed, whether they are in fact followed or not. Moral rules, in this sense, are very different from rules which define customs and practices: one can find out

empirically what rules people advocate or observe, but, as Hume and G. E. Moore insisted, one cannot determine by such empirical study whether these rules really ought to be followed—that is, whether they are moral rules. (*Encyclopedia of Philosophy:* s.v. "rules," 232)

These remarks presuppose that morality has to do with rules (or principles) and that there is some criterion for distinguishing moral rules from rules of custom. The encyclopedia sets a division of labor between philosophers and social scientists: Philosophers set out the criterion, social scientists empirically investigate the customs. The remarks presuppose a metaphysics of human nature and group life and a philosophic method.

In the enlightenment orientation, there are two aspects to the distinction between moral and customary rules that are important for sociologists to understand. The first is set in terms of the distinction between autonomy and heteronomy, and it concerns the way in which the moral rules affect an individual's decisions and actions. An individual acts autonomously when he or she freely and rationally chooses the rule that governs his or her behavior. In contrast, a person acts heteronomously when his or her behavior is conditioned by custom or arises out of socialization. In this aspect, genuine moral decision and action is contrasted with mere customary behavior. Both involve rules. Both take the individual as the source of decision and action. But the way the rules enter is different. Philosophers analyze rules and reasoning allegedly involved in autonomous moral action; sociologists describe rules and behavior allegedly involved in heteronomous moral action.

The second aspect concerns the nature of the rules: The form of moral rules is different from that of customary rules. In one of its phrasings, Kant's categorical imperative gives a criterion for distinguishing genuine moral rules from other rules: Act always so that you could consistently will your maxim to be a universal law. As a criterion, the imperative is a second-order principle that we are to use to criticize our rules of practice. Philosophers have put this by saying that genuine moral rules or principles must be universalizable. Although Kant believed that the imperative defined one morality for all rational beings, most analytic philosophers would not require that all human groups have the same rules. But though the rules might have different content, to be moral rules they would have to satisfy the universalizability criterion. And to be morally rational, group members would have to give reasons in terms of the moral rules and principles, accept reasons in those terms, and criticize the rules they use by some version of the categorical imperative. This argument acknowledges the fact of cultural difference while preserving the moral unity of mankind.

Contemporary philosophers working in principle ethics downplay or ignore the claim that philosophers are supposed to analyze the a priori framework for human morality. However, they keep the definition of moral rationality, and they keep the a priori, conceptual method. Faced with the moral diversity of the United States, many of them have retreated to analyzing the principles and rules of "public morality" in the United States. Public morality is the morality of obligations and rights that we are said to share in the United States (or perhaps in the West), in contrast to various religious or ethnic or communal or individual moralities. For the most part, it is what Lawrence Kohlberg (1971) called "the official morality of the United States" (level three, stage five of his developmental scheme). Ruth Macklin's remarks (quoted above) on "paradigmatic characteristics of the philosophical enterprise" describe this sort of work in applied ethics. The "official morality" shares the liberal, secular humanist metaphysics of individuals as the source of decisions in a society that is an aggregate of ideally free, rational atoms.

There has been sustained criticism of this approach. In fact, when Winch wrote that "all specifically human behavior is ipso facto rule governed," he did not mean that the governing rules exist in some reified conceptual or linguistic form that is open to "objective" analysis by sociologists and philosophers. Quite the contrary. His point, following Wittgenstein, is that the meaning of the rules is made by group members in action together, as they apply the rules in living their personal and group lives. In some ways, this is close to symbolic interactionism. [13]

In his statement on the metaphysics of interactionist sociology, Herbert Blumer says,

> A gratuitous acceptance of the concepts of norms, values, social rules, and the like should not blind the social scientist to the fact that any one of them is subtended by a process of social interaction—a process that is necessary not only for their change but equally well for their retention in a fixed form. It is the social process in group life that creates and upholds the rules, not the rules that create and uphold group life. (1969, 19)

This statement puts the focus not on the rules and principles but on their creation and retention. More than that, it offers a metaphysics of the human world in which the creation of moral theories and vocabularies is shown to be a political act, not simply a conceptual one. With such a metaphysics, we need an empirical method, not a conceptual one.

Howard Becker writes in more general terms of ways in which rules and definitions of all sorts operate in the process of creating and maintaining social structure.

> Interactionist theories of deviance, like interactionist theories generally, pay attention to how social actors define each other and their environments. They pay particular attention to differentials in the power to define; in the way one group achieves and uses the power to define how other groups will be regarded, understood, and treated. Elites, ruling classes, bosses, adults, men, Caucasians—superordinate groups generally—maintain their power as much by controlling how people define the world, its components, and its possibilities, as by the use of more primitive forms of control. They may use more primitive means to establish hegemony. But control based on the manipulation of definitions and labels works more smoothly and costs less; superordinates prefer it. (1973, 204)

Rather than rules and principles defining the morality of a group, the proper group members are "morally bound to accept the definition imposed on reality by a superordinate group in preference to the definitions espoused by subordinates" (Becker 1970, 126).

Here we see the question of scholars' authority and our place in the ruling apparatus. In the United States scholars are members of a superordinate group. Philosophers (and other academics, of course) have significant "power to define," as Becker puts it.

The political consequences of an unexamined "power to define" are blatant in applied ethics. For example, analytic philosophers regularly define the moral problem of abortion as a conflict of rights: the right of the woman to determine what happens in and to her body versus the right to life of the fetus. Despite much criticism, that definition is still the one that dominates introductory texts and classroom discussion. It formulates the central moral issue of the social problem of abortion in a way that limits debate. It leaves in limbo those who oppose or support public policies on abortion on moral grounds of love, sexuality, or the good of mankind, rather than on the basis of rights. In "clarifying the moral issue," the analytic philosophers silence others.[14] To the degree that they do so, they define public morality, not analyze it—a problem that is analogous to the much-discussed issue of sociologists defining social problems. But philosophic method and metaphysics obscure this fact, making it difficult to face the responsibilities of an elite defining the public morality.

The scholarly error can basically be seen as a false understanding of human nature and human group life. These philosophers analyze the products of group life—rules and individuals are both products. In doing so, they ignore the process by which the products come to be constructed as products. They study group life as if it consisted of objects, not actions; rules and individuals, not collective making of meaning. These mistakes lead to their faulty method. They also, of course, lead to moral failure. Although the analytic philosophers have always been outstanding at criticizing their intellectual work within their disciplines ("the notion of logical analysis turned upon itself and committed slow suicide"), they have traditionally ignored the social organization of knowledge and their place in it.[15] With their expertise justified by the enlightenment orientation, analytic philosophers have refused to discuss their actual place in the ruling apparatus. For them, the large questions of scholarly authority and responsibility are moot.

Today, many of the vanguard workers in philosophical ethics have rejected the old rules-and-principles view and are devising new approaches to moral theory. Because I am seriously recommending that philosophers become sociologists (and vice versa), I'll describe some of the new work on narrative, to make links between philosophy and sociology.

## NARRATIVE, CHARACTER, AND THE SELF

The premises on the rational and moral unity of mankind collapsed along with the enlightenment orientation. The new premises include the thesis that the human world is structured by language in ways that vary with convention and forms of life: There is no way to get at the world outside of language, either to compare language with the world or to compare different forms of life (or even scientific paradigms) with each other. There is no neutral, outside vantage point for an observer to take. One way the premises are interpreted in the new ethics is by emphasizing narrative language.

Over the past generation, narrative has become increasingly important as a scholarly method in history, women's studies, psychology, political science, and even in some quarters of sociology (see Polkinghorne 1987). Jerome Bruner has elevated narrative to one of the two basic modes of human cognition, the other being the logico-scientific mode that is used in the morality of principles and rules, the mode presupposed in the enlightenment orientation (Bruner 1986). In contrast, narrative is said to be historical and contextual. Alasdair MacIntyre is a major proponent of the narrative approach.

MacIntyre uses narrative as his own philosophical method, telling a story of intellectual arguments from the Middle Ages to the present as a way of defining and criticizing the enlightenment orientation.[16] He also claims that narrative is the way human beings explain the moral doings in life: Man is a storytelling animal. MacIntyre prefers to talk about intelligibility rather than rationality, and he claims that we make things intelligible through narrative. Our human nature differs from the beasts' nature because we converse and tell stories, and because we have histories and biographies. He says,

> Every moral philosophy offers explicitly or implicitly at least a partial conceptual analysis of the relationship of an agent to his or her reasons, motives, intentions and actions, and in so doing generally presupposes some claim that these concepts are embodied in or at least can be in the real social world. (1984, 23)[17]

His analysis is that narrative (in history and biography) relates agent to motive, intention, and action.

Richard Bondi states a principle of the narrative approach when he says, "Human beings are creatures formed in communities marked by allegiance to a normative story [or narrative]. This formation can best be discussed in the language of character" (1984, 201). Human nature is said to be essentially historical, and character and community necessarily linked. Human beings require "a narrative to give our life coherence" (Hauerwas 1977, 27).[18]

This approach in ethics seems compatible with C. Wright Mills's well-known discussion of vocabularies of motive. Motives, Mills says, are explanations given in answer to questions about a person's activity. The search for "real" motives is mistaken.

> Rather than fixed elements "in" an individual, motives are the terms with which interpretation of conduct by social actors proceeds. This imputation and avowal of motives by actors are social phenomena to be explained. The differing reasons men give for their actions are not themselves without reasons. (1963, 439–40)

Using narrative as the mode of explanation in moral theory makes philosophical sense of Mills's remarks. We may need a conceptual analysis of the relationship of an agent to his or her reasons and motives (as MacIn-tyre says), but we must proceed by seeing how the relationship is socially constructed in the making of the narrative. We need empirically adequate concepts, theories, methods, and a stock of good empirical studies.[19]

If we insist on empirical adequacy, we begin to see how "narrative" operates in creating and maintaining the social order. In interactionist field studies, we find that some people have the authority or power to de-fine the terms in which their own and other people's stories are to be offi-cially narrated. This authority must be taken into account.[20] There are as many errors in speaking of the narrative of a community as there are in speaking of the rules or principles of a community, and Blumer's advice is as good here as there: The processes of human group life must be known, and scholars should not take the products as self-evident. This is true whether we call the products rules or narratives.

If we say the moral world consists in action interpreted through nar-rative, then we need scholarly methods, concepts, and theories suited to studying such a world of action. We need to find out what the narratives are and how they are constructed in specific cases. This requires methods, concepts, and theories of an empirical science. But the science cannot be empirical in the enlightenment sense that either narrative or construc-tions exist as neutral data. In the rest of this section, I'll mention some of the interactionist concepts and theories that I find useful to moral theory.

It is in theory guided by field studies that the symbolic interactionist tradition is most valuable—including its accounts of the self, character, and virtue and vice. Studies of deviance are prime examples, particularly because they give us concepts to guide the study. For example, Lemert's notion of secondary deviance shows how a self and human character are formed in the labeling process, that is, in the course of acquiring the biog-raphy of a deviant (Lemert 1951).

The notion of a career has been useful in a multitude of field studies. Erving Goffman was only sometimes a symbolic interactionist. But his widely quoted remark from "The Moral Career of the Mental Patient" states how the dual nature of the self is captured by the concept.

> One value of the concept of career is its two-sidedness. One side is linked to internal matters held dearly and closely, such as the image of self and felt identity; the other side concerns official position, jural relations, and style of life, and is part of a publicly accessible institu-tional complex. The concept of career, then, allows one to move back and forth between the personal and the public, between the self

and its significant society, without having to rely overly for data upon what the person says he thinks he imagines himself to be. (1961, 127)

Goffman calls his paper "an exercise in the institutional approach to the self."

In "Moral Passages" (Chapter 5), I used research by Prudence Rains to talk about a network of careers that may chart social options available to different people within a group. Rains did several field studies in the late 1960s, which she reported and discussed in her book *Becoming an Unwed Mother*. They included studies of mainly white and middle-class young women at a home for unwed mothers and of black, mainly poor teenagers at a day school for unwed mothers.

Rains's studies make it clear that narratives and biographies were indeed constructed as accounts of the young women's behavior. They show that the social workers involved had tremendous influence in "coauthoring" the narratives of the mostly white, middle-class women, and very little influence in coauthoring the black teenagers' personal biographies. In the case of the black teenagers, certain narratives were recorded in official places—with the police, the schools, the social-service agencies, and the registry of births. One of the teens said of officials, "They keep records."[21] The black teens had, in effect, at least two biographies—the one they lived in the home neighborhood and the one in the official records. And, of course, all of them had many more "narratives" than that. Unitary life histories are for public figures, and for them only as they appear in school history books.

There are other new approaches in ethics that stress narrative and the historical nature of the self. Under the rules-and-principles ethics, the moral notions of responsibility and care were neglected in favor of obligations and rights. Carol Gilligan's work (1982) is probably the best known of the efforts to make notions of responsibility and care central.[22] Gilligan developed the responsibility-care orientation by criticizing Lawrence Kohlberg's principle morality of obligation and rights. The latter imposed male gender dominance. Gilligan saw that moral reasoning was being socially constructed in the Kohlberg "laboratory" and classroom. But in spite of that criticism, she herself ignored the processes by which narratives are made. It is within these processes that systematic relations of gender, and of age, race, class, ethnicity, and so on, are constructed.[23]

On the other hand, with the help of moral theorists, it may be possible to answer some of the criticisms aimed perennially at interactionist work. One common complaint has been that the tradition emphasizes the social at the cost of the personal—the public at the cost of the internal self and its creativity. An analogous criticism is that the tradition emphasizes the cognitive at the cost of the emotional. Some moral theorists and some feminist theorists offer help here.

Richard Bondi cirticizes some of the "narrative" moral theories because they do not give a way of speaking about the self as we experience it, which is at the same time the self in relation to the world. As a first step toward correcting the defects, he sets out "the elements of character" that must be accounted for and analyzed. They include the human capacity for intentional action; the involvement that affections and passions have with moral action and character; the subjection to the accidents of history; and what he calls "the capacity of the heart," "that intimate mix of memory, imagination and the desire for union we experience as marking the center of ourselves" (1984, 204–5). Bondi is setting out a program rather than giving a finished analysis, but it is a program that is important for both sociologists and philosophers.

Other philosophers have other offerings. For example, Annette Baier has written on the importance of trust as a moral concept that is essential to understanding community (1986). It is also important for interactionists to understand the moral notion of responsibility. The old "principle morality" and the old "rules and norms" sociology dealt with obligations and sanctions. Responsibility is receiving renewed attention in philosophy, and it is a moral notion that fits better with an ethics of narrative and character (Ladd 1970; Whitbeck 1983).

At this point, we need to turn more directly to interactionist metaphysics and method and its relation to scholarly authority.[24]

## METHODS AND MORALS

The enlightenment world was one of objects and concepts that could be objectively observed and neutrally reported. In contrast, the postanalytic philosophers and the symbolic interactionists agree that the human world is a world not of objects but of action and interpretation. Our question here is, What is a morally and scientifically responsible way to study such a world, given our social positions as scholarly authorities within the ruling apparatus? This is the double question that concerns responsible methods and metaphysics to serve as a basis for responsible work by members of our disciplines for members of the society as a whole. On the one hand, it is a question of honesty in our vocations; on the other, it is a question of responsible service—I hope we are serving the people as members of the ruling apparatus, rather than serving the ruling apparatus (or our own little disciplinary segments of it).

The methods and metaphysics of symbolic interactionism are those of an empirical science—but not an empirical science as defined within the enlightenment orientation. Our first movement toward meeting the double question is to see what sort of empirical science symbolic interactionism is.

Herbert Blumer's statement of the basic premises of interactionism characterize the empirical world that social scientists and philosophers study as scholars.

> Let me begin by identifying the empirical social world in the case of human beings. This world is the actual group life of human beings. . . . The life of a human society, or of any segment of it, or of any organization in it, or of its participants consists of the action and experience of people as they meet the situations that arise in their respective worlds.
>
> . . . The empirical social world consists of ongoing group life and one has to get close to this life to know what is going on in it. If one is going to respect the social world, one's problems, guiding conceptions, data, schemes of relationship, and ideas of interpretation have to be faithful to that empirical world. (Blumer 1969, 35, 38)

Blumer talks about respecting the social world and having concepts and methods that are faithful to it. The methods Blumer names include direct observation, field study, participant observation, case study, interviewing, use of life histories, use of letters and diaries, public documents, and conversation (Blumer 1969, 50). These are methods that are learned, used, criticized, changed, and developed, that is, they are scientific methods, not procedures carved in stone. Among these sociologists, the methods are examined continually to see whether they allow researchers to remain faithful to the empirical world. They are also examined to see whether they allow researchers to be respectful of the subjects and cognizant of their own authority in the research situation.[25] The methods are the basis of gathering data, even for dissident sociologists like Dorothy Smith. Criticism comes from "traditionals" and feminists alike. But we must be careful about what "data" means.

Within the enlightenment orientation, the problem of data is an ontological and epistemological one: There must be neutral, observable facts and distinct language and concepts if science is to find out the truth about the objects of the world.[26] This is because the enlightenment truth is one to be discovered. In contrast, as I said at the beginning of the chapter, the interactionist truth is enacted. Under interactionist ontology, facts are enacted through political and social processes.

To a limited degree, the enlightenment notion of truth has been overcome in philosophy and sociology. For example, when Thomas Kuhn discusses revolutionary science, he describes processes by which the facts and truths of a new paradigm come to be enacted within a scientific discipline. Kuhn clung to the enlightenment approach by assuming that scientists had authority to enact truth for the larger society. He did not explicitly analyze scientific authority in *The Structure of Scientific Revolutions*.[27] Enacting facts and truth requires authority of one sort or another. It requires authority to define the world and authority to have the definitions officially accepted. These are startling claims only if we cling to an enlightenment view of facts and truth.

Much interactionist work concerns how truth is enacted among the folk—studies on deviance and social problems fall into this category. Take, as an example, Prudence Rains's study on unwed mothers mentioned above. In the late 1960s in the Midwest, the truth that unwed motherhood was deviant was enacted among her white middle-class subjects by the efforts of families to conceal these pregnancies, by the existence of maternity homes that guarded the secrets, and by the social and economic systems that made it very difficult for the families to raise an "illegitimate" child while preserving the young mother's future options. In the black Chicago neighborhoods, the truth of a girl's having a deviant (or incorrigible) character was constructed by social workers, police reports, and a whole coordinated edifice of action and record keeping.

Today, unwed motherhood is deviant in some communities but not others. Teen pregnancy has emerged out of secrecy and become a social problem. The social problem has been enacted as a fact by thousands of political and scholarly efforts. This does not mean that "if we believe it true, then it is true." Enacting truth is not a matter of mere belief and attitude. Enacting truth means living together so that our worlds, our lives, and our characters are made in certain ways.

The emphasis on enacting truth is connected with knowing how to get along in our collective life rather than knowing that some proposition is true or some fact exists. The enlightenment tradition was obsessed with "knowing that." The analysis of scientific theories and concepts and scientific truth was slave to that obsession. In contrast, the interactionist tradition requires that "knowing how" be taken seriously. Consider Howard Becker's notion of a folk concept.

Folk concepts give meaning to our activities in the sense that they help us know how to do those activities together. Becker says, in fact, that folk concepts are shorthand terms people use to organize the way they do things together (see Becker 1970, 92). They convey a conception of a distinctive way of organizing what we do, including characteristic activities, typical settings, cast of characters, typical careers and problems. The folk term suggests that all these things hang together in a neat pattern. In some interesting cases, like "profession" or "discipline," the term carries with it a justification that rationalizes the social and political place of the work and those who do it. In others, like "lesbian," "drug dealer," or "pregnant teen," the term carries a justification for treating such people and activities as deviant.

Folk concepts are used by us folk to point to what we do, and to coordinate what we do together (in the sense that even a war requires coordinating both sides). Folk terms point out activities that "the folk" take to be the same, in the sense that they know how to do the same thing again. The shorthand folk term may suggest certain neat patterns, but that suggestion is persuasive and used in explanations and arguments that ultimately involve authority, not criteria. Through folk terms, we enact truth and make our communities and our characters.[28]

In discussing how the folk enact truth, I have implicitly made a distinction between the folk ways of enacting the truth that are being described by sociologists, and the ways of enacting truth that sociologists use in doing the describing. In the enlightenment orientation, this is usually set as a normative distinction between the value-laden ways of the folk and the objective, rational ways of the scientist or philosopher. In philosophy, it has sometimes been set as a distinction between unruly ordinary language and precise scientific or philosophical language.

It is obvious that scientists and philosophers are members of the folk, and their ways can be studied. Studying ourselves as members of the folk is essential to our methods and morals. But here I am making a distinction between the ways of the folk that we are describing and the ways that we are using in doing the describing. This can't be reduced to a distinction between the language the folk use versus the language we use in describing them. It is a question of authority and modes of action. To act responsibly, we have to take on the double task of criticizing our methods as well as understanding our authority as professionals, that is, as enactors of truth within the folk society.

If we accept the premise that truth is enacted, then our understanding of concepts and theories must change accordingly. In the enlightenment view, truth is discovered about a world of objects open to neutral observation. Truth is embodied in language, not in action. Scientific concepts must be defined so as to clearly distinguish their instances, ultimately in terms of observation. The definitions have to give necessary or sufficient conditions for the term's application—the movement for operational definitions was one extreme manifestation of this approach.[29] If terms do not give us criteria for telling when an event happens or fails to happen, we will be unable to confirm or falsify our propositions.

The enlightenment account of scientific concepts will not do for a world in which truth is enacted. In contrast, Herbert Blumer calls the sociologists' concepts "sensitizing concepts," or "sensitizing instruments." They are not the sort of concepts that define necessary or sufficient conditions for their instances. With sensitizing concepts, Blumer says, "we seem forced to reach what is common by accepting and using what is distinctive to the given empirical instance." This, he said, is due not to the immaturity of sociology but to the nature of the empirical world, which is its object of study (Blumer 1969, 148).

In his 1987 book *Qualitative Analysis for Social Scientists*, Anselm Strauss lays out some methods appropriate to developing adequate concepts. In contrast to the abstract conceptual analysis of the philosophers, Strauss insists that analysis is synonymous with interpretation of data (1987, 4). The interpretation, and the progressive data collection, must pass through stages of evolution structured according to an ongoing process of coding and memo writing. "Coding" is his general term for conceptualizing the data.

Developing rich and complex concepts with which to discuss a field study, through coding and memo writing, is the focus of Strauss's idea of grounded theory (1987, 26). That is, "theory" in this sense is not an abstract set of universal laws to be tied to observation by definitions of its terms. But it is genuine theory in the sense of giving a general picture of human group life and social structure—as general as the data allow. Theory in a particular field study may use concepts or categories developed in other studies. For example, the concept of a career (and its associated theory) is used in many studies. But the concept must be developed and tested within the present study just as if it were new and derived from the coding of present material. Strauss himself warns against assuming the "analytic relevance of any face sheet or traditional variable such as age, sex, social class, or race until it emerges as relevant" (1987, 32). They too must earn a way into the grounded theory. By using these methods, the community of field-workers continually test theory and develop a system of concepts useful for showing patterns across cases.

At this point, enter the skeptical chorus: To whom are those patterns useful? To whom are they the same—according to whose concepts, rules, theories, practices, language, conversation, or narrative?[30] The answer is that, initially at least, they are patterns according to the researchers' concepts, theories, practices, and so on. Given the reseachers' places of authority in the social organization of knowledge, the concepts may be extended to the rest of the folk through the educational system, the media, and other institutional means. This is how folk understanding changes according to the scholarly way of enacting truth. Initially, the patterns are useful to the researchers, but if the research is successful, they must ultimately be useful to the folk as well, and the folk ways of enacting truth and doing things together. And, at this point, we meet the other side of the double question—the question of responsible service to the people as members of the ruling apparatus.

According to the enlightenment orientation, we do responsible work by sticking to the facts and concepts and leaving the values and policy decisions to the appropriate officeholders. Rejecting the enlightenment orientation leaves us face to face with our moral and political tasks. If the enlightenment approach allowed us to be blindly partisan as a group, we now run the danger of being self-consciously partisan as individuals.

The individualistic metaphysics of the enlightenment orientation has collapsed within the disciplines. But its individualistic, secular humanism remains behind as the folk ethics of most of us scholars. I say folk ethics here because it is an ethics most of us use even when we criticize it. Robert Bellah and Richard Rorty (and many others) individualistically choose to become patriots, then use their authority in advising us to polish up the old stories of the American tradition to serve up to schoolchildren. Other scholars individualistically choose to become feminists or Marxists or minority advocates, then use their authority in espousing whatever cause they feel is appropriate. In their research, these scholars may raise issues and give criticisms that are essential to our work—I am not questioning that. I am saying that we should not reject the old, enlightenment orientation in our methods and metaphysics, then unself-consciously presuppose it in an ethics that has us "choosing" liberalism, Marxism, feminism, or whatever as basic "values" to direct our individual work. This is self-deception, because truth is not enacted by individuals choosing basic values. Values are not ideas on which we act individually—even though our folk concepts may explain them in that way.

Philosophers and other scholars have, of course, influenced the folk explanations and, perhaps, the course of history. In commenting on an earlier version of this essay, Jerry Schneewind argued that inventing moral theory and vocabulary has been, socially and politically, an important philosophical task. He wrote to me concerning Kant's contribution:

> Imagine a society where people weren't well educated and didn't have time to think about politics but are coming to be in that position. Suppose their sole vocabulary was one that stressed individual subordination to the law: to the king, to the pastor, to God. And suppose someone said, "Think of yourselves as making your own laws. All our moral terms can be explained that way. And you then can see that you can't be ruled by just anyone, because you rule yourself first."
>
> There's a political and social point to the Kantian vocabulary; people could use it for definite situated purposes. (Jerry Schneewind, letter to author, fall 1988)

I agree that what Schneewind says is important. Philosophers have filled and will continue to fill political and social roles. And so will sociologists and all the other varieties of humanists and scientists. My point in this chapter is that when we are exercising our authority as members of academic disciplines, we must be morally and intellectually honest about what we are doing. We must consistently extend our sound scholarly methods and judgments into our action as authorities enacting truth in the social world.

Kant devised a moral vocabulary that contributed to social and political changes in the making of the modern world. His moral theory (and its successors) has been a cornerstone of the enlightenment orientation. The most difficult task we scholars face now is overcoming the enlightenment orientation in our work lives, leaving behind the Kantian moral theory and its relativistic, modern successors that I discussed above. To serve others, we have to begin by serving ourselves. We need a moral theory that is useful to us, given our positions of authority, and one that is consistent with our new metaphysics and method. None of the philosophical theories I have mentioned in this chapter will do. They do not take into account the processes by which moral and empirical truth are enacted. The new theory must be one that makes scholarly sense and that can be enacted as we try to do responsible service as scholars and teachers and policy advisors. Making the moral theory requires changing ourselves and our work.

I have argued that, for reasons of good scholarship, sociologists and philosophers should work together. Symbolic interactionism (broadly understood) offers an appropriate metaphysics and method for studying society and making philosophical moral theory. But in the end, I believe that symbolic interactionism requires that we change ourselves and our world. Enacting a new moral theory is the real reason that philosophers should become sociologists (and vice versa).

## Notes

1. I was trained as an analytic philosopher, and I started becoming a sociologist in 1974 when I attended Howard Becker's class in field methods. After that, my sociological training was a kind of informal apprenticeship. I pursued it with the intelligent, patient, and generous help of Howie Becker, Arlene Daniels, Judy Wittner, and Joseph Schneider. In this chapter, I have been helped by comments from the audience and my commentators at the 1988 Stone Symposium of the Society for Symbolic Interaction; I was also helped by the philosophers of the Propositional Attitudes Task Force at Smith College. I owe special thanks to Jerry Schneewind for his comments on the penultimate draft.

2. This last, at least, is the way it appears in Karl Popper's presentations. See Jarvie 1984 for a discussion in these terms.

3. Thomas Kuhn's criticism addresses the internal question of authority in scientific revolution, and he reduces it to disciplinary politics and careerism (Kuhn 1970). He never deals with the question of scientific authority in the society at large, and, in that sense, he does not escape the enlightenment orientation. I say more about this in Chapter 4.

4. I am using "symbolic interactionism" in a broad sense here. In my use the term includes work by some of the ethnomethodologists and by some sociologists who can't really be classified by school. More strictly, symbolic interactionism has philosophical roots in the American pragmatism of the early twentieth century. It should be attractive to philosophers because an important segment of the philosophical vanguard looks back to the pragmatist philosophers Peirce, James, Dewey, and Mead in search of a new foundation for philosophy. But to settle questions of authority and method, we must follow the pragmatist philosophical tradition forward to one of its natural outcomes in a sociological tradition of today. In this normative sense, becoming a sociologist requires working within a research tradition that has corrected and extended the original, philosophical ideas of its founders by making them empirical. It requires working within a tradition whose members create new ideas out of the tradition and correct and extend them in the course of empirical research. What I have just given is, of course, a normative as well as a descriptive characterization of symbolic interactionism—a gesture in the direction of a disciplinary tradition.

5. The distinction between internal and external, once used in history, philosophy, and sociology of science, relies on an enlightenment orientation. I am using it for pedagogical reasons here, not because I believe it constitutes a valid distinction—quite the contrary.

6. My discussion of Dorothy Smith's work in this context comes out of correspondence with Joseph Schneider. Smith's work raises issues that are crucially important to all sociologists and philosophers, not just feminist ones. On the other hand, there may be questions of warrant that Smith needs to address. For example, the institutional possibility of making a sociology for women seems to rely on conventions of autonomy in the scholarly disciplines, which are entangled with individualist, voluntarist notions of science. For feminists, the questions of warrant include the warrants given by a feminist political movement or by "women." See Chapter 12 for some discussion of these issues.

7. For criticisms arising out of the study of social problems, see Spector and Kitsuse 1977 for a review. Gusfield's discussion of Merton and Nisbet in Gusfield 1984 is of this sort.

The labeling theory of deviance was developed in criticism of the enlightenment orienta-tion—that is the implicit basis of Becker's *Outsiders*, for example. There is conflict in these writings because the enlightenment orientation justifies our authority (as I say in the text) but also because as intellectuals, we tend unconsciously to accept a secular humanist morality that is in fact closely tied to the enlightenment orientation. We need a morality based on interactionist sorts of principles (see the last section of this chapter).

8. For a very good, brief overview of the transformation, see the introduction to Baynes, Bohman, and McCarthy 1987, written by Thomas McCarthy.

9. From the logical positivists, the legacy was precision in the philosophy of language and philosophy of science. In other quarters, and particularly in ethics, the influence came from Great Britain, and it included the British "ordinary language philosophers."

10. The paper contains outstanding examples of workaday philosophical work in its various gradations. In her own work, Macklin pays attention to cultural and legal data, however.

11. The term "postanalytic" is inadequate and even misleading, but no single term will do the job. The introduction to Baynes, Bohman, and McCarthy 1987 contains a tax-onomy of philosophic positions that is exact and enlightening but much too complex to use in this chapter.

12. Rorty borrows the phrase from Michael Oakshott.

13. In *The Idea of a Social Science*, the point is less clear than it ought to be because Winch uses simple, hypothetical examples, and he pays little attention to the political nature of the interpretation and application of the rules. To make sense of Winch's (and Wittgen-stein's) recommendations about rules, we need a way to understand the process of applying rules, and that requires an empirical method, not hypothetical examples. In a nutshell, that is why I believe philosophers must become sociologists. I argue this at greater length in the text.

14. Philosophical critics have long made a point of saying this. See, for example Hauerwas 1981 for a philosophical criticism by a theologian, Whitbeck 1982 for a criticism by a feminist philosopher, and MacIntyre 1984 for a widely read effort. See my criticism of the approach (Chapter 3). Meyers and Kittay 1987 contains papers that offer criticisms from a variety of standpoints. As we will see, some of the critics run into difficulties that resemble those the analytic philosophers face.

15. In this they have been supported by distinctions made within the enlightenment orientation—the distinction between justification and discovery and the distinction between internal and external studies of science.

16. His way of judging one position (or conceptual scheme) to be rationally superior to another is to appeal to the history of arguments within a tradition—the rationally superior is the best so far. This line of thought sounds dangerously like the self-congratulatory stories of scientific progress in the West, with the latest being the best so far. Much turns on the em-pirical adequacy of the way the narrative is constructed and the way the authority of the narrator is taken into account. MacIntyre published *After Virtue* in an effort to meet criti-cisms that he didn't pay enough attention to social history (see his remarks on Abraham Edel's criticisms, in the Afterword to the second edition of MacIntyre 1984). I believe Mac-Intyre does not succeed.

17. MacIntyre's is one of the most widely discussed "new" answers to the question, "What is morality?" He pursues many of the questions that Elizabeth Anscombe raised in 1957 in "Modern Moral Philosophy," though from his own more "sociological" angle (An-scombe 1981).

18. Danto 1985 has an interesting discussion of narrative. He still seems to believe in objective facts that can be found out, however. Polkinghorne 1987 gives an overview on the growing importance of narrative in a variety of disciplines. "Moral Passages" (Chapter 5) discusses problems with a model that assumes agents' motives, intentions, and the like are given in the moment of acting or deciding.

19. Consider MacIntyre's remarks on accountability and the interlocking nature of narratives: "Narrative selfhood is correlative. I am not only accountable, I am one who can always ask others for an account, who can put others to the question. I am part of their story, as they are part of mine. The narrative of any one life is part of an interlocking set of narratives. Moreover, this asking for and giving of accounts itself plays an important part in constituting narratives" (1984, 218). There are empirical questions that concern the moral and scientific acceptability of his new theory. Who may ask whom for accounts, and in what terms are the accounts given? Can deviants ask for an account of the respectable (or of the police)? Deviants might ask, but they would certainly not receive answers in their terms. That, after all, is why Becker's book is ambiguously called *Outsiders* (1973). See also my discussion below, on Prudence Rains.

20. Feminist historians (and others) have called this "the periodization problem," the double claim that historians have periodized history in terms of men's experience (a methodological claim) and that history and the narratives of group life have been defined in terms of (higher class) men's experience. See Dye 1979. This is relevant, of course, to Dorothy Smith's discussion of the ruling apparatus and a sociology for women.

21. Rains's studies also show that in the case of the middle-class teenagers in a maternity home, the narratives were not recorded in official places. A conspiracy among family, schools, maternity home, and officials kept these nice, middle-class girls' records clear. MacIntyre speaks of life narratives as being "coauthored," and he says the self inhabits a character whose unity is given as the unity of a character (1984, 217). Maybe so, but we need empirical study to see who does the coauthoring, and to see whether there really is unity of character. Without empirical study, the philosophical theory quickly goes astray.

22. But see also Noddings 1984 and a multitude of other feminist writings.

23. This paragraph is an edited version of a portion of Chapter 5.

24. Joseph Schneider and Jerry Schneewind made comments on an earlier draft that I used in the revision of the next section.

25. Dorothy Smith and other feminist sociologists are particularly sensitive to these questions, but the issues arise in one form or another among many sociologists. See, for example, Stacey and Thorne 1985; Stacey 1988.

26. The data problem is faced fairly directly in the interactionist tradition in a number of discussions of social problems. See Spector and Kitsuse 1977; Rains 1975; Woolgar and Pawluch 1985; and Schneider 1985.

27. Quite a lot is implicit in Kuhn 1970, however, and his discussion of textbooks is particularly important. See my discussion in Chapter 4. Interactionists offer case studies in science that serve as a basis for analyzing the place of scientists and other scholars in the ruling apparatus (see references in Clarke and Gerson 1990).

28. This is as good a place as any to express my wariness about Smith's term, "the ruling apparatus." Smith is making a sociology for women in a political sense, as a feminist much influenced by Marxist themes and politics, and so she selects out elements of social organization that are integrated into a centralized authority, albeit of a many-faceted sort. As professional scholars, we are part of that ruling apparatus. As an interactionist sociologist, however, I see authority operating systematically in all kinds of situations, not all of them linked in interesting ways to centralized authority. I think Smith would agree, of course, and her focus on the ruling apparatus is a mark of her feminist politics. I have my own feminist politics, but in this essay, I am trying to speak to issues that directly concern sociologists and philosophers in their work, whether they take themselves to be feminists or not.

29. Philosophers have struggled with this problem in philosophy of science and philosophy of language. In the "transitional years" of 1965–75, it often emerged as a problem of meaning change, the point being that if the necessary or sufficient conditions for application of a term change when the scientific theory changes, how can we say that a later theory falsifies an earlier one? Paul Feyerabend was famous for his arguments here, but W. V. Quine's arguments against reference have similar import. Rescue efforts were made by Saul Kripke

(with his notion of rigid designators), Hillary Putnam, and many others. Rorty 1979 reviews some of the efforts and gives a bibliography.

30. Enlightenment relativists are part of the chorus, but so are numberless postanalytic philosophers. For an argument directed explicitly against interactionist social problems research, see Woolgar and Pawluch 1985, which reveals how difficult it is for interactionists to leave behind an enlightenment orientation. These questions of sameness are crucial to philosophers and symbolic interactionists. I thank Joseph Schneider for keeping me on the mark here.

# TWO

## WRITING FEMINISM

# 7

## Making Do
(1989)

"The personal is the political" is just a slogan, until it is made into a politics. What does the slogan mean for an Irish working-class woman who made good? What kind of politics grows out of love and anger?

The question is a personal one for me, but it is embedded in a political question that has haunted the women's movement. In its most pointed phrasing, it is an accusation, "The women's movement is white and middle class." How is it possible to have a movement for all women in a nation that is marked by class, race, age, cultural, and religious privilege and the privileges of "being normal"? How is it possible to write feminism using the elite means and methods of the academy?

The answers lie in the thousands of decisions and actions of a movement that succeeds in taking those questions seriously. Without such a movement, my politics cannot be made, and I must find a way to live with the divisions among my own and the contradictions in my life. We do not have such a movement. We do not know if such a movement is possible. We have to make do with what we have. My own answers, such as they are, lie in the story of what has been given to me and what I have done.

I was given the gift of swimming in the waters of the Movement of the 1960s. It began for me in 1962, when I chose to go to a demonstration in San Francisco against the House UnAmerican Activities Committee. But my story isn't about acts I chose to do. It is about the political flood tide that carried me and millions of others.

The world was new to my eyes, a world of folksingers singing politics, students going south for voter-registration campaigns, and increasingly, the double movement of resistance against authority and resistance against the Vietnam War. Our roommate left for the Peace Corps, and my daughters and I read her letters full of triumphs and struggles. I was taking a seminar at Berkeley when the Free Speech Movement broke out, and I helped (modestly) to import it to Stanford. My daughters were in Los Angeles with their grandmother when the Watts riots exploded, and for the first time (but not the last) they heard rifle fire in neighborhoods hidden behind police barricades. It scared us, but we felt raised up to be part of history.

The cloister of my graduate training and the crowded world of politics were not the only places I lived. I shared the worlds my daughters and other family members lived in. My youngest sister had come to California in 1962, and she was living in a lesbian neighborhood of the Haight-Ashbury district. She was there still in 1966 when it became *the* Haight-Ashbury, lodestone of runaways. She and her friends changed with the times, and she moved to a hippie house, a San Francisco Victorian with warrenlike rooms filled, top to bottom, with tripping soul seekers, fogs of incense, ragged blankets, and dirty dishes. I have some beautiful photographs of her, in a picture book called *Hippie High*. She gazes into space, tripping, at the time of the first "Love In" at the Panhandle of Golden Gate Park. In the book there is a photograph of a crowd of hippies sitting cross-legged on the grass. The camera's eye is on a young woman standing alone in their midst. She is dressed only in a sheer cotton Indian shirt, her little nipples pointed up, her arm raised, her head back, swallowing a stream from a Spanish wineskin. A moment on the edge of the Garden, already stepping into Gomorrah. A moment of crossing where innocence meets corruption.

We were all so young, it was all so new, that we could not see what we were making of ourselves and our worlds. But soon, on the streets of Berkeley, there were young women sprawled on dirty sidewalks, wearing shabby Indian bedspreads for saris, nursing lethargic babies. And in the Haight, there were flower children, ragged and drugged and crazy and lost, some of them soon to be dead, seeking God on sidewalks deep in filth.

I was spared this, not because of my vision of corruption, and not because of my principles of politics. I was spared this because of my daughters. They were mine to care for. Out of the chrysalis of a working-class marriage, I had become the brave little mother, standing tall, arms lightly encircling the pretty daughters, bearing witness against war whilst American Legionnaires threw eggs at a line of marchers. I was spared it as well because of my career. By this time I was a professional—but a professional of those times. I had become the pretty young professor who could be mistaken for a bright graduate student, a pal to the boys, a support for activist students. These were my defenses, and they protected me in those danger-

ous years. But with time I became other things, on that border of innocence and corruption.

My little family moved to Chicago in 1967, and it was Chicago that
made my political self. We were there when rock and roll went electric
and throbbed through the city. We were there during the riots, on the safe
side of the barricades. We were there to see, time and again, the Illinois
National Guard encamped in the parks. We were there for the double
shock of assassinations in the spring of 1968—Martin Luther King, Jr.,
and Robert Kennedy. The Chicago police began beating peace marchers
that spring, and the Red Squads snapped photos and tapped phones. That
summer we were there for the Democratic Convention. We were there
when we finally gave up hope and trust in the elected officials of the
United States.

We lived our lives in crowds then, peaceful, loving, kindly crowds
that offered protection not riot. We were on the edges of the network of
groups planning things; consulting; marching; shutting down the universities; raising bail; holding concerts; publishing fliers, posters, streetsheets,
underground newspapers as slick and prosperous as the straight ones. We
were part of the Movement. We became one with that larger "we," the we
that would overcome some day. We moved with our own.

I became a draft counselor and a faculty member that protesting students could count on. I became a parent that high-schoolers could count
on, when my daughter worked organizing sit-ins against the war and the
dress codes. As time passed I became more and more involved with the left-
wing groups doing grassroots organizing, believing in self-determination for
the people of the Chicago neighborhoods as well as the people of Vietnam. In January 1972, I finally took the plunge. It was after the killings at
Kent State and Jackson State. After Black Panther leaders Fred Hampton
and Mark Clark were slaughtered in their beds in a predawn attack com-
manded by the Illinois attorney general's office. It was after the Chicago
Seven were tried at the Federal Building in the Loop, after masses of us
demonstrated for them outside Cook County Jail—corraled in by blue-
helmeted, armed police, while inside, thieves, pimps, rapists, and drug
dealers cheered us on. It was after all those things that I joined the white
working-class sector of the Rainbow Coalition and went to work with a
community-organizing group.[1]

Among ourselves we called it simply, "the organization." In 1972 it
published a newspaper (biweekly printing of 15,000) that was an organizing and educating tool. Most of us who worked with the organization went

out on the streets and sold the paper, using the occasion to talk politics with people in the neighborhoods. Among the standing programs to "serve the people" were the free health clinic, a lead-testing program, and a legal program. Sprinkled heavily throughout the year were special events—a peace rally aimed at working-class people, veterans, and servicemen; rock concerts and dances; speakers from other parts of the Movement; and smaller, localized events aimed at bringing in members. Work groups and study groups were ongoing.

The politics of the leadership were stained by the best and the worst of the times. There was the sophisticated naïveté of calling black and brown people, and peoples of the third world, "the vanguard" of our revolution. We embraced Mao's Cultural Revolution without benefit of facts (which were mostly unobtainable to us anyway). We supported guerrilla fighters everywhere, whether in Angola or Northern Ireland. Our organizing methods were soaked in sex, drugs, and rock and roll. But for all the machismo of the vanguard thinking, we sat and listened and learned from black and brown people. We worked together with the Young Lords and the Black Panthers and numberless other groups to find ways of "serving the people," and we shared goals, strategies, tactics, and educational methods. On our own turf, we listened to people in the neighborhoods. We helped them organize their fights against slumlords, the police, the courts, the health system. We had our homes there in the neighborhoods.

The leader of my first study group was a warm, sympathetic, working-class man—at forty, he was the oldest member of the organization.[2] He said to me, early in that spring of 1972, "Kathy, you've come home." Tears flooded my eyes when he said it. The pain of the loneliness of all my long years among academic professionals opened up inside me. I had come home.

It healed me, that work. I was healed of the class disdain between my father's side of the family and my mother's side. I was healed by knowing that what I saw of the world in my childhood was a valid perception, not to be dismissed by "those who knew better" as uneducated, unscientific, resentful, ignorant, redneck, Catholic, or any of those things.

My heart was there in that work, in a way my heart had never been anywhere but with my daughters. I gave myself to the work. I knew it was my work. There was no distance, no question, between me and the work. While it lasted, it was my life and my home.

I had come home, in the only sense in which I could come home. I came to be with people who knew my class experience and took it seriously. They shared my anger and they shared my love. They shared my hope to change the world—"The new world is ours to build" was a banner that ran across the top of the newspaper we published. I shared the fight. I shared the political work and the parties. For years my friends were there and my heart was there. But I couldn't share the world of the working-class people we were organizing. The truth is that I had been educated out of it. I had left the love and anger of my own working-class neighborhood not by changing the world but by moving up in it. That is the contradiction in my personal life, as it has been the contradiction faced by members of the working class in the United States for a hundred years. Neither the Movement nor the organization found a political solution to the contradiction. But even so, my work with the organization healed me.

It was this healing that has given me the basis of my politics and my philosophical work. This healing brought together love and anger so that, eventually, I could begin to see the world and to see how to live in it. "Eventually" is an important word in that sentence, for I became a casualty of the war at home. Before I could see how to live in the world, I had to pass through the cataclysm of the natural death of the Movement, the collapse of the organization, the decay of the dream, the ugly bones of a revolution without a future.

Through these times the women's movement was growing. In Chicago, many women had deserted the men of the Movement to make their own autonomous organizations. The Chicago Women's Liberation Union (CWLU) was the most successful. The women's unions were scattered in cities of the Midwest and the East. They tended to be federations of small work groups or study groups, and the women had a commitment to show respect for all women's viewpoints and experience, to overcome hierarchical structure, dominance, and authority. The point was to let each woman speak because women had been silenced, and their knowledge of the world had been made invisible. The world had been named by men. My feminist politics got its intellectual base from conversations and interviews with one of the organizers of the CWLU Abortion Referral Service—some of which I reported on in "Moral Revolution" (Chapter 3) as my interview with Jane. My last act as a member of the organization was to go with some of the women members to the Socialist Feminist Conference at Yellow Springs in the summer of 1975.

When I moved my life to Massachusetts and my job at Smith, I sought out grassroots, nonhierarchical, community-organizing groups.[3] For a year, I was with a work group of the Valley Women's Union. I began to see that anarchism, with its understanding of human nature and society, offered a basis for ethics that was quite different from those with which philosophers chose to work. Anarchist theorists of the grand tradition had not paid much attention to the effect of their work in ethics—like Marx, they tended to speak in moral terms or even to substitute social mores for the laws of the state.

I wrote "Anarchy and Morality" (Chapter 8) in October 1976 while I was a houseguest in Austin, Texas, visiting with Bob Solomon and Katie Marshall. I was a crazy revolutionary then, and it was a crazy piece. But its craziness let me say something about an anarchist ethics—a feminist ethics—that no philosophy paper has allowed me. Tight arguments are strangleholds on vision.

Beginning in the winter of 1978, I was with a communalist anarchist group that tried to bring together town and gown in Amherst. Martha Ackelsberg and I were assigned the job of writing a position statement for the group. Then, with Shawn Pyne, we began to work through what anarchist feminism would mean for a feminist philosophy. At that time Shawn was living in a women's cooperative household and working with a collective that operated a free clinic. She was our activist member. Together we wrote a long, ungainly paper called "Anarchism and Feminism" that was wonderful for its discussions of Shawn's clinic. We read it as a trio to large audiences at North Carolina State and at Smith College. Martha and I distilled it into the essay called "Anarchism and Feminism," which is Chapter 9 in this book—for the Black Rose speaker series in Boston, where we read it in October 1978.

In "Anarchism and Feminism" the discussions of the consequences of hierarchy and privilege give some background for the tension between upward mobility and class identity. The climb up the ladder of success seems to be the most direct route to economic, political, and cultural goods in the United States—the route for individuals, families, ethnic groups, and seemingly, for women and minority races. That's what "equal opportunity" and "meritocracy" are all about. The rub is that these goods depend for their definition as well as their distribution on class, race, and gender dominance in our capitalist democracy. For there to be some people at the top of the ladder, there must be a mass of people at the bottom supporting them, whether the "ladder" is the hierarchy in a family, on the job, or the class system itself. The tensions have clouded feminist politics.

When we wrote the paper, it may be that feminist politics clouded our discussions. We did not expand the discussion of self-development and anarchist respect to show the import for large-scale social change. I still like the way that we related discussion of self-development to the hierarchical organization of social groups and the nation itself. But we left implicit the implications of anarchist local change for the larger capitalist democracy. Anarchism offers interesting routes to regional self-sufficiency and self-determination in economic, educational, cultural, medical, and defense realms.[4]

The anarchist principles of respect allowed me to see the radical implications of Carol Gilligan's ethics, in "What Do Women Do?" (Chapter 10). In that chapter, I argue that feminist ethics requires an appropriate sociology, and I use the work of two feminist sociologists to make my case. I believe that some version of symbolic interactionism offers the appropriate sociology for feminism and for anarchism as well. In "Autonomy and Respect" (Chapter 11) I argue that Diana Meyer's liberal feminist idea of autonomy and self-development requires a new sociology if she is to avoid class dominance and disrespect for "traditional women."

At the very moment that I first came to the organization, in winter of 1972, I began working with the Society for Women in Philosophy—SWIP as we call it. SWIP began with the Women's Caucus of the American Philosophical Association. Nancy Holmstrom and Irvene Brawer sent letters to women listed in the Directory of Philosophers, urging them to attend a meeting at the December 1970 sessions of the American Philosophical Association (the APA). More than a hundred women came to the meeting—a remarkable number, given the small size of the philosophy profession and the tiny percentage of women within it.

In the early days it was a battle to bring departments, administrators, the APA, and even philosophical friends and colleagues to see women's professional concerns as legitimate. And yet, in 1970, women constituted only 7 percent of those teaching philosophy in the United States (440 women; 6,120 men). Women made up only 5 percent of full professors, but 20 percent of lecturers and instructors. In departments awarding Ph.D.'s in philosophy, only 3.5 percent of the faculty were women. During the 1960s, 7 percent of Eastern Division APA members were women but the percentage of women holding office or giving papers at the conferences was far, far below that.[5] It took years to convince the philosophy establishment that these figures indicated that sex discrimination was somehow being practiced.

In May 1971 those attending the Women's Caucus meeting changed the name to the Society for Women in Philosophy—societies had the privilege of getting on the APA agenda with a free meeting room, and caucuses did not. By May 1972 SWIP was on the APA agenda with a free meeting room.

From the beginning, SWIP has had a double focus: bread-and-butter issues of eliminating sexism from the profession and scholarly issues of creating feminist ways of doing philosophy. The cradle for the new philosophy was not in the APA meeting rooms but in the weekend regional conferences we held, fall and spring, in the East, Midwest, Southwest, and Pacific areas, and at times in other areas that our enthusiasm defined. We held them (we still hold them) without outside funding, relying on the generosity of the colleges for meeting rooms and the kindness of local residents for places to sleep.

I cannot tell you what a joy the early SWIP conferences were. For the first time, we were able to stand and talk philosophy with other women. The sound of our women's voices filling a room was a wonder. We listened to one another give papers, with respect, and we gave criticism and comment, with respect. Standing in groups at our cocktail parties we saw that we were different—no guarded posture, no shielding ourselves from roving male eyes. The APA meetings had been male hunting grounds in which we had been the prey. At those meetings we could not unglue ourselves from men, or if we did for a moment, other men came up and burst in on our talk as if it were nothing of importance—"women's talk." I cannot tell you how it felt to be in those meetings stuffed with gray-suited, insecure, self-important men, or in "smokers" choked with the stink of tobacco and spilled beer. I did not know myself how it was until I heard the sound of women's voices filling a room, until I could stand and talk philosophy without guarding myself from roving eyes.

I say this, and it is true. And yet I worked with SWIP in the way that my father worked to get a union into Fletcher's mill. I worked for affirmative action and for overcoming gender bias in philosophy at the same time that I worked with the organization in the Rainbow Coalition. I did the liberal work of reforming my profession to get equal opportunity for women to rise up the ladder, at the same time that I worked in the neighborhoods to overcome the class and race system. I did not acknowledge the contradictions, though they showed in the fragmentation of what I was doing. SWIP was part of my job. My politics were part of my life. I did not come home to SWIP, much though I loved the women and the work.

In those earlier days, I could overlook the contradictions because of the intimate connections between academic feminists and the many parts of the larger Movement. Feminist work in the academy then seemed to go hand in hand with activist work in the neighborhoods. We all seemed to be fighting capitalist patriarchy. Both kinds of work seemed to involve revealing the kind of society we all lived in.

Being a feminist cannot be defined in terms of a person's beliefs or the theories he or she holds. Feminism is a commitment to take women seriously. One of the first and most important places feminists took women seriously was in the classroom. Some of the women's movements methods and findings were brought into the academy with the early women's studies courses and programs. For example, in 1969, graduate students got together with faculty at Roosevelt University to organize one of the first women's studies courses in Chicago. Jenny Knauss and Judy Wittner were among the women who toiled through dusty library stacks in search of material on women for the courses, rediscovering women's history. At Chicago Circle, graduate student Holly Graff and others were helped by faculty member Sandra Bartky as they rediscovered the theory and research of women on women. It was not simply content that made a difference. Many of the early courses were collectively taught, by faculty and students, and they emphasized participatory methods. In SWIP we had session after session on feminist teaching. We shared our experiments and struggled to change the classroom into a respectful place.

Feminist philosophers are also committed to taking women seriously in their research. For example, in 1972, at the first Eastern SWIP regional conference, Caroline Whitbeck read a paper called, "The Maternal Instinct," in which she proposed a different self-other relation than the usual, oppositional, dualistic one of Western philosophy. She examined human nature by writing about the experiences of pregnancy, labor, childbirth, and nursing. She spoke of love of the baby as eros—an understanding of "the other" quite different from the male example of erotic love for a woman.[6]

In the early days (and even today in many places), taking women seriously meant taking a tremendous career risk. Graduate students could not find dissertation advisors for topics in feminist philosophy (it is still difficult today). The usual philosophy journals would not accept philosophy papers that used gender as a category of analysis—"not directed at a philosophical audience" was one reason they gave.[7] Feminist philosophers were denied tenure on grounds that they were "no good," when in truth they were simply not doing philosophy according to the methods and topics judged legitimate by the tenured professors. Overcoming these things, and creating feminist philosophy, required massive efforts on many fronts. Oceans of ink flowed in letters explaining why feminist philosophy was really philosophy and why the graduate student, or the applicant for a job, or the candidate for tenure, was really doing excellent and important work. Protests had to be organized. Feminist journals had to be founded, and presses that were willing to make feminist anthologies had to be discovered. Mary Vetterling Braggin forged a relationship with Littlefield Adams and let feminist philosophy see the light of the printed page through a series of anthologies. In a grand coup within the establishment, Sandra Harding and Merrill Hintikka laid the manuscript of *Discovering Reality* on that altar of respectable, unreadable philosophy, D. Reidel. They managed to have it accepted and published on quite feminist terms.[8] But *Discovering Reality* was accepted as the 1980s dawned. By that time, through the work and sacrifice of thousands of feminists, Women's Studies had become an established part of the academy. Battles had been fought on the fronts of all the disciplines in humanities and social science, and the multidisciplinary nature of feminist work had been accomplished.

"Making Knowledge" (Chapter 12) reviews some of that work. It took Elizabeth Potter and me several years of conversations with each other and with other feminists to find out what to write in that essay. It was written for a multidisciplinary anthology designed to take stock of the impact of feminist work across a number of disciplines in the humanities and social sciences. The impact has been considerable, in research and in teaching.

Chapter 12 closes with questions about the relationship of the feminist revolution in the academy to all the people of the world. "The personal is the political" is just a slogan until it is made into a politics. The question is what sort of politics academic feminism is. The answer has to lie in the nature of its connections with all people, not just with its success in the academy. A politics is something people make together, day to day, in the process of making our worlds. That is what "the personal is the political" meant in the earlier days of the women's movement, and it found expression in the local, grassroots, nonhierarchical organizations like the women's unions and the rap groups. Some academic groups, like the National Women's Studies Association, have tried to preserve those practices. But success in academia militates against them. Surviving in academia requires that one take on the coloration of the environment. Even entering academia requires learning the trade. And so we lecture rather than listen. We explain things to others and teach them our language. Our institutions place us as leaders rather than followers.

As times have changed, the contradiction has sharpened between working to improve the position of women in the profession and working to overcome the oppression of the class, race, and gender systems in the United States. The opportunities that the Movement offered for mitigating the contradiction have long since gone.

~

My own frustration as a feminist academic has been that only a handful of my feminist coworkers hear what I say about class and politics. More than once a woman from a working-class background has come to me after I have spoken out and we have opened our hearts, as if my public comment were a private communication between the two of us. Many times I have sat in feminist groups (once even at a women's union meeting) and seen a Marxist feminist look us over and then say, with disapproval, "We're all white middle-class women here." As if she never imagined that a working-class woman could "pass." As if the real working-class women were all down in the factories, waiting to be liberated.

The worst case of this prejudice that I know happened in the free clinic run by the organization. I heard about it from a slender, very attractive, intelligent, well-spoken young woman. She said that one of the male leaders in the organization had refused to believe that she was a working-class woman. She was furious about it: "He thinks working-class women are all stupid, fat, speak bad English, and wear dumpy clothes—or dress like whores."[9] This ignorant bigotry allows some working-class women to "pass." In her day, my mother "passed" when she got the chance. It's a mistake to think of this "passing" as nothing but false consciousness or identification with the dominant classes. As a matter of clearheaded, utilitarian survival, passing has major impact on the way people treat you and the opportunities that are open for working-class people as well as people of color.

The prejudice is not always so blatant. More times than I can number, feminist academics have become angry with me, have instructed me that I was mistaken when I said class bias was operating in our group, have closed me down, shut me off. This deafness is a class and race deafness due to a failure of politics, a failure of theory, a failure of practice, and, for feminist philosophers, a failure of feminist philosophy. Women of color have shouted their throats raw against that deafness.

The deafness is sometimes cultivated. Feminist theories that are built on our opposition to "the patriarchy," theories that define the violent, oppressive nature of "all men," theories that motive monger in the name of all women, those sorts of theories make us stone deaf to our own privileges of class and age and race and all the rest. They shut our ears to the voices of one-half of humanity. They stop our noses to the smell of the sweat of men and women who cook and serve the breakfasts for our meetings, who make our beds in the hotels and clean our toilets in the universities, who work in the fields that we may have food, who pump our oil and slave on fishing vessels and weave the cloth and sew our frocks and sell us our Cuisinarts. All these people are under our noses, but in these feminist theories they are silent, invisible, odorless.

As academics, as members of a professional class, we live off the work of these people, accepting privileges due those of our rank in a nation marked by class, race, age, cultural, national, and religious boundaries of privilege and power—and a hundred other boundaries as well. We must not pretend that we do not. We can only try to train ourselves in humility and try to hear others; work with others in their projects and not only on our own—according to their visions, not only our own. We need, once again, to try to use a common tongue, to use others' methods and others' meeting places, in others' neighborhoods and not only our own. We need to recognize the humanity of those whose labors support us, be they woman, man, or child, of whatever color, religion, culture, or state of "normality." We need to recognize their humanity in their terms, not simply our own. Even with the backbreaking burdens of an academic career, the challenge to academic feminists is to find a humble, effective way to do these things. The first step lies in knowing ourselves.

Others have words of wisdom that help me live with these things.

Jane Addams believed that genuine experience should be the basis of life and politics, and that social perspective and sanity of judgment come only from contact with social experience. She wrote,

> There is a conviction that we are under a moral obligation in choosing our experiences, since the results of those experiences must ultimately determine our understanding of life. We know instinctively that if we grow contemptuous of our fellows, and consciously limit our intercourse to certain kinds of people whom we have previously decided to respect, we not only tremendously circumscribe our range of life, but limit the scope of our ethics. (Addams 1907, 9–10)

Addams's aim was to give truth social expression. But such a truth is not to be found waiting in some philosopher's "good of the whole," or the standpoint of all women, or of the proletariat. It cannot be captured in a position statement or a party platform or a personal life plan.

Mohandas Gandhi offered other wisdom. He wrote that society is based on violence, and living in it, we cannot altogether escape violence. The meaning for me is that there is no politics that leads us to the peaceful innocence of the Garden, no politics for all women, no revolution for the sake of the future of all humanity. If we think there can be, if we believe we are the intellectuals of such a revolution, we deafen ourselves to the violence that we ourselves make in living our lives. There is no purity of heart. The best we can do is stand in humility before our violence and mitigate it to the degree that we can. The best we can do is to know and respect others as we act together with them. Reconciling love and anger has required that I accept the terrible pain of that truth.

For my own life, I have Thomas Merton's remark on his own life: "I have had to accept the fact that my life is almost totally paradoxical. I have also had to learn gradually to get along without apologizing for the fact, even to myself" (Merton 1974, 16).

## Notes

1. I'm using some rhetoric here, but it isn't empty. The Movement version of the events I mention was supported in later investigations and court decisions.

2. When I first worked with it, "the organization" was a cadre organization, with a membership of cadre and a "family" of nonmembers—people with special skills or education and others who "helped out" but were unsuited to be cadre. One motive for the division was an effort to protect the place of working-class people in the group. Many higher-class white radicals were interested in joining, and they would have swamped the locals. There was also a class bias operating: prejudice against professionals and the higher classes that was more pronounced in some of the leadership than in the rank and file cadre and the "family." The cadre leadership were nearly all from college-radical backgrounds. My working-class background and my gender made me more palatable, and I was the only academic working closely with the organization until it changed form a couple of years later. It then took a more general form, and the "family" became members and the leadership opened up. The shift meant that educated radicals took a more prominent position; the change was not simply one of form but of content, method, and goal. This change was forced by historical change in the political circumstances, as was the dissolution of the organization two years later.

3. The phrase "moved my life" is peculiar, but I use it because the facts are complicated. I accepted the Smith job in the fall of 1971, to begin teaching in fall of 1972, that is, I made the Smith commitment before I began working with the organization. By juggling unpaid leaves, visiting appointments, and so on, I managed to spend most of my time in Chicago, from 1972 to 1975. By 1975 the organization was breathing its last, and my life in both Chicago and Massachusetts was in a shambles. I am once again grateful to my daughters for holding things together for me.

4. We do give a large number of references in the chapter to books discussing these things.

5. These figures are from a report of the APA Committee on the Status of Women in the Profession. One of the resolutions at the first Women's Caucus meetings was to fund such a committee at a level appropriate to its tasks.

6. Prime examples are phenomenologists Jean-Paul Sartre and Emmanuel Levinas.

7. This was a reply I received from the *Philosophical Review* when I insisted on a reason for the editor's instant rejection of "Moral Revolution" (Chapter 3) (without sending it out for review). That essay argues that the dominant philosophical approach in ethics is mistaken and that a paradigm change is needed. In the originally published essay, the method I use to make the arguments is justified at tedious length, on the grounds that an argument for paradigm change cannot usually use the methods of the dominant paradigm. The essay as published in this collection is an abridged version that omits those lengthy arguments.

To be fair here, I should say that both *Signs* and *Feminist Studies* rejected "The Man of Professional Wisdom" (Chapter 4) as not being directed at their feminist audiences.

8. The coup was made with the help of Jaakko Hintikka, who himself had come to see the validity of the feminist approach. I mention it as only one example of the help that some establishment men extended to feminists in the academy.

9. During the various periods when I was dating, it was not unusual for a man to express surprise that I came from a working-class background. I spoke middle-class English, and my mother had taught me to dress stylishly, and she had provided me with the materials for a background in Shakespeare and the classics of Victorian literature!

# 8

## Anarchy and Morality
(1976)

Anarchism has almost always been taken to be a political theory. When it is criticized and dismissed, it is taken to be a political theory in the sense of a strategy for bringing about the postrevolutionary, communist society. The critics shake their heads. How utopian to think that the first act of the people after they overthrow the state should be to destroy the state and live stateless! Critics call up visions of tribal wars, banditry, and economic chaos. The war of all against all.

Some critics encourage us to leave aside this silly romanticism and take a "hard-headed" socialist position. Marxism-Leninism, for example. Marxist-Leninists call anarchists utopian, and they should recognize what utopian thought is. Their utopian communist society is supposed to be attained by the strategy of overthrowing a capitalist bureaucracy and the dictatorship of a military-industrial elite and replacing it by a socialist bureaucracy and the dictatorship of a communist party elite. Attainment of heaven by taking a detour through hell.

I think that far from being a harebrained utopian strategy, anarchism offers the means for a rational strategy. A strategy, after all, is no good unless it stands a likely chance of reaching the goal we want it to reach. But the rational strategy, which we may come to with the help of anarchism, is to be understood in crude terms. If the revolutionary strategy of anarchism as a political philosophy is that, upon seizing state power, we should instantly destroy the state, then anarchism as a political philosophy doesn't offer much in the way of rational strategy. But underlying the revolutionary political philosophy of anarchism is a revolutionary moral philosophy and a revolutionary theory of society. To see what anarchism has to offer in the way of rational strategy, we need to put the focus on anarchist morality.

When Anglo-American philosophers do ethics, they talk a lot about obligations, about acts that are right or wrong, about principles that justify actions. Sometimes they talk about rights and freedoms. Almost always they take obligation as a central moral concept. Most of us, when we get self-conscious about ethics, talk in the same terms. Sometimes we must do this because it is tactically necessary. For example, sometimes it is tactically necessary to talk of rights, perhaps to argue effectively against restrictive laws. But other times, it is not. Anarchist ethics is very different from this other kind of ethics—I could call it bourgeois ethics, but because that would in some ways be misleading, let me call it instead archist ethics. "Anarchist" means without law or rule. "Archist" means with law or rule.

Anarchist ethics is very different from archist ethics. The essence of the difference does not lie in the fact that the anarchist and the archist make different moral judgments—for example, that the one considers punishment to be morally abhorrent in all cases, and the other considers punishment to be morally just in some cases. The essence of the difference lies in the fact that the basic form of anarchist ethics, and the basic concepts used, are different from those used in archist ethics. They are different in the way that Einstein's physics is different from Newton's. One thing this means is that as anarchists, we will lead ourselves into incoherence if we thoughtlessly use the methods and concepts of archist ethics to do our moral reasoning—though as I said, sometimes we must do this thoughtfully, as a matter of tactics.

Let me represent archist ethics first through some remarks made by John Stuart Mill. So far as our purposes go, he picks out most of what is essential. Mill insists that the morality (or immorality) of an individual action is a question of the application of a moral law or principle to an individual case. Moral obligation is also decided in terms of a moral law, and it carries liability to sanctions. This is true in questions of any sort of moral act, including just acts. Mill says,

> The truth is that the idea of penal sanction which is the essence of law enters not only into the conception of injustice but into that of any kind of wrong. We do not call anything wrong, unless we mean to imply that a person ought to be punished in some way or other for doing it; if not by law, by the opinion of his fellow-creatures; if not by opinion, by the reproaches of his own conscience. . . . It is a part of the notion of Duty in every one of its forms that a person may rightfully be compelled to fulfil it. Duty is a thing which may be exacted from a person, as one exacts a debt. (Mill 1951, 45)

Not all archist philosophers are as up-front as Mill is about the connection between duty, compulsion, and punishment, but this does not at all mean that Mill has the model wrong.

The very statement of Mill's position, with its talk of punishment, with its talk of morality on analogy with penal law, with its powerful, co-ersive authority hidden under the pronoun "we," that statement is thor-oughly repugnant to anarchists. But I believe what Mill says is correct about the concepts of duty, obligation, and principle morality. The rela-tion with punishment and authority is intrinsic. Anarchists cannot simply reject Mill's talk of punishment and exacting a debt and keep the talk of morality as having to do primarily with moral laws, obligations, duties, praise, and blame. Anarchists must reject the entire system of ethics.

But what of an anarchist system of ethics?

The first and major moral point to be made out of anarchism is that the whole human being is the basis of ethics. Not an abstraction like the human being as an end, or the human being as a citizen, or the human being as an economic unit, or the human being as a moral agent obligated to decide on her actions under the moral law. It is the whole human being with her needs, desires, and loves; her anger, her hunger, and her glory; her children, family, friends, and neighbors; her work; her place in her community, her relations with others. Whole, unique human beings can-not be defined in a system of moral principles.

It is paradoxical to suppose archist ethics can deal with whole human beings. Isn't ethics defined by the principle "What's right for me is right for any similar person in similar circumstances"? Doesn't ethics work only for classes of people and classes of acts? How can I judge myself or others if we insist that people are unique moral beings? How can I show respect for them if my principles do not apply to all morally similar persons in morally similar circumstances? This is the crux of the matter.

In archist ethics the genuine moral principles are supposed to guaran-tee respect. Kant says that when we choose a principle, we must be able consistently to will that everyone follow it. John Rawls (1971) designs his moral standpoint to include everyone's moral standpoint. He does not have to find out the unique facts about others to include their perspectives in his perspective. He assumes we are similar in morally relevant respects. The utilitarian ethics does require us to know the facts—we need to know the real consequences for happiness of real people. But like the other ar-chists, the utilitarian sits alone, deciding our moral good by the principle of the greatest happiness of the greatest number. He does not ask whether each of us goes along with the principle or not.[1] Archist ethics has each of us alone in the moral standpoint, like an agoraphobic spider in a web, translating other people's worlds into its own arachnid terms. Of course we cannot make archist ethics into one that respects whole, unique persons.

The solution is to admit that morality takes place *in media res*, not making judgments in one's private conscience. Anarchist ethics is for people out in the world working together. The emphasis is on action, in ethics as in politics. If we want to find out other people's perspectives, we have to ask them, ask others, and see what we all do. We have to discover what their happiness is, and our own, in the process of making it together. This is because the basis of the ethics is the whole person. The whole person is present in the action.

Now this emphasis on action solves the seeming paradox of taking the whole human being as the basis of ethics. People are unique and complex, and there is no way anyone can have a set of principles that respects the uniqueness and complexity. There is no exhaustive list of empirical statements that can tell us the whole truth about a whole person. That is why John Rawls (like many other philosophers) tries to base his ethics on what we have in common, on the posit that we are similar in morally relevant respects. That is why utilitarians presuppose that there are psychological laws that describe how we are similar in respects relating to our happiness or goodness. The primary location of archist ethics is inside the head of a congressman.

In the primary location of anarchist ethics, the whole person is there with us in action. We do not need an exhaustive list of empirical statements. We have the person. When we have a question, we ask. When we seem to be mistaken, the person objects. We hear his or her criticisms and hopes, and the person hears us. We weigh the moral activity together, as we go about doing it. Secondary locations must preserve these features to whatever degree possible.

The emphasis on action solves another problem. Whole people are not complete objects whose meaning (or traits) are given. There cannot be an exhaustive list to tell us the whole truth because the whole person is in the process of creating herself and her world, together with others. Defining our "similarity in morally relevant respects" or defining us in terms of psychological laws is both immoral and unscientific. It misrepresents our nature as beings who, at every moment, make ourselves and make our communities. The archist model is the wrong model of moral knowledge.[2]

To know another person is to *know how* to live and work with her. To know another person in a moral sense is to *know how* to respect her. This is why nonhierarchical social groups are important to anarchists. They offer hope of knowing and respecting others. Respect must show in action. It is respect that calls for the nonhierarchical social forms that the anarchists love. It is respect that requires nonhierarchical forms that will let us know one another and know the truth of our world. The primary archist model for human social life is the centralized state. The primary anarchist model is the decentralized, nonhierarchical group.

Anarchist ethics shows in practice. So we should look at some cases.

The first thing to realize is that much of our lives is lived within decentralized, nonhierarchical groups—particularly the informal ones of friendships, social groups, work groups, neighborhoods, playgrounds. Nonhierarchical groups are obviously common and familiar. Some of the more formally organized, nonhierarchical groups exist in nearly every community in the United States. Alcoholics Anonymous and its related groups like Alanon and Alateen are prime examples known to millions of people.

In the past anarchists have self-consciously promoted nonhierarchical groups as a means of revolutionary change. The aim was to educate people to the nature of the capitalist, class society and to show them that we in fact make ourselves and our world in action. One of the most famous strikes in U.S. history, the Lawrence Textile strike of 1912, was seen as a step in anarchist revolutionary change.[3] The strike began spontaneously when workers walked out after a wage cut, but soon it was guided by the Industrial Workers of the World (the IWW or "Wobblies"), an anarchosyndicalist group. The strike involved men, women, and children who worked in the mills as well as those at home. As the strike went on, the people saw how the authorities reacted—the mill owners, the police, the priests, and the governor, for example. This taught them something about their society and raised their consciousness. They also saw the massive support they received from people in the northeastern states. They learned about themselves and others through acting.

The workers and their families organized a system of relief committees, which provided for food, fuel, clothing, and sometimes even rent. That is, they created alternative social forms to provide for their needs. They acted on their beliefs and had a chance to test them out in action. They learned that the world isn't given to us like an object; we make it and change it. Most of all, they learned how to manage their world through nonhierarchical, cooperative groups. This was the sort of strategy that anarchists used. The case shows how anarchist morality finds a location in a revolutionary movement.

Anarchist morality also operates in workplaces, and in the women's health movement there has been a sustained effort to make nonhierarchical, collective work groups. Hierarchical work groups (public schools, factories, bureaucracies) are designed for inequality of decision-making power, and they have corrective mechanisms that tend to keep the power unequal. Nonhierarchical collectives are designed for equality, and they have corrective mechanisms that tend to keep the power equal. Nonhierarchical collectives offer an example of a primary location of anarchist ethics. They show that the primary location isn't restricted to face-to-face, momentary situations and that it ideally has an appropriate structure that guards respect.

The Vancouver Women's Health Collective was designed to share information, power, and responsibility among workers at the collective.[4] There was a "division of labor" at the collective in the sense that there were various jobs people did—taking charge of the desk, doing pelvic examinations, putting together the agenda for meetings. But the division of labor didn't mean that one person did one limited task forever. Newcomers received on-the-job training for all jobs, and workers rotated the jobs. The idea was not simply to give the workers a variety of skills. By working through all the jobs they knew what was going on in the collective, they could exercise more responsibility, particularly in decision making.

Decisions and policy at the collective were not made by executive order. They were made by consensus, in meetings of the whole work group, and they ranged from questions of how to arrange the furniture, to how to allocate and rotate jobs, to what the priorities of the organization should be (Kleiber and Light 1978, 36). In consensus decision making, every member must have equal opportunity to discuss the issue—at the collective they sometimes had "rounds" in which each member in turn spoke her feeling at that point in the process.[5] In consensus decision making, the group process has to encourage honesty. This means that the people involved must have skills at consensus decision making. It is at least as highly skilled a process as executive decision making, and no one doubts that executives in hierarchical organizations need training. In fact, using the legalistic reasoning of archist ethics also requires skills and particular kinds of decision-making organization. Anarchist ethics also requires skills, but of a different sort.

Work collectives offer only one example of a primary location for anarchist morality. There are also locations in public policy and community decision making. These cases show most starkly the difference between anarchist and archist models. The prime archist model seems to be a group of legislators individually making up their minds and then voting on a law for people to follow or on a decision for someone to carry out. The example of a charette is quite different.

The charette is a social form that brings people together to make decisions on projects that affect their community.[6] It has been successfully used in the United States, in community planning about schools, for example. It is designed to work for people having very different—even hostile—perspectives and world views. It is designed to educate everyone in the process of the decision making, not only about other people's perspectives but about technical matters like the engineering and educational requirements for school buildings, and the place of school complexes in the social life of the community. A charette is systematically constructed to collect and sort out ideas generated by people directly interested in a project (Thayer 1973).

The point is to bring together interested people. They are divided into small groups for discussion. Each group is planned to include people whose interests are diametrically opposed. People move back and forth among groups until they find the one they are most interested in, or until they decide to leave the whole process.[7] At intervals, the groups report back to the body as a whole, so that conflicts among different groups can be raised and worked out. People may not end up agreeing with one another's viewpoints, but at least they stand a good chance of understanding one another and showing respect. The final decisions benefit from the creative thought and criticism of many people, and the eventual project has community support.

In the charette, the decision is created, not deduced. In the process of creating the decision, people's beliefs and understandings change, their social relations change, their community changes. In the process of the charette, the definition of the moral situation comes into existence. It is not predefined by authority, whether the authority of an expert or leader, or the authority of principles.

The charette gives us a different picture of people doing things together. It is a good example for anarchists to learn from. Some older anarchists felt that once we got rid of the state and its coercive laws, we would have a society that runs on mores. We then have moral obligation to one another under our moral principles, rather than legal obligation to the state under coercive laws. I want to say no to that. Instead of allowing manipulation by the state or by the ruling class, mores and moral principles allow manipulation by public opinion, by the gossips of the village, by the men of the women, the whites of the blacks, the old of the young, the dominant of the subordinate. The charette is an example not of people judging one another and holding one another to their obligations but of people creating mutual respect as they create the future together.

These examples also let us see that we do not need to talk of obligation and duty, principles and blame. Suppose someone at the Vancouver Health Collective or the Lawrence strike committee doesn't do his or her assigned work. What then? What do we gain from saying those people failed their obligations? Would we want to blame and punish those people? I would hope not. We might, like the Vancouver Collective, come together to discuss what happened. Some of us might even be furious. We might yell and get red in the face. We expected something that didn't come through. We were disappointed. Our group project suffered bad consequences. And so we are angry.[8]

How does this description differ from one in terms of blame and obligation? Well, it takes my anger as my anger. It doesn't pretend that there is some God-given (or reason-given) moral law that those people have violated, that is, that they have done something bad so I am justified in berating them. It doesn't give me the edge over them by standing me on the platform of Reason. I may mention principles in talking to them, but I don't use principles to stop my ears, shut their mouths, and force them to repent.

My anger is simply my anger. And if I have a criticism of them, then I must work with them, and they with me, until we come to a resolution. Part of their understanding of me requires their seeing and knowing my anger in this situation. They know where I am at. My anger is part of myself revealed to them. I have no need to hide it under the justification that they failed in their obligations. But this means that I can know where they are at as well. If I put aside my self-righteousness, I can hear what they are saying, and what's more, they can say it. We can work through the anger together.

This means that in an anarchist morality, I am taken as myself and you are taken as yourself, without justification. We face each other naked. Naked at least of the trappings of justification, blame, praise, punishment, and reward. Naked of those rationalizations, those mystifications. As an anarchist, I am only myself, I can give you only myself, take from you only yourself. But in giving myself and taking yourself, we give each other a world in which respect is possible.

This brings us back full circle to anarchist politics. Our American Declaration of Independence (an archist document written in 1776) says that we have the right to revolution. Now, rebellion or revolution or insurrection is at the core of anarchist politics. But it would be wrong to understand this as a right to revolution.[9] For the anarchist, we would do better to talk of a freedom to rebel. And this freedom is a thing within the person and the group. Within me, it arises out of my respect for myself and for others. Trampled by authority, respect for myself and others causes my gorge to rise. I am consumed by the anger of rebellion. The freedom to rebel is not something outside that justifies my action. It is an anarchist virtue. It is a virtue worth analyzing—as Plato analyzed the virtue of justice or temperance. Certainly it involves the virtue of courage. Certainly it involves the virtue of self-respect—for it is the trampling of respect that sparks the spirit of rebellion. Certainly it is involved intimately with the core anarchist respect for other whole persons. I have not analyzed it. I only know that it is at the center of anarchist virtue and that it is the guardian flame of what is morally best in all of us human beings. Anarchists love nonhierarchical social forms because they let us act with these virtues.

I say these things about anarchist morality because of the anarchist understanding of human nature and human society. Human beings are always in the process of being created as human beings. Human society is always in the process of being created by human beings working together. This is why, unlike Marxism or fundamentalist Christianity or Islam, anarchism does not prescribe the way to the millennium. This isn't because it misses the route. It is because the millennium is a corpse, and anarchism has to do with life. Living human beings and living human society are always growing, always creating, always incomplete, always in process and ferment. The peaceful, changeless society where we've got it all right is a human nightmare, not a human dream.

In a world that we are always creating, the best strategy is to find ways to help us create it well. In a world that we make together, the best strategy is to educate ourselves and one another so that we can know ourselves and the facts of our world. Acting successfully in such a world requires that we respect one another. Anarchist morality gives a hope of letting us learn how to do these things as we gradually change ourselves and our world.

## Notes

1. In her comment on my "Respect and Impartiality" (paper presented at American Philosophical Association Eastern Division Meetings, December 1979), Mary Gibson said that in uniting all perspectives, utilitarianism eliminates the morally crucial fact that they are the perspectives of different persons. She went on to say, "A third approach attempts to combine the full information available to Utilitarianism's sympathetic observer with the distinc-

tion between persons insisted upon by Rawls. It is a proposal of Thomas Nagel's suggesting that we imagine that the impartial observer chooses, not on the assumption that he/she will experience all lives together, but will actually split into so many distinct individuals, living each life 'from the inside' so to speak, having just those relations to other lives that actual persons have." She notes that the difficulty is that having set the proposal forth, it is by no means clear how to implement it. She goes on to say that my own suggestion is that the only way to proceed is in actual practice, that is, by allowing people to speak for themselves.

2. I don't mean that there are no valid psychological laws. There may well be—and there certainly are valid biological laws that apply to us. My point is that these laws cannot define us for moral purposes, particularly not the moral purposes of the archist philosopher who sits in his office and defines the moral world.

3. I discuss this example at greater length in Ackelsberg and Addelson 1987.

4. This example is from an unpublished paper, which was written in 1978 for an issue of *Feminist Studies* on anarcha feminism. That issue died in the fetal stage, in part because it was difficult to shape anarcha-feminist work into the standards of academic socialist feminists, in part because the editors were chronically overworked. I finally wrote up the case in Ackelsberg and Addelson 1987. The data is from Kleiber and Light 1978.

5. On the surface, as a way of running a workplace, nonhierarchical collectives may seem "less efficient" than hierarchically organized workplaces. However, if we calculate in the effects of misunderstandings, rebellions, protests, and foot-dragging in hierarchical workplaces, the balance looks very different. On the plus side, the Vancouver Collective methods led to new and creative and workable solutions, as well as satisfaction among the workers.

6. This example is taken from my paper "Respect and Impartiality."

7. If people are so intensely hostile at the beginning that they can't get anything done in their group, then subcommittees are formed and assigned facilitators who can help work out points of special hostility.

8. I had some good, helpful conversations with Bob Solomon about this topic.

9. I suppose that saying we have a right to revolution allows us to justify revolution at a given time. It gives a person something persuasive to say in an argument.

# 9

## Anarchism and Feminism

WITH MARTHA ACKELSBERG AND SHAWN PYNE
(1978)

## I. IN SEARCH OF A TRADITION

> Every art or applied science and every systematic investigation, and similarly every action and choice, seem to aim at some good; the good, therefore, has been well defined as that at which all things aim.
>
> —Aristotle, *Nicomachean Ethics*

Asking what the point of an activity is, gives us a way of evaluating some things people are doing. For example, if we ask what the point of doing science is, we can probably agree that the ultimate point is to give us all scientific knowledge and to contribute to people's having good, fulfilling lives. We can then evaluate what our scientists are doing by seeing whether they make that point or not.

We can ask, What's the point of our all being gathered together in a democratic, capitalistic, bureaucratic United States? And the answer to that seems to be that the point of our people's activities being organized in that way is to bring them to having good lives. A good life means having enough to eat and a roof over your head, of course. Once those are given, it involves more. In the past, supporters of "the American way of life" have explicitly argued that *our* way is the best way to achieve that goal— and they point to our high standard of living and our liberties as evidence.

We think the basis of feminist criticism in the United States has been that our society does not, or cannot, make good, fulfilling lives for all our people. This is the most fundamental criticism we can make of our society: It fails to fulfill the point of its existence. Different feminists have made the criticism in different ways. Betty Friedan's *Feminine Mystique* (1974) was a force in starting the "second wave" of the women's movement in the United States early in the 1960s (the first wave was in the late-nineteenth and early-twentieth centuries). That book is an analysis of how and why the United States doesn't allow a good life for middle-class women. Betty Friedan says,

> Equality and human dignity are not possible for women if they are not able to earn. . . . Only economic independence can free a woman to marry for love not for status or financial support, or to leave a loveless intolerable humiliating marriage, or to eat, dress, rest, and move if she plans not to marry. But the importance of work for women goes beyond economics. How else can women participate in the action and decisions of an advanced industrial society unless they have the training and opportunity and skills that come from participating in it? (1974, 371)

Betty Friedan is a liberal, and most of us here are probably not liberals. But we believe that all members of what came to be called the women's liberation movement acted fundamentally out of the belief that our "democratic, capitalist, bureaucratic United States" does not and cannot fulfill the point of its existence. It cannot give people full lives, and so it must be changed.

If we can criticize whole societies for not fulfilling the point of their existence, we can also ask about revolutionary movements. We can ask if, at any given moment, they are acting so as to fulfill their goals. And we can ask if in fact their goals are good goals. There are two parts to any movement for change. One criticizes the existing society for not fulfilling its aims. The other is a creative part that moves the revolutionary movement toward fulfilling its own goal. On this creative side, feminists have spoken for and worked for making a society in which people have a better possibility for good lives.

On the critical side, most feminists in the United States take hierarchy and privilege in our society to be main factors preventing people from having good lives. Hierarchy involves patterned ways of interacting and behaving. In a hierarchy, people (or at least the roles they fill) are ranked, and interactions among them occur through this ranking. The interactions are not all one way. Those below can provide some information to those above. Those below, at times, are *allowed* some independent decision power. But the word *allowed* is crucial. According to the structure, all decisions are made from higher-up points and filtered down. Generally, too, status, prestige, money, and greater degrees of freedom accompany higher-up positions.

In developing analysis and strategy for confronting hierarchy and privilege, feminists have turned to a number of different political traditions. Some (for example, Betty Friedan) begin with the liberal tradition, looking at what it has to say about hierarchy, and then adapt its methodology and approach to the question of women's subordination in society. Others turn to the Marxist-socialist tradition and attempt to modify its approach to incorporate subordination on the basis of sex, as well as of class. Still others (for example, radical feminists) have rejected both approaches, and argued that an analysis and strategy adequate to deal with women's subordination must be developed on a totally new basis. We will argue that while each of these perspectives has something to contribute to the development of feminist theory and practice, the tradition with the greatest potential for contemporary feminism is that of communalist anarchism.[1] But first a look at the others.

Writers in the liberal tradition view hierarchy as a necessary condition of social life. They argue that coordination is necessary, and that the most efficient form of coordination is hierarchical organization. Liberals also believe in "meritocracy," which they describe as a system in which jobs go to the best qualified. When liberals turn a critical eye toward our society, they see that the most highly rewarded jobs tend to be held by white, upper-class males, and that many highly qualified women and non-whites never make it to the tops of the hierarchies. They then suppose that something has gone wrong with the system of "sorting" people into these hierarchies. They attribute this "unfair" sorting to various kinds of discrimination on the part of those hiring, or those making up qualifying exams, and so on. Their practical solution to the problem seems relatively straightforward: End discrimination and adopt equal opportunity as a goal.

Now, most advocates of social change work for equal opportunity to some degree. For example, the three of us have had to fight the equal opportunity fight within our workplaces and professions, for ourselves and for others, but we do not have "equal opportunity" as our prime goal.

The problem with equal opportunity as a prime goal is that, in our society, equal opportunity means the opportunity to become *unequal*. It does not challenge the *system* of privilege; it merely aims toward the more sex-blind or race-blind distribution of that privilege. As we will see, hierarchy and privilege can be shown to be significant obstacles to many people's realization of their goal of a good life. A movement that accepts such privilege cannot accomplish the goal of changing society to give all women (let alone all people) good lives. Thus, liberalism does not seem to be an adequate starting point for the feminist movement.

Socialists, on the other hand, do see hierarchy and privilege as bar-
riers to people's leading full and good lives. And they see that hierarchy
and privilege to be based in economic structures—in particular, in industrial capitalism. They argue that capitalism—the inequalities built into it,
and the social and political hierarchies that grow out of it—is the central
factor preventing people from realizing good lives. This perspective has
important consequences for both analysis and strategy. Marxist criticism
treats class and economic factors as the most crucial, "the primary contradiction." Marxists derive all other conflicts and contradictions in society
from those fundamental relationships. Strategically, this means that people
committed to social change must work together to overcome the economic
structures of capitalism. Through that struggle, they also will be working
against all hierarchies, social, political, or sexual.

This socialist tradition poses problems for feminists, at least in part
because of its focus on the one "primary contradiction." Many contemporary feminists have attempted to modify the tradition. They argue that
sexual power or domination is an independent source of hierarchy and
privilege, and that it will not necessarily disappear when capitalism is
overthrown. They have also criticized the sexism of socialist movements,
both in this country and in others. They have, in the process, begun to
create a new tradition—of "socialist feminism." [2]

Still, we want to argue that this tradition, too, must have its limits.
On the theoretical level, one cannot simply add another, independent
source of domination or oppression without changing the initial theory in
a fundamental way. And this theoretical problem is reflected in a very real
practical problem for socialist feminists. What should be the focus of their
organizing efforts? In fact, experience shows us that the analysis has led
some socialist feminists to a reverse elitism—college-educated, middle-
class women taking up factory or waitressing jobs, and focusing their work
on *organizing* poor and working-class women. In doing this they dis-
count or ignore the reality of middle-class women's experiences of subordination. The problem flows directly from the socialist tradition they attempt to adapt. [3]

In developing some of these same criticisms, radical feminists have
argued that neither tradition provides an appropriate starting point for
analyzing and overcoming women's subordination. Instead, they argue that
hierarchical patterns of behavior and interaction such as the desire to put
oneself first, to dominate others, to give orders, and so on, are essentially
*male* characteristics. [4] Through the exercise of their male power, men have
structured these characteristics into the very fabric of our society, so that

they infect our social, economic, and political life. Along with the socialists, and in opposition to liberals, radical feminists reject the claim that hierarchy is necessary to human society. But, unlike socialists, who see hierarchy as derivative from economic relations, the radical feminists trace it to male dominance. They point out that the hierarchical structures themselves encourage the development of aggressive, competitive behavior that makes good lives impossible for many. They argue that it is male privilege that must be eliminated. Hierarchical patterns of behavior will then follow them to oblivion, and people will be able to realize their goal of a good life.

The battle cry of the radical feminist is that women of all races and classes must unite to overcome sex oppression first and foremost. As a practical matter, however, black women find they must unite with black men in fighting racism, and working-class women find they must unite with their men in overcoming their class oppression. Radical feminism ignores the importance of class- and race-dominance structures and gives no reasonable way for black and working-class people to overcome the structure of their subordination. For this reason, many black women call radical feminism racist—because it looks upon all women as if they were the same, that is, as if they were all *white*.

While each of these traditions has some things to offer to a feminist analysis and strategy, each also raises problems for that analysis. In particular, each can be criticized for leaving out the perceptions, the lives, and even the movements for change of some large groups of people (including women) in the United States. To base a feminist strategy on either of these perspectives requires that many women put aside their own perceptions and lives and oppression, to work for someone else's. We feel, however, that instead of trying to modify these traditions to make room for all women, feminists would do better to turn to another tradition, the anarchist tradition, which has an analysis and strategy more clearly suited to both the theoretical needs and the existing practices of the feminist movement.[5]

What is anarchism? There is no one, monolithic version of anarchism to which all who call themselves anarchists would subscribe. As is the case with liberalism and Marxism, there exists a tradition to which many thinkers and activists have contributed and which is still undergoing development. We see ourselves in this tradition—and, in particular, in the communalist-anarchist tradition of Bakunin, Kropotkin, Goldman, and the Spanish anarchists. Even these people and groups differed among themselves. But the main lines of the tradition that all share are (1) a criticism of existing societies, focusing on relationships of power and domination; (2) a vision of an alternate, egalitarian, nonauthoritarian society, along with claims about how it could be organized; and (3) a strategy for moving from one to the other.

The particular form and content of these criticisms and strategies have changed, of course, over time. As Western capitalist societies have become more complex during the one hundred years since massive industrialization began, understandings of those societies—of the ways in which domination and subordination function, and of the movements that have arisen to overcome those relationships—have changed as well. In fact, part of our purpose in writing this chapter was to suggest a more complete anarchist analysis that uses developments in many of these areas. For example, the analysis of domination and subordination, which we will present in section II, owes much to the insights of sociologists and social psychologists, who have studied the impact of workplace organization on working people. It owes much to women in the women's movement, who have contributed to an understanding of the operation of male dominance, the role of the family, and possibilities for nonhierarchical, cooperative forms of behavior. It owes much to developments in the natural sciences and to their impact on the ecology movement. And it owes much to the black and poor people's movements of the 1950s and 1960s—and to many other sources as well. Our analysis of strategies for struggle to achieve a better society, which we will present in section III, owes much to the struggles of the many subordinate groups that have attempted to understand and overcome their subordination within the past thirty years—and, especially, to the women's movement.

But before we begin these presentations, let us say just a bit about what sort of a society we, as anarchists, envision—or, to put it better, what kinds of perspectives would underlie the organization of such a society.

One is that human freedom is a social product: Freedom and community are compatible, but communities need to be structured in particular ways to support and make possible that freedom. That means that the structure supporting that freedom must be egalitarian—that is, there should be no need for hierarchies of authority and privilege. Instead, society, including work structures, will be arranged to foster relationships of reciprocity and cooperation (what anarchists have traditionally termed "mutualism"). Thus, there would be no need for economic inequalities or differential work incentives. The institutions in and through which people interact will encourage them to cooperate with one another, not to compete. Each will come to recognize that the fulfillment of the self need not be achieved at the expense of others. Spontaneous organizations, set up by people to meet their own needs, replace centralized, hierarchical patterns of coordination. To be sure, leaders may arise in some situations, but the right or authority to "command" a situation should not inhere in roles or offices to which some people have privileged access. Diversity, and a plurality of perspectives, is to be the watchword. Finally, instead of conquering nature, people should orient themselves to finding new ways to live in harmony with our physical surroundings.[6]

So far, this vision may not seem very different from one offered by Marxist socialists. But, as we will see in section III, anarchism also has some important things to say about the process of social change. In this perspective on change, it differs significantly from both the liberal and the Marxist traditions, but it has strong connections with feminist practice— especially much of the practice of radical feminism. The anarchist perspective requires that means be consistent with ends. It requires that the process of revolution take place in and through structures that reflect the sorts of relationships in which people aim to live. The organizations through which people struggle to achieve their aims must not undermine those aims. It implies a new concept of revolutionary practice, which consists in creating new forms of communal-social existence, new ways to meet people's needs,[7] forms through which people can overcome their own subordination.

We will be looking more closely at anarchism—at its implications for feminism and at the implications of contemporary social movements for it—in the sections to follow. Once again we will be arguing that this perspective—and the criticism of hierarchy and domination from which it stems—provides a much firmer grounding for feminist theory and strategy than does any of the other traditions.

## II. DOMINANCE AND SUBORDINATION

More than two thousand years ago, Aristotle said that for human beings to have a good life, they must realize a complete development of their abilities in their activities.[8] Of course they must have an adequate supply of external goods, too: food, clothing, shelter. Most of us would probably agree that a complete development of abilities in activities is needed for a good life. We would also want to turn it around and say that a fulfilling life requires that there be activities open to a person that permit complete development of his or her abilities.

Many people in the United States today would agree with something like that characterization of a good life, and some of our psychologists have related this idea to the idea of maturity, the child moving toward such a development as he or she grows older.

These psychologists have certain hypotheses about people in "our culture." They claim that we tend to develop from a state of passivity and dependence as infants to increasing activity and independence as adults. They say we tend to develop toward being able to act in many different ways in many different kinds of situations, while at the same time we develop deep, long-term interests. They say we tend to develop from being in a subordinate position in family and society to one of equality with peers, or superordinacy with others. Finally, they say we tend to develop an awareness of self and self-control, and control over our lives, leading to a sense of integrity and self-worth.

That is a *normative* definition of maturity. It is not properly respectful of children. And it is not available to large groups of people in our society, for reasons we will discuss. But its desirability is empirically supported in what people in our culture *feel* is important and what bothers them when it is lacking. We may take it as specifying to some degree what is needed to realize one's abilities in activities and thus have a good life.

It is clear from the description that people need to be able to develop various abilities and, along with that, a sense of competence and self-confidence. We will begin with this characterization and look more directly both at the conditions necessary for that to be achieved, and at the ways in which hierarchy and dominance and subordination can be used to help or hinder that process of development.

First, we will look at an informal, nonhierarchical situation (a Sunday-afternoon picnic) in which one person gets to develop his competence and self-confidence by being dominant in the situation, putting others in a subordinate position in which they are forced to behave in ways the psychologists we quoted would call "immature."

We will then look at some social situations in which there is an explicit hierarchical structure, to see how dominance and subordination are made "legitimate" through the roles in a hierarchy. The most severe formally structured situation we will consider is what Erving Goffman calls the "total institution" (1961). After looking at the ways total institutions structure roles, we will examine family and workplace hierarchies, as less extreme examples of hierarchical social structures. In each of these cases, we will discuss how people holding dominant positions in the hierarchy get to develop abilities that seem important to living a good life, while those in subordinate positions are forced to develop characteristics that most people consider disadvantageous in achieving that goal.

These are all *situationally* caused disadvantages due to a person's role in a hierarchy. We want to show, beyond that, that these structured hierarchies in fact underlie dominance and subordination in the broadest sense: the dominance of higher class over lower, of male over female, of adult over child, of white over nonwhite, of human over nonhuman. It is this broad sense, not restricted to particular family, work, or other hierarchies, that is most important to anarchist feminists. We will try to indicate how this very broad dominance depends on hierarchical social structures and how it is enforced by the state and economic coercion, which supports those hierarchies. The hierarchies themselves give a basis for the centralization that allows the state and economic coercion to operate. Centralization also allows reality itself to be "officially defined" through the viewpoints of members of dominant groups, so that the viewpoints and the very selves of members of subordinate groups become invisible, lost to official history, lost to official politics, but, as we will see in section III, *not* lost as a force for social change.

## An Informal Situation

Let's suppose that it's a beautiful, warm Sunday afternoon in Indian summer. We're all going to the house of a friend who has a big pleasant yard. Duke shows up with a volleyball and sets up his portable net and enthusiastically gathers us to play volleyball. Emmylou and Doctor John want to play a little music and have everybody sing and dance, especially because the children can do that, too; but Duke carries the day. He refreshes us on the rules and tactics of volleyball, and we all start playing. He's a pretty good player, and he begins playing not only his own position but Emmylou's and Doctor John's too, shouting, "I'll get it," so that they back off. Gradually, Emmylou and Doctor John stop covering the outer parts of their territory and become tentative and unsure in their moves. Eventually, they become demoralized and passive. Duke is in a superordinate position and gets practice at making long-range plans and at having command of a situation. He has succeeded in getting everyone to take part in an activity that allows him to exercise and develop *his* abilities—particularly athletic ones. He has control over this part of his life, at least, and gets a sense of integrity and self-worth out of the afternoon.

Emmylou and Doctor John gradually move into a subordinate position in which they feel they have little ability to control things, and they develop feelings of lack of self-worth. They also get no practice in having command of the situation, but a lot of practice in being subordinate.

The point is that in these situations, the dominant person gets to develop abilities needed to have command of a situation, as well as other abilities. The subordinate person tends to be put in a position where "immature" action is required. He or she develops the abilities needed for a subordinate and does not get to develop a wider range of abilities.

The volleyball game was an informal situation, where domination and subordination were "enforced" by force of personality. One way of looking at hierarchies is as systems of interaction that require and reinforce those relationships of domination and subordination—not on the basis of personality, but through their *formal* structure and organization. We face these kinds of hierarchies everywhere—for example, school, professions, government, family, and work.

Unlike the Sunday-picnic situation, a hierarchy involves a group of people who regularly do a certain set of activities together. Each person's part in the activities is conditioned by conventional understanding of roles, by explicitly set out job descriptions, or by rules of one type or another.

## Total Institutions

What Erving Goffman calls "total institutions" are extreme examples of such formal, hierarchical systems that enforce dominance and subordination. To understand what happens to people in these institutions is to see the extent of hierarchy's impact. "Total institutions" include nursing homes and orphanages, mental hospitals, prisons, boarding schools and army barracks, convents and monasteries. Goffman says,

> A basic social arrangement in modern society is that the individual tends to sleep, play, and work in different places, with different co-participants, under different authorities, and without an over-all rational plan. The central feature of total institutions can be described as a breakdown of the barriers ordinarily separating these three spheres of life. (1961, 435)

Instead, there is a single source of authority (the staff). Staff members plan all activities for subordinates (the "inmates"). These activities take place according to a schedule. They are set about by rules, which all people classified into the particular subordinate group must follow. Even the most personal events, such as going to the bathroom or brushing one's teeth, wait upon the schedule and the authority. For example, in nursing homes, a resident must wait until the aide gets to her, and then go through the morning's wash, bathroom, and dress-up according to the rhythm of the aide's job. The resident is not allowed to follow her own life rhythm.

In the context of a total institution, the staff often sees the inmates as secretive and untrustworthy, and they in turn see staff as condescending and high-handed. So far as self-opinion goes, Goffman says that "staff tends to feel superior and righteous; inmates tend, in some way at least, to feel inferior, weak, blameworthy, and guilty" (1961, 436). The *official point of view*, however, belongs to the staff, not only because both groups take the views or interests of the institution to *be* those of the staff, but because the staff writes up the reports on the inmates and has the power to judge and punish. Inmates are coerced, pretty directly, into acting as subordinates.

In total institutions, the inmates cannot take part in activities that allow them to have control over their lives, and they are prevented from having the opportunity for self-determination, which is necessary for adults. The movie *One Flew over the Cuckoo's Nest* shows adults forced to act like children. To visit a relative in a nursing home or in prison is to see how total institutions prevent people from having activities that use abilities they need to act "maturely." They have to learn to act like subordinates.[9]

## The Family

Goffman overstated his case when he suggested that all other people in modern society tend to sleep, play, and work in different places, and under different authorities. Housewives and small children tend to sleep, play, and work in the same place, as do agricultural workers, or those who live in "company towns." For many *small* children, the family functions like a total institution, and it may suit them no better than nursing homes suit their great-grandmothers.

For most people, however, the family is not a total institution in Goffman's sense. Most women, for example, spend a substantial proportion of their time outside the household, acting in different contexts, and under different authorities (in the workplace, the supermarket, interacting with teachers at school, etc.). Children have the opportunity to play with other children, according to rules and procedures they set for themselves; and older children leave home for school. (While it is true that school is another hierarchical institution, the point here is that it is a different one.)

Nevertheless, there are some aspects of life in total institutions that operate in families and other hierarchies as well. An "official point of view" helps to maintain the subordination of women, for example: The woman who is a housewife may be dominant over her children and in certain work realms it's "her kitchen." But there is an official point of view that also defines which activities are valuable and important (Dad's work is more important than Mom's; Dad's sports are more important than Mom's hobbies). And it designates some activities as "work," and others as simply "doing what mothers do." These activities, and the evaluations of them, are supported—in ways we can already begin to see—by other institutions and practices in our society.[10] We'll return to this below.

The family hierarchy trains both women and children in how to be subordinates, in the family and outside it. That training is then reinforced by schools and by work hierarchies. Both within and beyond any particular work hierarchy, economic and state coercion are used directly to enforce continued subordination.

## The Workplace

Let us look at the workplace as an example of hierarchy, to see how these interconnections are made and maintained. Many work hierarchies in our society are governed by what were originally developed as principles of "scientific management."[11] Over the past hundred years, the structure of work in the United States has become more "scientized"—and more hierarchical—as part of the economic, social, and political changes that have accompanied industrialization.[12] We will examine the nature and impact of these changes in greater detail below. In any case, some type of principles of scientific management now govern the organization of much work. Under these principles, work is *specialized*: Different people do different tasks. There is a chain of command: a hierarchy of authority, with those higher up controlling, directing, and coordinating the activities below. Since individuals on the bottom have to be motivated to do their part, those higher up have the formal power to hire, fire, reward, and punish. This power is legitimated by the rules of the hierarchy. Argyris says of this plan of organization:

> The impact of the principles is to place employees in work situations where they are provided minimal control over their workaday world; (2) they are expected to be passive, dependent, and subordinate; (3) they are expected to have the frequent use of a few skin-surface shallow abilities [because of the specialization]; (4) they are expected to produce under conditions leading to psychological failure. (1977, 267) [13]

We might also notice some other things about this pattern of organization. Specialization not only *divides* tasks, it also values them differentially. So, planning and "mental" tasks are separated from "carrying out" tasks; the former are considered more important, and those who do them are more highly valued and rewarded. Not only do they have *control* over their subordinates, they also get more satisfactions and rewards from their jobs.

### Discrimination or Subordination?

Liberal social critics (including feminists who base their criticism of hierarchy on liberal theory) might look at these hierarchies and acknowledge that they prevent some people from developing their abilities. But these critics tend to accept this limitation because of their understanding of the relationship of work hierarchy to the structure of society as a whole. From the liberal point of view, one aspect of that relationship is the claim that "one's work is not one's life." So, a liberal critic might say that people can develop themselves in other situations—through hobbies, or "leisure time activities," for example. In this view, the good life takes place in a person's "private life." Anarchists, as well as Marxists, have long argued that work is a central part of human life and self-expression, and that one's work cannot be separated from one's life. Workers seem to agree, because there are studies showing that workers want to enlarge areas of their lives in which their own decisions determine the outcome of their efforts, and they try to do this even in the workplace. [14]

Although we share the belief that work is an important, and inseparable, part of one's life, we do not base our criticism of hierarchy on that claim alone. There is a second aspect of the liberal view of the relationship between work life and social life that is also important to consider. And that is the connection between work hierarchy and societal patterns of dominance and subordination. We mentioned above that people in higher positions in the work hierarchy get paid more, are accorded more respect, and so on. When we look around at our society, we also notice that the tops of these hierarchies are full of white, higher-class, males, and that the bottoms are disproportionately full of nonwhites and females. [15]

Liberal theory assumes that hierarchies exist to take advantage of different "talents" and abilities, and that they ought, therefore, to be filled according to "merit." If groups of people are disproportionately represented in these hierarchies, that is a sign—in this view—of a poor distribution of people, probably caused by discrimination. So, a feminist basing her arguments in liberal theory would fight to end sex discrimination so that talented women could rise to the top on equal terms with white men. She would suppose that nonwhites would form their own interest groups to stop discrimination against themselves. If discrimination is stopped, then the hierarchy would be "fair."

This view of what is wrong with hierarchy is too limited. To talk of *discrimination* as the cause of male dominance, or white dominance, is to presuppose that it makes sense to talk about ranking people on some unitary scale according to their abilities. It is to presuppose that there *is* such a thing as a meritocracy, that those at the top deserve to be there because they are more able than those at the bottom. It is obvious, however, that we need lots of different kinds of people with different kinds of abilities to make the world go round. [16] There isn't any unitary scale along which to rank people's abilities, and there isn't any meritocracy. The features of hierarchy itself create the illusion that there is one. [17]

Within hierarchies, different work is defined as having different value. Those at the top do the work labeled "planning and direction," and that work is considered more valuable than the work of those at the bottom, which is labeled "manual," or "carrying out the plan." Officially, labor done by those at the bottom is devalued, whatever its actual contribution to the work of the hierarchy. A striking example here is the difference in value attached to the work of doctors as opposed to nurses, or administrative staff as opposed to aides, in a hospital.

An acceptance of hierarchy is an acceptance of a situation in which some people have opportunities to develop the abilities psychologists associate with maturity, and others are prevented from doing so. But it is more than that. Because, as we have also seen, people at the tops of hierarchies also obtain other advantages, and these work to enforce subordination of children, women, nonwhites, and people of the lower classes in society at large. Work hierarchies exist in a relationship of mutual reinforcement within a larger system of domination and subordination.

*Economic Coercion*

Work hierarchies reinforce patterns of domination through economic coercion, such as the power to hire, fire, give raises, or dock pay. Aside from adding to feelings of control (and to the feelings of lack of control on the part of those lower down), this structure rewards those higher up in other ways as well. Their work is considered more valuable, and they are accorded status and respect in society at large. Often they are paid more, and at greater intervals (they are paid monthly, with large bonuses annually; while "manual" workers are paid daily, or weekly). So, higher-ups have greater control over cash flow, more opportunity for saving and investing, and more chances to develop some of their abilities. They have more chances to own a home, thus more control of their home space. The opposite, obviously, is true for those lower down. Being paid less means that workers and their children have less opportunity for formal education. Working one's way through Greenfield Community College isn't the same as being sent to Harvard with an allowance.

Our society is not patriarchal in a strict sense, but many of our practices and policies presuppose that the norm is the male-headed family.[18] The fact that white men have "better jobs" than others reinforces their claim to "head" their families. In the past, the expectation that the man is head of the family justified paying women less at work. That fact, in turn, ensures that women on their own, or female-headed families, will not be able to "do as well" as male-headed ones. This economic coercion works to keep women in a family situation, and it supports male dominance across classes. Similar patterns exist for black workers, which also support racial domination.[19]

*Status Groups and Domination*

Those near the tops of hierarchies associate with one another during work times *and* during social times. They and their families associate with families of others at a similar level. This forms status groups. Members of these groups have access to a lion's share of the resources that allow people to develop many abilities (travel, art, attendance at Ivy League universities, music lessons, or internships in Washington). They also have access to the knowledge, influence, and power held by others in the status-groups network, so that they can learn to get things done, as well as do them themselves. Because of the family basis of status groups, in the future, places at the tops of hierarchies will be disproportionately filled by children of high-status families.

### Centralization and Domination

Hierarchy reinforces and perpetuates relations of domination and subordination by aiding centralization. Both economic and political (state) coercion operate by using hierarchies to maintain subordination.[20]

Centralization consolidates both power and status. Economic centralization made possible more effective management control over workers in the developing industrial system. This control was in turn supported by centralized political power; and, ultimately, it supported greater political centralization. For example, hierarchical organization of government and political parties made possible the centralization of political decision-making power in the hands of a fairly small number of people (not all of them elected officials). That power could then be used—both directly and indirectly—to protect the interests of those in positions of economic power; and to frustrate any attempts at change by less powerful economic groups.[21]

In addition to these patterns of relationships are the more subtle connections between the hierarchies, which reinforce a particular point of view and, in turn, maintain subordination. Hierarchical organization of the military, of business, and of "organized labor" centralizes decision making in those areas. Dwight Eisenhower's warning about the "military industrial complex" was a warning about the centralization of power that resulted from joining the tops of certain business hierarchies with the military. But even in nonwarlike domains such as baby-food production or copper mining, "spokesmen" from top offices in the industry represent the official viewpoint of that industry and give "facts" or advice to the government. The official view of "organized labor" or the "value-neutral" truth of science and the academy also come from the mouths of a small number of people—and there is no built-in way for anyone else to respond (except, seemingly, through other large, centralized organizations such as Common Cause, etc.).[22]

## Dominance and the "Official Point of View"

In this way, broad social control (not merely control in a single work or government hierarchy) is centralized to the benefit of a comparative few. As we've all noticed, the few are predominantly higher class, white, and male. Newspapers, television, history books, novels, and statuary report the words, deeds, and bodily forms of these men.[23] Their viewpoints come to define "official reality" and put limits even on the raising of alternative perspectives.[24] Their behavior comes to define the criteria by which both valuable work and admirable abilities and manners are judged. This devalues the work and styles of women, nonwhites, working-class people, and the young. It also operates to keep these people from rising in individual hierarchies, or from challenging the existence of hierarchies at all.

Rosabeth Kanter's work suggests that the homogeneity of people at the tops of hierarchies results not only from this singular definition of what's valuable and important but also from the uncertainty in the definition of what constitutes success in a managerial job. The fact that managers spend most of their time communicating with one another leads them to select other managers who are, at least, similar to them in certain characteristics:

> The structure of communication involved in managerial jobs generated a desire for smooth social relationships and a preference for selection of those people with whom communication would be easiest. . . .
> One way to ensure acceptance and ease of communication was to limit managerial jobs to those who were socially homogeneous. Social certainty, at least, could compensate for some of the other sources of uncertainty in the tasks of management. (Kanter 1977, 58)

Uncertainty about management tasks, and the vast volume of communication involved, are both aspects of hierarchial organization. As a consequence of these, however, people who have *different* ways of operating or communicating are labeled hard to communicate with and are excluded from managerial positions on that basis. Thus Kanter reports, from management's point of view: "Women were decidedly placed in the category of the incomprehensible and unpredictable. There were many reports that managers felt uncomfortable having to communicate with women. 'It took more time,' they said. 'You never knew where you stood'" (Kanter 1977, 58). Nonwhites and working-class people are also hard for these white male managers to understand. And so they, too, find themselves disproportionately unrepresented in management positions.

~

Total institutions, the family, schools, and work hierarchies all offer ways for those who are dominant to define reality in terms of their "official point of view," and for them to exercise control over others in society through the imposition of this point of view as the *only* one. When members of subordinate groups engage in activities that threaten that definition of reality (showing them to be able and competent, for example) members of dominant groups either define those activities as unimportant, or else absent themselves from the arena. Higher-class white men avoid the streets of working-class or nonwhite neighborhoods where working-class or nonwhite men are dominant, even when there is no physical danger. Some husbands rigidly avoid sports and cultural activities in which their wives are adept and knowledgeable. Doctors may not be present when nurses or aides sit around with one another and discuss *their* understanding of patients, or of the medical hierarchy in which they all participate. This way of behaving is one way in which members of dominant groups define reality.

There is another side to the story, however. People in subordinate statuses, women, children, nonwhites, and those of lower class, *do* develop abilities and have knowledge that members of dominant status groups do not. The "official" definition from the dominant viewpoint stereotypes these people as subordinate "through and through." But people who may act as subordinate in one setting do not necessarily have their whole selves defined through that behavior. In fact, they may share another view of reality, a view often quite different from the "official" view. This provides them with opportunities to challenge both the "official" view of reality and the existing distribution of power and privilege in society. In order to survive, they must know the official point of view; but they also know, firsthand and in the utmost intimacy, wherein it is false.

The question we turn to now is how the viewpoints of subordinate people are to be used in a strategy for social change. How is this power of subordinate people to be released? How can subordinate people overcome their subordination?

## III. OVERCOMING SUBORDINATION

Feminists criticize our society for not achieving its point, for not permitting many people to develop in what we consider mature, self-actualizing ways. Feminist say that hierarchies and patterned relationships of domination and subordination prevent many of us from realizing these goals. We have already compared the criticisms of hierarchy given within the liberal, the Marxist, and the radical-feminist traditions with that of the anarchist tradition. Now we want to look at the movements to change those conditions, to see if they can achieve their aim of allowing all of our people to work for good, fulfilling lives. This means looking not only at their criticisms of our society, and not only at the vision of some future society. It means looking at the *process* of change embodied in the movements themselves.

Let's look in more detail at some of the anarchist principles we mentioned earlier. One important anarchist principle is that means must be consistent with ends. The process of revolution must be consistent with the point of the revolution. We cannot hope to establish a society that achieves its point by using an organizational structure that undermines the point. Hierarchical revolutionary organizations do just that.

One reason that hierarchical revolutionary organizations are objectionable is pretty obvious: When people get in positions of power, they find it next to impossible to relinquish it. But that is a symptom, not the disease. The real reason is that there is no way to overcome longstanding patterns of domination and subordination except by overcoming them. We can't "learn" how to act in nondominating ways in an organization based in hierarchical structures. We can not learn to think and act for ourselves in those Marxist groups in which the leadership works out theory and plans strategy and hands down orders to the cadre, who then try to go out and organize us masses. Nor can we learn to think and act for ourselves in liberal groups in which the leadership of an "interest group" carries out lobbying and political pressuring for a constituency whose participation consists in donating funds or writing a letter on request. If we have been subject to subordination, we can learn to think and act for ourselves only by doing that: by joining together in organizations in which our experience, our perception, and our activity guide and make the revolution.

Anarchists traditionally have talked about this kind of revolutionary activity as "propaganda by the deed," or as "spontaneous organization." By that we do not mean activity that begins and ends in tossing bombs into banks or tossing monkey wrenches into assembly-line machines. We are referring to a strategy of direct action. Propaganda by the deed refers to ways people organize. Spontaneous organization is a way people join together to meet their goals.[25]

Propaganda by the deed refers to what we could call exemplary action, action that draws adherents by the power of the positive example it sets, and changes people in the process. An instance of propaganda by the deed is KOPN, the community-operated and collectively run radio station in Columbia, Missouri. The Amherst Food Coop is an example, as is the New England Federatoin of Cooperatives. Other examples include the New Words bookstore in Cambridge, the Cambridge Women's Health Center, Bread and Roses restaurant, and the Community Health Care Project in Florence, Massachusetts.

They are activities that arise from people's day-to-day needs and experiences. They represent ways in which people can take control—not over other people, but over their own lives. Participation in such activities allows people to develop a sense of competence and self-confidence. It *empowers* people, and fortifies them to act together. It is propaganda in another sense: It "speaks" to anyone else who might be around and willing to notice. It demonstrates by example that nonhierarchical forms of organization do and can exist, and that people can achieve valued goals in and through them. To communicate such a message believably is no small feat.

Spontaneous organization refers to another aspect of this phenomenon, emphasizing that both the *form* the organization takes and the *goals* people establish for it are not determined by some revolutionary cadre from above but by the people whose needs are expressed in it. Spontaneous organization shows in *practice* that people who have experienced subordination are—to put it most crudely—still capable of thought, still capable of action, and still capable both of knowing what their needs are, and of figuring out ways to meet them.

We should not be utopian about spontaneous organizations. An earlier anarchist, Enrico Malatesta, had some words of caution about worker co-ops:

> I recognize the extreme usefulness that co-operatives, by accustoming workers to manage their own affairs, the organization of their work, and other activities, can have . . . as experimental organizations capable of dealing with the distribution of goods and serving as nerve centers for the mass of population. . . .
>
> [But] in my opinion, cooperatives and trade unions under a capitalist regime do not naturally or by reason of their intrinsic value

lead to human emancipation but can be producers of good and evil. (*Umanitá Nova*, April 13, 1922)[26]

Anyone who has worked with a spontaneous organization knows firsthand that there must be a constant struggle against the "shopkeeper spirit," against reproducing hierarchy within the organization, against reproducing white, higher-class, or male dominance within the organization. The problem isn't a simple one of carrying over attitudes of the larger society. We all must continue to live in the larger society, and the spontaneous organization must succeed in that context. The success can never be more than partial, and the spontaneous organizations themselves are always experiments in trying to understand and develop nonhierarchical, decentralized ways of doing what we need to do and what we want to do.[27] Within them, subordinates always face a struggle to overcome their own subordination, and to educate and change themselves and the members of dominant groups who work with them.

Still, there are many examples from our own recent history that might help to illustrate the power of propaganda by the deed and spontaneous organizations. Many women say that some of their most important experiences in the women's movement were in consciousness-raising groups. Those groups enabled women to talk (instead of being silent), to recognize that they had *ideas*, and that they had *grievances*—and, more importantly, perhaps, that their experiences and their grievances were *shared*. Through talking with other women, we were able to recognize what seemed to be our personal failings as consequences of larger patterns of domination and subordination. And the "simple" fact of recognizing that changed our reality. It is not surprising that so many women felt strengthened by consciousness-raising sessions and motivated to act. Acting together—on the basis of needs and goals we *defined for ourselves*—strengthened us further and gave us the power to continue, even against obstacles. Out of this came the self-help movement; community clinics; a variety of feminist, collectively owned and run businesses; and feminist journals and women's studies programs. These practices of the feminist movement are good examples of anarchist strategy. Though they are far from perfect, they demonstrate that new forms of meeting needs are possible. They *change* people—both participants and observers—in the process.

In addition to propaganda by the deed and spontaneous organization, anarchists have traditionally talked about decentralism. Part of the reason for urging a decentralized society lies in the monstrous effects of centralization. In part, anarchist arguments against centralization have been arguments against the state, any state with police and military force, courts and prisons, including the socialist state. We suggested in section II that state coercion is an important mechanism for keeping certain groups subordinate.

In part, anarchist arguments against centralization have been against our capitalist economic system, which centralizes power in the hands of the minority who have control of the wealth. This centralization allows economic coercion to keep some groups subordinate.[28]

In the process of the anarchist revolution, using the experience of our own lives as the basis for understanding and action, we come to understand decentralism as we build it.[29] We do this in building spontaneous organizations, particularly in the form of community control, worker ownership and control, tenant control, and consumer control, as well as the co-op organizations and networks. These help create the understanding of what decentralism is in practice. If they are politically strategic, they also operate against centralized political and economic power.

By now, any liberal or Marxist feminists probably have two serious questions about this spontaneity and decentralism. They are serious questions for us, too, so let's ask them.

First, a question about spontaneity. We've talked about spontaneous organization of health centers, food co-ops, restaurants and other businesses, and consciousness-raising support groups. What *political* relevance do these things have? What makes them have revolutionary force toward changing our society? Do they just take up people's energies and give them some new hobbies and leave our coercive society unchanged?

Historical and sociological data show that "spontaneous" protest actions by people in subordinate positions are aimed at what *they* perceive to be the cause of their oppression, and what *they* perceive to be that part of the cause they can act effectively against.[30] Anyone who has been involved in these protests, and anyone who has talked seriously to working-class people, black people, young people, or women about their subordination knows this. Tenants strike against landlords, young people act against local police or teachers and principals. Nearly always, these people are correct that what they act against is really *a* cause of their problem, and that it is really a factor they have a chance at being effective against. It is rarely the ultimate cause, for more ultimate causes are hidden from view and protected from protest. Tenants cannot touch bankers or financiers very well, students have more trouble acting against the government and industry, which shape their education—although in the late 1960s both groups managed this.

But this problem of reaching more ultimate causes isn't to be solved by a group of trained Marxist cadre dropping in to do propaganda by the word and taking over leadership, nor is it to be solved by liberal professionals in community organizing who take over leadership. People learn from their experiences and from the experiences of others in similar situations. What works is a network of communication among groups of people in similar situations so that we may learn from our own and others' successes and failures: visits to other places and visitors from other places, and a network of communication. That is education to consciousness. In the process of engaging in these activities, people learn strategy. We have very good examples of this sort of thing from the black and poor people's and youth movements in the 1960s; and in the women's and ecological movements in the 1970s.

This answers part of the question—that posed by Leninists who claim that average people, left to themselves, will never develop an understanding of ultimate causes and will never "progress" beyond what Lenin termed "trade union consciousness." But there is another aspect to the issue of the *political* relevance of these organizations: What makes them revolutionary organizations rather than cooperative clubs? If we recognize that there are some kinds of organizations that might just let people feel better, while maintaining—or even reinforcing—dominance, how do we distinguish among organizations? Of course no revolutionary strategy comes with a guarantee that it will not be co-opted. Still, it might be helpful to know what types of organizations are less subject to that threat, or are most likely to contribute to the overcoming of subordination.

There are at least the beginnings of an answer in what we have said so far. If the point of social change is to overcome subordination, so as to enable people to live good, fulfilled lives, then those organizations that contribute to people's actually exerting such control are those that fulfill a revolutionary purpose. It is the *process* that is crucial. Organizations in and through which people are able to exercise some degree of control over the conditions of their life—and through which they can, together with others, experience the *changes* as of their own doing—must, of necessity, be "revolutionary." Such organizations are not making people simply feel better. In fact, as people struggle to improve their conditions, they may actually become more aware of their subordination, and thus feel "worse" about their situations. What these organizations do, however, is to develop in people a sense of their own power. If there can be *any* measure of the "progressiveness" of an organization or strategy, it must be that.[31] Even that, it is true, is no guarantee against co-optation. But at least it gives us a way to begin talking about strategies and evaluating them.[32]

The second question is about coordination. Spontaneous organization makes sense as a way of developing consciousness and strategy when the people working in the different spontaneous organizations see their work as similar or compatible. But how can we link people in spontaneous organizations that are dissimilar and perhaps even antagonistic—not only in their members' perceived goals but in their modes of relating to one another? Many feminists perceive some left groups that include either black or white males as the most macho, sexist, male imperialist things we have ever come up against, and we find it impossible to work with them. It was for this reason that there was great debate in socialist-feminist women's unions over "autonomous" women's groups—linked externally with "mixed" groups. It is one reason why some radical feminists are separatists.

So what is our anarchist solution to this "linkage problem"? Before talking about that, we need to clarify just what the problem is.

Liberal, Marxist, radical, and anarchist feminists offer different solutions to the linkage problem because they ask different questions. They even *perceive* the linkage problem differently because of their differences in political and social theory.

Liberal feminists see a plurality of competing interest groups. To overcome what they perceive as discrimination against women, they work to organize women into an interest group that can use political pressure to get the state to use its coercive power in their favor—thus the recourse to legislation and the courts. NOW, for example, takes its constituency as an interest group and usually has operated on the principle that it will fight for issues of interest to *all* women—and this has led to charges of racism when NOW has refused to move on issues most seriously affecting the interest of third-world women. If liberal feminists ever notice a problem of linking subordinate groups, they tend to see it as a problem of a coalition of interest groups that have a stake in a particular issue.

This pluralist thinking is enormously difficult to overcome. We find ourselves slipping into it. We find it underlying the thinking of many, many Marxist feminists. We all grew up with it.

Marxists in general attempt to escape from this thinking by emphasizing the centralized power of the bourgeois state and the centralized power of capitalism. This leads them to ask the question, How can we *organize* a unified force to overthrow the unified, centralized force of the state? Asking the question leads us straightaway to seeing centralized revolutionary organization as the solution. The problem of antagonistic subordinate groups is allegedly solved by a vast superstructure of theory, which places the interests of one subordinate group in the vanguard, behind which members of all the other subordinate *and* dominate groups are supposed to range themselves. In fact, this has never worked in the United States, even on a small scale.

Now, what we've said here is that there is a serious problem somehow involved in these antagonistic subordinate groups. The liberal suggestion preserves hierarchy and domination. The Marxist suggestion, at best, is a theoretical one that has never worked here; at worst, it is a suggestion that preserves centralization, hierarchy, and dominance. What do we have to say, as anarchists?

We are not grand strategists. We do believe that the anarchist principles of decentralism, propaganda by the deed, spontaneous organization, and self-determination are the best ones for making the revolution and forming the revolutionary society. This suggests a number of possibilities. First, we must not undervalue, or shy away from, *partial* successes. Even though we must not be utopian about the achievements of spontaneous organizations in our society, it is important to recognize just what such organizations have accomplished and to attempt to learn from both their successes and their failures.[33] To speculate a bit further, if we don't focus all our attention on the centralized power of the state, we may find strategies that let us work together in smaller, non-national units—for example, northern and central New England and the Maritime states of Canada share a great deal and form a certain kind of natural, economic, and cultural unit. The science-fiction book *Ecotopia* describes such an anarchist society created when northern California, Oregon, and Washington secede from the United States.[34]

Second, we can recognize the tactical or strategic necessity of engaging in joint *actions* with other subordinate groups, on specific issues—even if the general goals, structures, and methods of those groups are such that we would not *join* them. We have in mind here, for example, the broad coalitions formed to struggle against restriction of access to abortion, or against sterilization abuse. In other words, a strategy of direct action need not force us into a totally separatist stance. Rather, it derives from an understanding of strategy and process that allows us to see what kinds of behavior are likely to do the most to overcome subordination.[35]

Finally, we must remember the point of all this: the overcoming of subordination. People act out of their own understanding of their subordination. We do not wish to rank those subordinates, or to argue which is "primary." To the extent that these groups—however different their structures and methods of operating—aim at overcoming subordination, there may be at least *some* basis for cooperation. But that method of cooperation must lead us to respect the experiences represented in each of the groups. There may, in fact, not be any way to resolve this issue immediately and completely. To the extent that all subordinate groups are struggling against the patterns of domination that maintain their subordination, even "uncoordinated" struggles have the potential to weaken those larger patterns and strengthen the struggling groups. We can learn from one another by talking, watching, or perhaps participating.

So, we aren't grand strategists, but we do know that no strategy is worth anything unless it *aims* at the goal of the revolutionary movement. It must show the right way to the right ends. If the end is the possibility of a good life for all our people, if the end is the overcoming of dominance and subordination, even if the end is only the overthrow of capitalism by the working class, the strategy must accomplish certain things. It must provide a way for people to gain revolutionary consciousness of their situation. It must provide a way for people who have been in subordinate positions all their lives to learn the skills and to acquire the abilities necessary to operate an industrial society. It must provide a way for people to learn to organize a new society that will not reproduce the oppressions they are fighting against. Finally, the strategy must be one that makes sense to people out of the experience of their own lives. Out of that, people will develop as effective tactics as our historical situation permits.

We believe that such a strategy is necessary for the feminist movement. We believe that anarchism offers that strategy.

## Notes

1. Kathy Ferguson makes a similar survey of political traditions in Ferguson 1978, especially 96–99. But she does not relate them to hierarchy in particular.

2. One of the best collections of such writings is Eisenstein 1977. For a careful statement by socialist feminists of the difficulty of uniting Marxism and feminism, see also Hartmann 1981.

3. Hartmann points to this problem as well in "The Unhappy Marriage of Marxism and Feminism." See Hartmann 1981.

4. See Dworkin 1977, especially "The Root Cause" and "The Sexual Politics of Fear and Courage."

5. Others who have argued for the relevance of anarchism to feminism include Kornegger 1975, and Ehrlich 1977.

6. Writings by anarchists on these topics are extensive. Some of the most easily available—and which address themselves to these issues—include: Goldman 1969; Peter A. Kropotkin, "Anarchist Communism: Its Basis and Principles," "Anarchism: Its Philosophy and Ideal," and "Modern Science and Anarchism," in Baldwin 1970; Michael Bakunin, "On Federalism and Socialism," "God and the State," and "The Paris Commune and the Idea of the State," in Lehning 1974. More recent writings include Guerin 1970, especially chaps. 1 and 2; Bookchin 1971; Carter 1971, especially chap. 3; and Ward 1973.

7. See, especially, Ward 1973. The experiences of anarchist collectives in Spain provide some examples of ways in which people organized themselves to meet their needs. See,

for examples, Gaston Leval, *Collectives in the Spanish Revolution* (London: Freedom Press, 1975); José Peirats, *Anarchists in the Spanish Revolution* (Toronto: Solidarity Books, n.d.); Vernon Richards, *Lessons of the Spanish Revolution* (London: Freedom Press, 1972).

8. Aristotle did not believe that it is equally within the capacity of all human beings to live a good, or fully realized life. Some people, he thought, are able only to meet their most basic, animal-like needs; while others are capable of developing varied abilities. Still, he was clear that the *fully* human life entails the exercise of a wide range of abilities.

9. On prisons, and the ways in which they deny the full range of inmates' personhood, see Jessica Mitford, *Kind and Usual Punishment* (New York: Alfred A. Knopf, 1973) and Peter A. Kropotkin, "Prisons and Their Moral Influence on Prisoners," in Baldwin 1970, 219–35. There are also many firsthand accounts that illustrate this point. For example, George Jackson, *Soledad Brother* (New York: Bantam Books, 1970); Malcolm X 1964.

10. See Broverman et al., "Sex-Role Stereotypes and Clinical Judgments of Mental Health," *Journal of Consulting and Clinical Psychology* 34 (1970): 1–7. Sara Ruddick and Pamela Daniels, eds., *Working It Out* (New York: Pantheon, 1977), provides numerous examples of the ways in which that official point of view penetrates into people's lives—even among feminists, both male and female.

11. There have been a number of interesting studies recently on work, its definition, and its evaluation—especially as regards male-female divisions. See, for example, Amy Bridges and Batya Weinbaum, "The Other Side of the Paycheck," and Rosalyn Baxandall, Elizabeth Ewen, and Linda Gordon, "The Working Class Has Two Sexes," both in *Monthly Review* 28, no. 3 (July–August 1976): 88–104; 1–9. Rubin 1976 discusses some of the ways in which subordination affects life in the working-class family.

12. We have relied heavily on Argyris 1977 in the discussion of psychologists' views on maturity, and in the discussion of scientific management. His essay has many good references. Braverman 1974 discusses the impact of contemporary refinements of scientific management on workers and particularly on the possibility of a working-class consciousness.

13. In addition to Braverman, we have found Katherine Stone's work on the steel industry to be helpful in understanding these changes in work organization. See Stone 1973.

14. See Argyris 1977, 263; and also A. Gorz, *A Strategy for Labor* (Boston: Beacon Press, 1968). Ely Chinoy's *Automobile Workers and the American Dream* (Boston: Beacon Press, 1955) could be taken as a counterexample: workers "putting up" with lack of control in the factory in hopes of earning money to live better in their "private lives." But even there, workers report frustration with the conditions of their work; and their ideal visions for their future include opening a shop of their own, where they could be their *own* boss, and exercise control over their work conditions.

15. Since, by definition, the bottoms of the hierarchies are full of working-class people, most liberals tend not to notice that. Thus, the meritocratic perspective, to be discussed below, makes working-class people inferior "by definition."

16. Younger children may know this better than older. The grading system in school, in which children are ranked according to their ability to perform on classroom tests, offers powerful propaganda for meritocracy. Those who refuse to perform according to school expectations end up having fairly clearly a double consciousness, simultaneously thinking of themselves as unworthy and stupid; and knowing that those who did well in school *aren't* better and *don't* have more merit and may, in fact, be *more* stupid in many ways: dupes of the system. Christopher Jencks et al. (1972) talk about the way this operates in our school system.

17. Richard Sennett and Jonathan Cobb (1973) have written about how this illusion of meritocracy is supported by both schools and work hierarchy; and also about the effects it has on participants. See also Jencks et al. 1972.

18. In one strict sense, a patriarchy is one in which the political as well as the economic units are male-headed families. For example, in Puritan New England, the male head represented the political voice of the whole family.

19. Chafe 1977 has a fine presentation of these interconnections, and of the parallels (and differences) between racial and sexual domination. We have benefited considerably from his analysis. (Public consciousness of these things has changed greatly in the years since this chapter was written. But the substance of what we say here still holds.)

20. Katherine Stone's study of changing work organization in the steel industry at the turn of the century demonstrates how work hierarchies were designed to enforce the subordination of workers, and how that subordination was further supported by political and other institutions. We have been helped a great deal by her analysis. See Stone 1973.

21. Martin Shefter's studies of the Tammany political machine in New York document these processes in informative detail. See, for example, Shefter's "The Emergence of the Political Machine: An Alternative View," in Hawley, Lipsky, et al., *Theoretical Perspectives on Urban Politics* (Englewood Cliffs, N.J.: Prentice-Hall, 1976), 14–44. W. D. Burnham's study of the 1896 election and its consequences points up the ways in which changing party organization prevented large groups of people from organizing to change either the distribution of power in society, or their immediate social and economic conditions. S. P. Hays demonstrates that the interconnections between economic and political forms was continued into the Progressive Era, despite the Progressives' rhetoric to the contrary, in "The Politics of Reform in Municipal Government in the Progressive Era," in A. Callow, ed., *American Urban History* (New York: Oxford University Press, 1969), 421–39. The point is to note that changes in organizational structure changed the ways in which people related to their political system, and, thus, the ways they had available to influence it. And, in particular, they laid the basis for the operation of laissez-faire policies in the early years of this century which, in turn, allowed for further consolidation of economic and political power in the hands of a few.

22. This structuring of influence in and through large-scale, hierarchical organizations has significant impact on resulting policies. Much recent literature in political science has examined those connections. Mills 1956, despite its flaws, opened many of these issues to thoughtful discussion. More recent examinations include Theodore Lowi, *The End of Liberalism* (New York: W. W. Norton, 1969); Grant McConnell, *Private Power and American Democracy* (New York: Alfred A. Knopf, 1966); J. David Greenstone, *Labor in American Politics* (New York: Alfred A. Knopf, 1969); and Matthew A. Crenson, *The Unpolitics of Air Pollution* (Baltimore: Johns Hopkins University Press, 1971).

23. The battles for black studies programs and women's studies programs have been fights by subordinate groups to alter this situation, as have efforts to change television programming, movie-making, and elementary-school readers.

24. On the ways in which the existing "rules of the game" operate to protect the power of some, and make difficult the raising of alternatives on the part of others, see E. E. Schattschneider, *The Semi-Sovereign People* (New York: Holt, Rinehart and Winston, 1960) and P. Bachrach and M. Baratz, "Two Faces of Power," *American Political Science Review* 56 December 1962), 947–52. Steven Lukes develops and enlarges on this position in *Power* (New York: Macmillan Co., 1976). One need not argue a "conspiracy theory" here. The point is, simply, that the rules of acting in our society already advantage some and disadvantage others. Taking those rules as given enables those who benefit by them to exercise a certain degree of control over reality even without conscious manipulation.

25. On "propaganda by the deed," see, for example, Peter A. Kropotkin, "The Spirit of Revolt," in Baldwin 1970, 34–43. On "spontaneous organization," see "Expropriation" in Martin A. Miller, ed., *P. A. Kropotkin: Selected Writings on Anarchism and Revolution* (Cambridge: MIT Press, 1970) and Kropotkin 1913. See also Ward 1973 for a more contemporary treatment.

26. We took this quotation from a poster published by New Moon, c/o P.O. Box 263, Somerville, MA 02143. Malatesta goes on to say that the cooperatives have to be animated by the "anarchist spirit." In times of mass movement, like the late 1960s in the United States, it makes sense to talk of being animated by revolutionary spirit, for the rhetorical

phrase takes its empirical content from the mass movement. We have no such mass movement now in the United States.

27. For examples of some attempts at cooperative, nonhierarchical organizations at the workplace, and analyses of their coping with many of these issues, see D. Zwerdling, *Democracy at Work* (Washington, D.C.: Association for Self-Management, 1978), especially the chapters on McCayseville Industries and Cooperstown Central. The book also includes an excellent chapter on "collectives" (closer to what we have called spontaneous organizations) as models of "economic and political change in the community," with discussions of the problems they face trying to operate within a bureaucratically structured, capitalist society (77–90).

28. See, for example, Bakunin, "God and the State," (especially 28–39); "Paris Commune" in Lehning 1974, 195–213; and "Federalism, Socialism, and Anti-Theologism," in S. Dolgoff, ed., *Bakunin on Anarchy* (New York: Vintage Books, 1971). Also, Peter A. Kropotkin, especially "Law and Authority" and "Revolutionary Government," in Baldwin 1970, 195–218 and 236–50; and Goldman 1969, as well as "Woman Suffrage" and "The Tragedy of Woman's Emancipation," in the same work.

29. Here, again, we are indebted to the women's movement, and we see its parallels with anarchism. Nancy Hartsock writes, for example, "We cannot work . . . with people who refuse to face questions in terms of everyday life or with people who will not use their own experience as a fundamental basis for knowledge" (Eisenstein 1977, 72).

30. See, for example, F. F. Piven and R. A. Cloward, *Poor People's Movements* (New York: Pantheon, 1978), especially chap. 1, and *The Politics of Turmoil* (New York: Pantheon, 1974); Alinsky 1969, especially part II; E. J. Hobsbawm, *Primitive Rebels* (New York: W. W. Norton, 1962); Thompson 1968; Flexner 1971; Rowbotham 1974; Brecker 1974.

31. A number of people have made somewhat similar arguments, though based on a different analysis of subordination, which have contributed to this presentation. See, for example, Andre Gorz on "reformist reforms" versus "structural reforms" in the labor movement, in *A Strategy for Labor*, especially part 1; Nancy Hartsock on "Feminist Theory and Revolutionary Change," in Eisenstein 1977, especially 66, in which she talks about feminist action as (quoting Gramsci), "action 'which modifies in an essential way both man (!) and external reality,'" and 71–73 on "organizations and strategies"; also Hartsock 1974, 10–25; and Bunch 1974.

32. This is the point, in fact, where many of our anarchist forefathers turned to the "anarchist spirit" to sustain the revolution, and protect activities and organizations from the threat of "reformism." (See Kropotkin, "The Spirit of Revolt.") Since we do not really have, now, a mass movement, we cannot be so sanguine about the power of such a spirit—or where it would come from. Our answers, obviously, are not foolproof. But then, neither is social change.

33. Here we can also look to the experience of Spanish anarchists during the Civil War—and the ways in which their experiences both were, and were *not*, recognized by those who participated in them. On the collectives themselves, see Leval 1975. On the evaluation of the experiences, see Richards, *Lessons of the Spanish Revolution;* also Ackelsberg 1976, especially chap. 6 and Conclusion.

34. Ernest Callenbach, *Ecotopia* (New York: Bantam, 1977).

35. Compare Nancy Hartsock's suggestion that feminists join with others to the extent that they accept the material of their own lives as a basis for action, "Feminist Theory and Revolutionary Change," 72.

# *10*

## What Do Women Do?
## Some Radical Implications of Carol Gilligan's Ethics
### (1985)

My basic question is this: What would an ethics be like that took women seriously as moral beings?

On the surface, this may seem like a question asked out of ignorance. After all, the main criterion in contemporary ethics is that a genuine moral system must apply impartially to everyone. Principles must be universalizable. The good of a moral system must be the good for all men, women, and children. And yet I believe that asking about gender leads us to question the foundations of philosophical ethics and the theories of social and political organization that are implicit in the ethical systems. Asking about race, class, age, culture, or other systematic distinctions leads to these questions as well. But here, in a discussion of Carol Gilligan's work, I'll take up the point of gender.

Theories of ethics are about what people do, in a very deep sense. And if morality is specified in terms of what men do—or rather what higher-class men are *supposed* to do—then we will not have an ethics that takes other people, including women, seriously. Let me give an example.

Philosophers have often set the problem of abortion in terms of a conflict of rights: the fetus's right to life versus the woman's right to decide what will happen in and to her own body. They distinguish two different contexts in which the moral problem arises, the policy context in which laws and national policies are decided, and the personal context in which a woman considers whether or not to have an abortion.[1] The analysis in terms of universalizable principles about rights is supposed to suit moral reasoning in both contexts. But, in fact, the analysis is made for the policy context. The policy analysis fixes the personal one. It does not suit the way many people conceive the problem of abortion—for example, it does not capture how Gilligan's subjects understood the moral problem of abortion, nor is it the way Kristin Luker's pro-life women understood it (Gilligan 1982; Luker 1984). There is a serious political bias here, for the philosophers' analysis favors some ways of solving moral problems over others. The modes it favors are officially sanctioned, "legitimate" ones within the established system.

To define the moral problem of abortion in terms of a conflict of rights is to use what Lawrence Kohlberg called, "the official morality of the United States" (Kohlberg 1971). That is a morality of the group *politically* defined, that is, the polity. The activities important to the polity have, historically, been those of men of higher class: governing, heading households, judging, and so on.

"The official morality of the United States" is one that is supposed to apply to all spheres of life, but it is formed in what has been called "the public sphere" (in contrast to either the personal or the domestic spheres). Until recently, in the West, the public sphere consisted of activities men were supposed to do. Ideally (in the writings of theorists, as least) they were to do this public work with practical wisdom, or justice, or whatever the key moral basis of the ethics turned out to be. In the United States, it is only relatively recently that political arguments about sex bias and affirmative action led us to say that public-sphere activities ought to be done by both women and men. There has been a change in what we do. Does it require a change in our ethical theories? There are at least three ways of answering the question.

The first answer is a simple, "Of course not." Genuine ethics applies to all people irrespective of gender (or race, class, age, or culture). It is simply because of flaws in the social order that higher-class men have dominated the public sphere and gained the opportunity to develop what we all *ought* to develop in order to reason correctly about moral matters. That is Lawrence Kohlberg's answer. So far as I can see, it is the answer most philosophers give, although they disagree over what is the proper basis for ethical systems. It is also the liberal political answer. The problem is described as discrimination, and the resolution lies in equal opportunity and affirmative action. We change (or add to) what women do and show that a woman *can be* as good as a man.

A second answer is that we must correct and supplement our ethical theories because they are morally and empirically mistaken: They define human moral nature in terms of male nature—or human morality in terms of the morality of the public sphere, or the male sphere, or in terms of what higher-class men do. This is a widespread feminist claim. A few feminists have supposed that the compensation here is to analyze women's moral reasoning (within the domestic sphere perhaps) and give equal time to their different but equally valid kind of moral reasoning. Sometimes readers take Carol Gilligan to be doing this sort of compensatory work, discovering a different voice that complements the long-known male moral chorale. And so the moral concepts of the "different voice" are different: care instead of justice, responsibility instead of obligation, commitment instead of impartiality. Because morality is deeply about what people do, this approach carries presuppositions about what men and women do.

The third answer is that our ethical theories are more radically mistaken. They mistake what men and women do, morally speaking, or even socially speaking. Our theories are mistaken in the underlying presuppositions about human group life. It is an error that concerns what men and women and children do. I believe philosophical ethics suffers from this radical error. If we follow through the implications of Carol Gilligan's work, I believe we will find this more radical error in the Kohlberg ethics. How can we begin to use her work to ask questions of such a radical nature? One way is to discover more precisely how it falsifies or confirms Lawrence Kohlberg's work. Because Kohlberg is explicit about the philosophical ethics *and* the sociological theory of society he uses, we should be able to see the deeper implications of Gilligan's research.

The sociological tradition that lies behind the Kohlberg ethics owes its fundamental insights to Kant—just as his ethical theory does. The sociological route goes back from Kohlberg to Piaget to Durkheim to Kant. To make his sociology, Emile Durkheim relativized and "sociologised" Kantian epistemology—in a nutshell, he said that to understand the structure of a collectivity's classification of the world is to understand its principles of social organization. Influenced by Piaget, Kohlberg shows a concern with the individual and his or her development that Durkheim did not. But, like Durkheim, Kohlberg supposes there is an intimate connection between human social organization and human moral classification— or moral reasoning. It is the basis of the development theory, which claims we develop moral reasoning and the moral categories through the interaction of our cognitive structure and the social structure. The human "collectivity," *homo sapiens*, shares the basis of the cognitive structure and the social structure, though not all human individuals or societies develop the full structures, and so some do not express the full human morality.

I believe the central mistake here is to speak of a *collectivity's* categorization of the world. Speaking that way presupposes that there is a privileged categorization scheme for each collectivity (or for all humans, if we stay with Kant, Piaget, and Kohlberg). It is the assumption of a privileged moral categorization that Gilligan's work ought to challenge.[2]

The challenge is more radical than it may appear at first glance. In the Kohlberg theory, the "privileged categorization" is one that all human beings ought to use, and that all do use who have reached full moral development. Philosophers like John Rawls develop privileged categorizations without saying that everyone *ought* to use them. Rawls's ethics is supposed to be one a person *may* use in the assurance that it is impartial, fair, represents all moral perspectives, and so on. It is a privileged categorization for that individual in the sense that the individual decides on actions that affect others and judges others whether or not they use or even understand the ethical system. Philosophical ethics, with its criteria of generalizability, impartiality, and so on, is designed to allow this kind of privilege. The philosophical criteria are not enough by themselves, of course. They require certain kinds of similarity postulates for support—postulates that human beings and situations are similar in morally relevant respects. The postulates, in turn, require a particular idea of a social science.

It is this kind of privilege that Gilligan's work ought to challenge and that a feminist ethics must challenge. In this chapter, I will try to show the challenge.

I will first discuss Piaget and Kohlberg in a way that makes their sociological presuppositions evident. I will then set out Carol Gilligan's innovations. Next, I will use some recent research by feminist sociologists Marjorie DeVault and Arlene Daniels to show what our society looks like when we put aside the privileged categorizations. They discuss women's work in terms of care, work that is hidden by the official categories, work of the sort that creates and maintains the social structure itself.

My conclusion will be twofold. First, the very categories that most philosophers (and some sociologists) use to define a human collectivity are biased toward the life experience of dominant groups—or rather, toward the way the work of members of some dominant groups is officially represented. Correcting the bias requires a different social science and a different ethics. Second, in many social circumstances, for women (and all people) to take themselves seriously as moral beings requires that they change the social collectivities in which they live. Aristotle said something like this when he brought together the moral and the political in discussing what the man of practical wisdom does. But it means something quite different when we say it of women.

# MORAL DEVELOPMENT:
# THE KOHLBERG VARIATIONS

Lawrence Kohlberg's studies of moral development have their roots in the "genetic epistemology" of Jean Piaget. Piaget is Kantian to the degree that he believes that we make an active contribution to constructing our knowledge of the world. But where Kant tried to set out the necessary forms of cognition by rational arguments, Piaget studies the genesis of structures of cognition and their transformation—by observing children. Kant did epistemology and metaphysics, Piaget does psychology. Piaget says,

> Knowledge is an interaction between subject and object, and I think the subject cannot be locked in by a structure given once and for all, as the apriorists would have it. . . . Structures are not given in advance, neither in the human mind nor in the external world as we perceive and organize it. They are constructed by the interaction between the individual's activities and the object's reactions. (Bringuier 1980, 19, 37)

It is adaptation, but adaptation with two poles: the pole of subject assimilation and that of object accommodation (Bringuier 1980, 43).

In his work on development of moral reasoning, Piaget studied children in more-or-less natural settings, using a more-or-less intuitive understanding of ethics. Piaget worked at his institute, detached from other professional researchers. Kohlberg was deeply embedded in the professional, academic search for truth. Accordingly, there are significant differences in the two men's work. Kohlberg's most controversial assumption is that development of moral reasoning continues into young adulthood. But another important difference is that he uses a more precisely formulated ethics developed by professional philosophers. His reason for doing so is that a psychological theory of moral development must be a theory of *moral* development, and as such it requires a philosophical analysis of the morality, as well as an empirical demonstration that human beings actually use the moral reasoning. His model for "genuine morality" is based on John Rawls's version of the Kantian ethics.

This genuine morality is a principle morality having to do with judgments, decisions, and reasoning, using moral concepts of right and wrong, obligation, rights, and the like.[3] It is constructed so as to be objective (in some interesting sense), impartial, just, and fair. Fundamentally, these things are argued on the basis of a generalization principle. There are various ways to state the principle.[4]

What is right for one person cannot be wrong for another, unless there is some relevant difference in their natures or circumstances.

What is right (or wrong) for one person must be right (or wrong) for everyone, if there is no reason to the contrary.

What is right for one person must be right for every similar person in similar circumstances.

The criterion of generalizability allows a categorization to be privileged in the sense that an individual may use it or install it as the group ethics, even though others in the group do not use it, understand it, or acknowledge it in fact. The various statements of generalizability and genuine morality assume it makes sense to talk about morally relevant similarities in people and circumstances. This needs to be supported by a similarity postulate of one kind or another.

Similarity postulates, like aspirin, come in different strengths. For example, Baysian-utilitarian philosopher John Harsanyi requires a very strong similarity postulate because he requires interpersonal utility comparison in his ethics (that one person's preferences be comparable to other people's preferences).[5] He explains his similarity postulate in this way:

> The principle that, given the basic similarity in human nature (i.e., in the fundamental psychological laws governing human behavior and human attitudes), it is reasonable to assume that different people will show very similar psychological reactions to any given objective situation and will derive much the same utility or disutility from it— once proper allowances have been made for any empirical observed differences in their biological makeups, in their social positions, in their educational and cultural backgrounds, more generally, in their past life histories. In other words, in the absence of clear evidence to the contrary, the presumption must always be that people's behavior and psychological reactions will be similar in similar situations. (Harsanyi 1976, 301)

Harsanyi assumes that differences relevant to morality can be defined in terms of biological and social science.

John Rawls allows greater scope to individual variation, because he allows people a wide range of tastes in selecting one's goods.[6] However, there are similarities that he must presuppose. He bases his ethics on what he takes to be common in different people's perspectives, using the device of the "original position," from which an individual decides on principles for a society without knowing what his or her position would be within it. He also assumes people share a psychological and social nature that can be captured in social sciences. Rawls, like Durkheim and Kohlberg, believes social sciences can be modeled on the natural sciences, particularly in giving us general, predictive laws.[7]

A similarity postulate is a theoretical statement, but it is empirical in the sense that it must be embedded in some science that allows it to be tested. Kohlberg performs this service for the Rawls ethics. He devises a testable theory of moral development, and a method of testing whether his theory is true. His method is to compose standardized "moral dilemmas," present them to subjects, and score the responses according to a standardized manual.

The most widely known dilemma is "The Heinz": A woman is dying of cancer. There is one drug available that might save her, but the druggist who discovered it charges ten times what it costs him to make; the husband, Heinz, cannot raise the money to buy it. And so Heinz gets desperate, breaks into the store, and steals the drug.[8] The interviewer asks the subject whether the husband should have done that, then probes the subject's reasoning and records the replies. Someone types up the responses, and someone with special training scores them.

According to Kohlberg's original accounts, the scoring places the subject on a scale marked according to six stages, organized into three levels of moral reasoning. The three levels are the preconventional, the conventional, and the postconventional. The conventional level reasoning corresponds more or less to what Kant called heteronomous reasoning. Postconventional reasoning corresponds roughly to autonomous reasoning—or at least to the kind of reasoning that many contemporary Anglo-American philosophers analyze as moral reasoning.

The distinction between acting heteronomously and acting autonomously is crucial to Kohlberg's moral-development theory. Moral development requires a shift from heteronomous reasoning, in which social rules are viewed as changeless and constraining, to autonomous reasoning in which the social rules are viewed as human constructions, ideally the outcome of mutual agreement and respect. Under autonomous reasoning, a person chooses to follow the moral rules freely, or "gives himself a rule." The key relationship is between an individual and rules (or principles).

The theory of cognition that justifies Kohlberg's test methods is a variation of Jean Piaget's cognitive psychology. The shift from one stage to another takes place according to a roughly Piagetian principle of interaction between subject and object. But just as Kohlberg's ethical theory relies on technical developments in philosophy, his theory of cognition relies on professional theories of society and socialization. Kohlberg (1969,

1981) says that the stage theory is interactional. Stages are equilibrations arising from interaction between the organism (with its structuring *tendencies*) and the structure of environment (physical or social). Thus moral stages are as much a function of universal features of social structure as they are products of the general structuring tendencies of the knowing organism. This approach requires twin similarity postulates: similarity in those at the subject pole, and similarity in features of social structure.

Piaget's original work was on the development of causal, relational, and formal judgments and reasoning in children. Those sorts of reasoning have to do with understanding the Newtonian properties of bodies: number, quantity, motion, space, and the like. Because of our current Western beliefs in the objectivity of the natural sciences, it is easy to believe that all children develop invariantly through the same stages of cognition about the natural world. After all, the biological endowment and the natural world both seem to be constants, no matter what society or culture a person is born into. There is similarity at the subject pole because people have similar biological endowments. There is similarity at the object pole because we face essentially the same "nature." It is a different paradigm from Kant's, but like Kant's, it argues universality of judgment forms.

When Kohlberg uses this cognitive theory to explain moral development, he supposes that we face essentially the same human social environment. I don't mean that what sociologists call norms, rules, and customs are the same (Kohlberg 1971, 155). But the social structure with which any human being's cognitive structure interacts is the same—I here use Kohlberg's reifying language (Kohlberg 1969, 348). We may say that there is a model of society that social scientists may find out, which is the very model that human beings construct in their thought and their actions, and which is the model that explains the development of human moral cognition.

Societies become objects of scientific knowledge in the same way that nature is an object of scientific knowledge. Society and nature are both human constructions, but they are both at root *universal* human constructions. Natural scientists explain a natural world that is already to a degree constructed, and social scientists do the same for the social world. Thus the model that social scientists seek to find in their investigations is the model all human beings use. Though as Kohlberg's results "show," not all human beings understand it to the same degree.

On Kohlberg's scheme, differences in people's understanding of the social model are reflected in differences in their levels of moral cognition. In earlier studies, only about 4 percent of subjects turned out to use the highest sort of moral reasoning—the kind Kant and Kohlberg and many philosophers take to be genuine moral reasoning. They were nearly all higher-class, white males, from urban environments, in industrialized societies. Males in isolated villages in Turkey and Yucatan tested out at preconventional or conventional-level reasoning. Working-class men in America also fell short (Kohlberg and Kramer 1969).

These results could be explained by the Kohlberg theory, and they might even be predicted from it. For, Kohlberg said, development of moral reasoning is fundamentally a process of restructuring modes of role taking. People who have more opportunities for role taking will rank higher in moral development. He claims that studies show that middle-class children have more opportunities for role taking in their families than do lower-class ones; that members of complex, urbanized industrialized societies have more opportunities than do members of rural, agrarian ones; that individuals central to the decision-making structure of a group have more opportunities for role taking than do those who are not. So the results that place white, higher-class males at the top in reasoning ability are not anomalous, they are predictable. One might even predict that women would place low.

In some studies women showed a tendency to test out at the conventional level of moral reasoning—at stage three, called "personal concordance morality." Kohlberg explained this result by the basic principles of his theory: "Stage 3 personal concordance morality is a functional morality for housewives and mothers; it is not for businessmen and professionals" (Kohlberg and Kramer 1969, 108). Presumably women did not have adequate role-taking opportunities to fully develop their moral reasoning. They confused moral problems with problems of interpersonal relations.

Is this blatant sexism? Well, Kohlberg does not say that women reason at stage 3 "by nature." Rather, Kohlberg's result is in one sense progressive: Women should have an equal opportunity to develop. It is anti-sexism of an ERA sort. In an analogous sense it is antiracist, operating against the eugenic theories that placed people of color and of non-Western culture "by nature" at a lower stage than Western whites.

The social structures important for full moral development are what he terms the secondary institutions:

> My general theory relates differential social experience, in terms of opportunities for social role taking, to a differential rate of moral development. Of particular importance for the development of later stages of moral reasoning . . . are opportunities for power, responsi-

bility, and participation in the secondary institutions of society (i.e., institutions of government, law, and economy, in contrast to the primary institutions of society such as the family, the adolescent peer group, and other small face-to-face groups). Also of importance to rate of development is higher education. (Kohlberg 1982, 518)

Kohlberg develops this at much greater length in Kohlberg 1969 (400–401).[9]

There are certain things we must note about his analysis here. You recall the Durkheim thesis: To understand the structure of a collectivity's classification of the world is to understand its principles of social organization. For Kohlberg, the collectivity required for genuine moral reasoning is an industrialized society. Within industrial society, he ranks the "secondary institutions" of government and business highest, not only socially and politically but so far as giving experience in moral reasoning goes: Individuals central in the decision making structure have more opportunity for developing their moral reasoning.

Kohlberg's similarity postulate says that people will develop in the same ways if they have the same opportunities for interaction in the society, particularly if they have opportunities in the secondary institutions of industrialized society. To support the postulate, Kohlberg has to presuppose that different societies progress along a similar path—he calls it a mild doctrine of social evolution. He also presupposes that those who have had opportunities in the secondary institutions of industrialized society are the ones who define the moral categories of the collectivity—the collectivity in the sense of their own society as well as all humanity. He supports a double hierarchical order. Some societies rank higher than others and, within a society, some groups rank higher in their use of moral reasoning.

Kohlberg's theory appears to be confirmed by his empirical studies on moral reasoning. One way to challenge his theory is to challenge his empirical results. That is what Carol Gilligan did.

## GILLIGAN'S DIFFERENT VOICE

According to her own story, Gilligan noticed that many women dropped out of a Kohlberg class on moral and political choice. When the women were contacted and interviewed, their moral thinking appeared to confirm the Kohlberg results that women confuse moral problems with problems of interpersonal relations. That is, their thinking appeared to confirm the

Kohlberg results *if* the standard Kohlberg categories were used. But Gilligan sensed patterns in the women's explanations, patterns that hinted at a different form of moral thinking. Gilligan took women's performance on the test as an anomaly—a phenomenon that the theory could not explain (Kuhn 1970).[10]

Her sense was reinforced by the fact that Kohlberg had set up his moral development scheme on the basis of an all-male sample. Gilligan decided to do a study based on judgment and action in a sample of pregnant women considering abortion (Gilligan 1984a). To test for a new type of moral reasoning, she needed a new type of testing method.

In her abortion study (1977), Gilligan made a major methodological change from the Kohlberg approach. She did not present ready-made dilemmas, because doing so would predefine moral reasoning and impose the investigator's categories on the subjects. If the investigator's definition of moral reasoning was biased toward male use, then women's reasoning might be made invisible, and, at the least, their answers would be distorted (Gilligan 1984a). So she used open-ended interviews and asked women about their own abortion experiences. She then used early interviews to construct a scoring manual with which to score the later ones.[11]

Kohlberg did not use a moral dilemma concerning abortion in his studies. The usual philosophical statement of the abortion dilemma frames it as a conflict between the right to life of the fetus and the right of the woman to control her body. That is a standard statement within the terms of Kohlberg's highest level of moral reasoning.

When Gilligan analyzed her interviews, she did not find discussions of the right to life of the fetus or of the rights of the woman. She found a "new moral language," in which the words *selfish* and *responsible* were used to define the moral parameters of choice. The language called attention to a construction of the moral problem as a problem of responsibility in relationships—not an obligation to fulfill an abstract duty but an injunction to respond with care and avoid hurt. The word *selfish* marked a morally problematic separation of others from self. The abortion dilemma became a dilemma of relationships in which self and other are connected and interdependent. This conflicts with the view of self and other as separate that underlies the understanding of moral problems as problems of conflicting rights (Gilligan 1984a). The question is, How does this affect the Kohlberg theory and the philosophical ethics and sociology that underlie it? Does it mean Kohlberg is mistaken in his similarity postulates? Does it mean men and women use different moral reasoning? Does it mean that one type of reasoning is appropriate for the secondary institutions of the public sphere and another for the primary institutions of the domestic sphere? We need an interpretation of Gilligan's results.

In her later papers, Gilligan conceptualizes the difference in moral thinking as a difference in orientation: The justice orientation that Kohlberg analyzed is different from the care orientation that she discovered (Gilligan and Murphy 1979). With proper scoring techniques, it was possible to distinguish elements of each orientation in subjects' answers to the Kohlberg dilemmas. When this was done, it appeared that while both women and men used both orientations, women tended to use the care orientation more, and men tended to use the justice orientation more. Furthermore, some dilemmas drew forth an emphasis on one or the other orientation. The Heinz brought out emphasis on a justice orientation, even from women. But hypothetical dilemmas about a woman facing abortions emphasized a care orientation, even among men.[12]

I want to state this in other terms because it is important. Gilligan does not claim to have discovered a new ethics that women use and men do not. Both men and women use both ethical "orientations." But philosophers and developmental psychologists have analyzed only one of them. And so their theories as well as their reading of evidence has been distorted. I believe that is Gilligan's claim.

Gilligan's new theory seems to postulate a new and different sort of human moral development. Like Kohlberg, she maintains that people move up through reasoning levels in the ethics of care; and so far as I can tell, these are invariant levels, and they are universal, in that all people would move through them given appropriate experience.[13] However, as I understand it, development through Kohlberg's levels takes place through opportunities in role taking and requires change in one's relationship to rules. Gilligan's requires changes in relationship between self and other.[14]

In Gilligan's ethics of care, one develops through three levels and two transitions. At level one, a person cares for herself, and for others only to the degree that they are included in her self-care. She moves on to level two by reflecting on past actions (they seem selfish) and by developing ability to maintain interpersonal relationships. Gilligan once dubbed level two a "maternal morality" in which the self finds worth in the ability to care for and protect others (Gilligan 1982, 79).

One moves into the transition to level three by seeing a "confusion between self sacrifice and care inherent in the conventions of feminine goodness" (Gilligan 1982, 73–74). One understands relationship as a dynamic process of interaction rather than as a bond of mutual dependence. At level three, Gilligan says, care becomes a universal injunction and a self-chosen ethic (Gilligan 1982, 90).

Gilligan's description of level three is certainly too close to the language of Kohlberg's justice orientation: "universal injunctions" and "self-chosen ethics." Elsewhere, she speaks in terms of transformed understanding of social relationships.

> Beginning with the assumption that the relationship is the fundamental condition of social reality, the ethic of care is contextual in its insistence on seeing connections. Moral judgement thus cannot be abstracted from the context of individual and social history, and decision making relies on a process of communication to discover the other's postition and to discern the chain of connections through which the consequences of action extend. Thus dialogue replaces logical deduction as the mode of moral discovery, and the activity of moral understanding returns to the social domain. (Gilligan 1983, 45)

She says the responsibility ethics is a "psychologic logic of relationships" rather than "the formal logic of fairness," which informs the justice approach. And it restores the concept of love to ethics. Furthermore, "moral problems formerly seen in philosophical terms as problems of justification come to be seen in psychological terms as problems of commitment and choice" (Gilligan 1982, 73).

There are two sides to this work of Gilligan's. One is the critical part—by treating women's scores on the Kohlberg tests as anomalous, she made a start on falsifying the moral-development theory. On the positive side, she apparently discovered a new kind of ethics that some human beings use and live by. But like all research that makes a major breakthrough, Gilligan's work leaves us with more questions than it answers.

The central question from the critical side is: Just what has Gilligan falsified about the Kohlberg theory? When she speaks of "two orientations" or a "Gestalt switch," it sounds as though she is simply supplementing Kohlberg's work (see Gilligan and Murphy 1979; Gilligan 1987). On this interpretation, Gilligan's work fits into the traditional philosophical ethics; it does not challenge it.

Kohlberg himself said that Gilligan's theory deals with ego development, not moral reasoning, and so there is no real conflict (Kohlberg 1982). Some philosophers have said that Gilligan is working in the ethical theory of the good and a morality of character, rather than the theory of the right and a morality of justice (Flanagan 1983). Owen Flanagan, Jr., and Jonathan Adler write that she intends a unity of the two.

> It is not ideal for morally mature men to operate solely with justice concerns and morally mature women with goodness concerns (the world somehow working out fine with this sexual division of moral labor), nor should people ever reason impartially [being concerned only with care and commitment]. Rather it is best for every individual to operate with both a theory of the right and a conception of good, each in its proper domain. (Flanagan and Adler 1983, 593)

The theory of the good concerns character, virtue, choice, responsibility, and action in determinate circumstances, as well as the good life and the good of society as a whole. In contrast, the theory of the right concerns moral principles, decisions, justification, reasoning, and obligation, as well as questions of rights, and justice. At first glance, the philosophical explanation seems to suit the difference between Gilligan and Kohlberg. But it overlooks difficulties with the social, psychological, and political basis of the Kohlberg theory. What of his similarity postulates and his "mild theory of social evolution"? Are we to accept all that baggage, and the traditional philosophical ethics to boot? I believe that Gilligan's contribution is more radical than that. The question is how to show that it is. The clue lies in Kohlberg's use of higher-class men and their work as the basis of genuine moral reasoning. Philosophers have often done this in the theory of the good as well.

Suppose we turn to the classic philosopher of the theory of the good: Aristotle. The keystone of Aristotle's theory is the man of practical wisdom, that man who can see what moral principle is appropriate in a determinate situation of action—that man who has the excellence of character to be able to do what is morally appropriate. After a sound childhood training, the man of practical wisdom develops his excellences by being a head of household and a citizen in a direct democracy. We might say that the man of practical wisdom has developed a craft through which he exercises his wisdom and acts to make a good life for himself and his society. Aristotle's man of practical wisdom was a *man* in the sense that his craft was a male craft. He did the things that male citizens did in Athens. Aristotle set out the keystone of his ethics in terms of what men do.

The Kohlberg theory was built on an implicit division of labor between men and women—implicit because it was concealed under the terminology of "primary, face to face groups" and "secondary institutions." It follows the old division between the public sphere (formerly men's territory) and the domestic (which was women's) (Elshtain 1981). In a way, Kohlberg's leading question in framing his theory was, What do men do?

To test the radical implications of Gilligan's ethics, I want to ask: What do women do? I don't want just to ask what women say they do. I want to have an appropriate empirical theory that lets me understand what women do. I believe the answer will shake the foundation of Kohlberg's—and the philosophers'—"genuine morality."

### What Do Women Do?

Marjorie DeVault wrote her dissertation on housework, particularly the aspect of organizing food and meals.[15] In her study she brings together the fact that housework is work (in fact, a craft that must be learned) with the fact that housework is a labor of caring for others. She used open-ended interviews and, to a small degree, participant observation in developing this notion of housework.

Other researchers have studied housework on the model of paid work, with its instrumental logic and its division of labor defined by authorities of the workplace, and ultimately of the economic market.[16] The model of paid work was developed out of rationalized models of secondary institutions, and so the work of care is submerged. On the other hand, people at home tend to see housework under a logic of care, so that housework as a craft is made invisible. It is hidden by being seen as a natural expression of caring, under virtues appropriate to women.[17]

DeVault says that the craft includes skills of management, planning, and coordination, but that the central principle that organizes work in the "project" of care is adjustment: adjustment to material conditions—including those of the marketplace—and adjustment to the needs of members of the household. It includes adjustment to members' activities and their preferences, and it means paying attention to them as individuals. She says that housework as care, "produces a group life, while preserving a sense of household members as unique" (100). Most important, "the heart of the work lies not in any given set of tasks but in the social relationships produced through the activities of feeding [and the other activities of care]" (102).[18] This is one way of shedding light on Gilligan's remark that "relationship is the fundamental condition of social reality" (Gilligan 1983, 45).

DeVault sees the project of care as producing a group (here, a primary group). She describes the process of making and sustaining a primary group that is embedded in the economic and political structures of the "public sphere." Women's work in this light has two inseparable aspects: making the group (and the uniqueness of individual members) through the craft of care; and doing so by working within the environment of the economic and political institutions of the public sphere.[19]

In a paper on Virginia Woolf's *To the Lighthouse*, DeVault analyzes women's craft in creating an event and a group by making a dinner party. The paper is called "Women's Invisible Work: Mrs. Ramsey's Craft," and in it, DeVault makes the point that the project of care is work, a craft of making relationships and groups, not simply a virtue of moral caring.

Mrs. Ramsey gives a dinner party. There are two sets of tasks essential to giving a dinner party: bringing together the diners so that they experience the dinner as an event, and seeing to the preparing and serving of the food. Here is Virginia Woolf's description of the assemblage at the outset, through Mrs. Ramsey's eyes.

> Nothing seemed to have merged. They all sat separate. And the whole of the effort of merging and flowing and creating rested on her . . . if she did not do it nobody would do it, and so, giving herself the little shake that one gives a watch that has stopped, the old familiar pulse began beating. (DeVault 1982, 4)

She gently prods others into talking with one another, she talks to a guest herself, and shortly the group has been united, "composed into a party round a table." To do this, Mrs. Ramsey must take part herself in the eating and the conversation, as a participant. But she must also keep an eye on all the guests to see that they are pleasantly engaged socially. And she must see that the food is properly served and that guests get what they need to eat. That is, she makes a group while paying attention to the uniqueness of each person.

She cannot do this alone, of course. Rather, she gives everyone an opportunity to do what they can in the way of socializing. All the guests know how to be guests, though not all do it well. When things go wrong, Mrs. Ramsey needs help—and every hostess knows that there are certain people who understand and can help and others who do not know how to help. For those who do not understand, dinner parties are mystified. If we do not ask about how dinner parties are made, we can be satisfied with descriptions of roles, customs, norms, and the like. We do not ask about the craft.

DeVault says that what others see as something naturally feminine in Mrs. Ramsey is in fact her craft—a kind of work she has learned to do and does well, work in which she is always "on call" (something that makes it difficult to see as a job). DeVault also says, "Distinctions between 'for-me' and 'for-others' are relatively clear for Mrs. Ramsey, but go unnoticed by others" (1982, 7). I would say that this is a well-developed understanding of self and others and of social relations, one that is required of a good hostess or a manager of any sort. DeVault concludes that this "women's work" has certain principles and character and a logic; most women have learned it, and they are troubled when it doesn't get done.

DeVault has discussed what women do, but she hasn't done it by giving an abstract model. Instead, she has given a description of an activity: housework and feeding a family. She used Virginia Woolf's description of giving a dinner party. Everyone knows about dinner parties (though they vary by class and culture). But Mrs. Ramsey and people who know how to give dinner parties understand them differently than do some of the guests. They understand that events, relationships, and groups have to be made and maintained, and they facilitate the making.

DeVault is discussing "primary face to face groups," which Kohlberg says give role-taking opportunities that give practice in moral reasoning at the conventional level. But she does not define them in terms of role obligations in the institution of the family. We can see this difference quite clearly if we move out of the homey level to a more public one.

DeVault studied activities in the "domestic sphere," with its "primary institutions." According to Kohlberg and the philosophers, when one makes the transformation to genuine moral reasoning, one moves to reasoning that takes all human beings into account: the whole society or the nation or all humanity. For this, he says, one needs role-taking opportunities in secondary institutions, presumably like Geraldine Ferraro had, or as women executives now have. This is the standard training ground for the man who uses genuine moral reasoning. What does "women's work" look like in the public social spheres?

Arlene Kaplan Daniels discusses women's work outside the home. She studied volunteer work among upper- and middle-class women on the West Coast. These were major-league volunteers—staging benefits for art institutes, operas, and symphonies, and high-toned fund-raisers for distinguished political candidates. Over a period of ten years, Daniels interviewed seventy women and did participant observation at luncheons, social gatherings, and philanthropic events. Some fund-raising work for good causes has become professionalized work. But much of it has not and still involves small gestures of hospitality and day-to-day efforts to create an ambience in which personal loyalties and commitment to a cause may all be fostered. Like housework, this work is also invisible, so that some parts of the work, for example, monitoring and strategizing, are not clearly seen even by the workers themselves (Daniels 1985; 1988, chap. 1). These women volunteers have political impact because they promote important causes and raise needed funds. But they are not simply the "behind the scenes helpers" in a male-defined world. They have independent organizations and influence networks. Their work provides an avenue for a sense of community solidarity to develop and grow—Daniels says it is a way for collective representations to be reaffirmed and to solidify. They give a new meaning to the term "our city." Publics are formed. The result, she says, is a combination of celebration and philanthropy. She concludes:

> It is important to underscore the importance of the work that goes into this combination of celebration and philanthropy. These celebrations require the hard work that creates the context in which community solidarity flourishes. The workers who become successful producers have skills and techniques developed through practice and experience. (Daniels 1985, 373)

This picture of the public world is very different from the official, rationalized picture that defines the modern world in terms of acting through government offices, making corporate decisions, and so on. This is not simply "behind the scenes" work that oils the official machinery. It is work that is hidden.

When I discussed the question What do women do? I discussed it in terms of "hidden work" of a certain kind: work of creating and maintaining social institutions and structures. How is it hidden? Kohlberg's theory hides it under the label "personal concordance morality." He hides it by taking an official description of moral reasoning to be "genuine moral reasoning" and defining all other sorts in its terms. The philosophers hide the work as well. They hide it in the abstract theory of the right that supports Kohlberg's theory, and they hide it in the theory of the good that turns the craft into a virtue.

The work is not hidden from those who do it, except in the sense that they may not clearly categorize it as work because it is hidden under official categories. And it is not only women who do this work. Children also do hidden work—work particularly hidden because of prejudices about children's place. Men do this sort of hidden work, even at dinner parties. They clearly do it in certain kinds of occupations. Administrators of the American Philosophical Association and local arrangements committees for annual conferences do it, and many of them are men. Politicians do it, with the help of their staffs: caring for loyal supporters, caring for their constituencies by finding out what they want and need, and then pushing for it. This goes on all the way from the president down to the ward captains, and with the latter, the care shows much more clearly because it is more direct. And when we see all that, we also see all the hidden work that most adults do in helping people find jobs or apartments or colleges or doctors. All the organizing of reunions and office potlucks. All the "putting in a word" that we do, the smoothing-out-the-wrinkles, the personal chat and hand on the shoulder. This is knowing how to make the institutions work.

Clearly it is a mistake to think that this hidden work is only the informal oiling of the wheels. Even the most formal of roles and the most rigid of institutions exist because of know-how. To fill a role is to create a role and, with others, an institution. It is a craft that is learned: a craft of doing things together (Becker 1986). It is a craft that allows guests and hostesses to make dinner parties. It is a craft that allows students, professors, secretaries, administrators, custodians, ground crews, cooks, and carpenters to make universities. It is a craft that allows clerks, justices, attorneys, clients, policemen, criminals, victims, prison guards, citizens, and legislators to make the legal system. All of this work of creation is hidden under the abstract talk of roles, institutions, rules, and reasoning. Hiding it has the political effect of supporting a dominant elite by supporting their official story. It supports their privileged categorization in ethics and politics.

Kohlberg's theory was built on an implicit division of labor between men and women—implicit because it was concealed under the terminology of "primary, face to face groups" and "secondary institutions." In defining "genuine moral reasoning," he described what some higher-class men do in justifying their actions and work and lives—they use the rationalized mode of the secondary institutions of the public sphere in industrialized societies. We cannot suppose that these modes of justification give an empirical description of the secondary institutions themselves. Rather, they are the modes that describe the institutions so as to support hierarchical structures of dominance. They are used to justify the dominant place in industrialized society of the secondary institutions and the people who make them up. And yet Kohlberg used this mode of reasoning to define genuine morality, and then he defined all different moral thinking as lower stages. He made privileged the mode that a dominant group uses to justify its dominance, and he used it to define the moral categories of the collectivity. He built his genuine moral reasoning, his highest level, not even on what men do but on how higher-class men (and some women) justify what they do.

Kohlberg's work quite straightforwardly supports a dominant group because his theory holds that everyone *ought* to use genuine moral reasoning, and that those who do not *ought* to be dealt with under its categories. Rawls and other philosophers argue only that a person *may* rationally choose their universalizable principles and be morally justified in using them to make decisions that affect others, to decide public policy, and to judge and train others. Kohlberg says, "All ought." Rawls and the philosophers say, "One may." But in the end, that is less of a difference than it seems.

Rawls's justification for his ethics uses the requirement of generalizability, supported by essentially the same similarity postulates and the predictive social science that Kohlberg uses.[20] Most of the criticisms I have made of Kohlberg apply to Rawls and many other philosophers. But with a twist. Because Rawls says only that one may rationally choose his ethics, the consequences on privilege follow from the fact (Kohlberg's fact) that it is an elite group that predominantly will choose the ethics—and use it to define the moral and political doings of the rest. After all, it is Rawls (and other philosophers) who offers the necessary philosophical justification for Kohlberg's defense of our hierarchical social order (see Kohlberg 1971).

The way out is to see the hidden work that creates and maintains the "secondary structures" through which the world is officially labeled and decisions are officially made. Those secondary structures, and the categories used within them, are concerned with governing the polity or managing a business enterprise, not with revealing what the processes are and who it is that does the work that creates and maintains the collectivity. Those structures are not empirically real, they are political constructions unsuited for explaining psychologically real, universal moral development.

The research of Gilligan, DeVault, Daniels, and many other feminists shows not only that we have left women out but that we have misunderstood both the social world and moral reasoning. The assumption that to understand the structure of a collectivity's classification of the world is to understand its principles of social organization is much more complicated than it first appeared. The "collectivity's classification" may be an official classification imposed by a dominant group, and its "principles of social organization" may be simply the picture officially painted by a dominant group. Both may be products of a political order.

In this light, we do well to read Carol Gilligan's remarks again:

> Beginning with the assumption that the relationship is the fundamental condition of social reality, the ethic of care is contextual in its insistence on seeing connections. Moral judgement thus cannot be abstracted from the context of individual and social history, and decision making relies on a process of communication to discover the other's position and to discern the chain of connections through which the consequences of action extend. Thus dialogue replaces logical deduction as the mode of moral discovery, and the activity of moral understanding returns to the social domain. (Gilligan 1983, 45)

It should be clear that to be a feminist ethics, Carol Gilligan's morality of care cannot be the complement of Kohlberg's genuine moral reasoning. It cannot be classified under the philosophical theory of the good versus Kohlberg's work in the theory of the right. It requires a different sociology and different similarity postulates. It requires these things in order to be a feminist ethics, and it requires them to be empirically adequate.

A feminist ethics requires a different sociology. The sociological model must show how social structure, institutions, role, norms, or whatever are products of human interaction. "Products" are not the basic units for analysis. The sociological model must tell us how to discover the processes by which the structures, institutions, roles, and norms are created and upheld in people's everyday interactions—including the processes by which some categorizations of reality come to be the privileged categorizations of a collectivity, and by which one sort of moral reasoning comes to dominance as genuine moral reasoning.

A feminist ethics requires a different set of similarity postulates from the traditional philosophical ethics. Traditional ethics is tailored to the requirements of objectivity and universalizability: What's right for one is right for all, what's justified for one is justified for all, even if only one uses the ethics. This sort of equality is fine for the legal system of a nation— nations after all are political entities governed by elites through the use of power. For the moral system of a collectivity, it won't do at all, for it breeds a moral blindness. It is the blindness that Aristotle showed when he defined character, virtue, and the good life in terms of what men do—and went on to define the lives of women and children on that basis. It is the blindness that Kohlberg showed when he defined genuine moral reasoning in terms of what a dominant male elite say they do—and went on to define all others on that basis.

What similarity postulates are suited for a feminist ethics? To begin our answer, we need to keep in mind that the roots of a predictive, universal social science (which Kohlberg and Rawls rely on) are the same as the roots of a universal, genuine morality. Feminist similarity postulates must be joined with a feminist sociology. That requires acknowledging that similarities are socially constructed by a process that is, in important parts, political. Similarities are, after all, among the categorizations of a collectivity, even when they are postulated by scientists and philosophers. A feminist similarity postulate would be empirical in the sense of uncovering the processes of constructing similarities and bringing them to consciousness, not in the sense of testing for objectively existing similarities.

We also need to take seriously the fact that Kohlberg's social science and ethics are suited for hierarchical societies and support them. The very idea of a universal, genuine moral reasoning supports elites in their dominance. It does so by pretending that a single individual can guarantee that his decisions are morally proper by reasoning all by himself. Or that a single individual can decide what is just or right for all of us by reasoning all by himself. Without reaching group understanding. Without working it out in practice. This is a warning that feminists must take to heart, and it requires some radical change of politics and theory. Many feminist arguments in the abortion controversy rest on a woman's right to reason by herself and come to a genuine moral decision. Some theoretical discussions about "all women" allow elite feminists to define women's nature and feminist politics, using privileges of class and education.

Feminist activists have often favored nonhierarchical modes of decision making. They have formed collectives, rotated offices, worked by consensus. These social forms must give content to feminist similarity postulates and to a feminist ethics. A feminist ethics must be rooted in the work of feminist activists (whether they be men, women, or children), not in the hierarchical orders of our present society.

I believe that the consequences of taking women seriously in ethics are radical indeed. They require a change in our social science, in our politics, and in our forms of social organization. By this I do not mean that we should try to run great nations nonhierarchically, nor do I mean that we should work for a low-tech, pastoral utopia. The first is contradictory; the second, in our world, is a dream suited for the well fed who lack responsibility for children, the elderly, the poor, and the sick. A feminist morality isn't a design for seizing the means of government. It is one that allows us to come to consciousness of the processes by which we make ourselves and our societies so that we can exercise care and love and respect in the making. Such an ethics takes women seriously by taking every one of us seriously.

An ethics that takes women seriously is an ethics for us all.


## Notes

This chapter was presented at a panel on Carol Gilligan's ethics at the meetings of the Pacific Division of the American Philosophical Association, in San Francisco, May, 1985. The philosophical core of the chapter was taken from "Respect and Impartiality," a paper I presented at the Eastern Division meetings of the American Philosophical Association December 1979. Mary Gibson commented on that paper. This paper (and my understanding) was much improved because of her comments.

1. Singer 1961 and Sumner 1981 discuss this at length, but it is common among philosophers who use a rights analysis of abortion.

2. Gilligan's work, as she sets it out, does not make the challenge. She takes the two moral "orientations" to be complementary, and she posits an apparently universal scheme of development in the care orientation (see below). To my mind this puts Gilligan in Copernicus's position. Some historians have said that Copernicus started the revolution in astronomy with his heliocentric theory, but that he himself remained an old-style, Ptolemaic astronomer—though history is a complex business, and other historians disagree. In this chapter, I'll be using Gilligan's work to make a more radical criticism of the philosophy and sociology that make up genuine moral reasoning, or the "official morality of the United States."

3. The other ethics these philosophers recognize is an ethics of character having to do with the good, virtues, and choice rather than decision. Kant is associated with the first sort, Aristotle with the second. See below, in the discussion of Gilligan's ethics.

4. My various statements of the principle are from Singer 1961, 31. Kant's categorical imperative (in one version) tells us to act only on that maxim that we can will to be a universal law—it brings in additional notions of maxims and willings.

5. Intuitionists who analyze the moral faculty in terms of judgment of cases need equally strong principles, though they would probably explain them differently.

6. The range appears to be too wide. See Gibson 1977.

7. Rawls 1971. Robert Paul Wolff criticizes this idea of a social science in Wolff 1977.

8. The pattern of active males and passive females is characteristic of the Kohlberg dilemmas that formed the basis of Kohlberg's theory.

9. And it sounds like the procedure Aristotle recommended for the man of practical wisdom, but altered to suit the modern, industrial state.

10. It is significant that Gilligan began her independent work in the United States, at a time when gender bias was an issue socially and politically. The change in political understanding meant not only that it was easier for academic researchers to notice errors in the traditional models; it meant they might be listened to when they pointed them out.

11. Personal communication with author, early 1985.

12. It also made a difference if the dilemma concluded, "X did this, was it right or

wrong?" or "What should X do?" The Heinz dilemma is of the former type. That sort shows an increase in justice-orientation thinking in subjects' answers. Whatever we think of moral-development theory, these results have to be taken seriously by philosophers.

13. I have asked Gilligan about this, and she has said that they are not developmental in the Piaget/Kohlberg sense. But I have not seen a different sense analyzed in her work.

14. The justice ethics Kohlberg used has been worked out in a multitude of philosophy books, and so he has been able to set out descriptions of his levels and stages in standard charts, suitable for psychology texts. Gilligan gives her levels and stages discursively. This is in part due to the nature of her ethics of responsibility, in part due to the fact that philosophers have not given detailed analyses of her type of ethics. Some philosophers are working on an ethics of responsibility. See Whitbeck 1983 and Ladd 1978.

15. She worked with Arlene Daniels, Howard Becker, and Dorothy Smith, in a way that uses Daniels's and Becker's field approach and empirical concepts to "operationalize" Smith's more abstract theories. See Becker 1971; Smith 1979; and Daniels 1988.

16. The paid-labor model takes seriously the fact that housework is work, but DeVault says, paid labor operates under instrumental logic, in which the employer has the right to define one's work and how one's work articulates with that of others. See also essays in Wallman 1979.

17. DeVault (1984a, 98) says that recent changes in household duties have clarified things somewhat. When one person has all the responsibility for the work, others never have to think about it. Even the one who does it—because so much of her thought about it is never shared—may not be fully aware of all that is involved. Her work can come to seem like a natural expression of caring.

Attempts to share housework mean that its underlying principles must be made visible, and recognized as work. The work must be seen as separable from those who have done it traditionally, instead of as a natural expression of love and personality.

18. This is a materialist analysis of how the relationships of reproduction are reproduced, but one far different from Chodorow 1978.

19. Dorothy Smith's "sociology for women" takes the standpoint of women in the second aspect, and she says the work of feminist sociologists is to show the macro structure as it appears in women's everyday lives and doings. See Smith 1987.

20. See Robert Paul Wolff's criticism of Rawls's idea of a social science in Wolff 1977.

## *Autonomy and Respect*
(1987)

An account of autonomy defines something important about humanity—perhaps a goal for human beings that allows them to develop their full humanity. Because we feel autonomy is important, there are certain criteria that we Americans insist that any philosophical analysis of autonomy must satisfy . . . or we might call them desiderata that the analysis should fulfill. Among them is the positive requirement that the analysis should yield a respectful account of people's selves and actions. Put in as a negative condition, the accounts must avoid gender bias, and age, race, class, religious, ethic, or national bias. Needless to say, philosophic accounts have more often than not failed these conditions even as they try to satisfy them. I believe that one main reason for the failure is that they use already-biased models of human action. They use biased models of the relation between human action and social structure and human history.

Philosophers recognize different sorts of autonomy.[1] Moral autonomy characteristically requires self-legislation: giving oneself a moral law to follow. The moral law is binding in the sense that morally autonomous people make decisions that are obligatory under the genuine moral law they have given themselves. Some people make their moral decisions according to what custom or the laws of their group require, and if they do so through fear of sanction or unthinkingly through their socialization, they make their decisions heteronomously. Instead of giving themselves a moral law they are given a law.

Moral autonomy of this sort has its classic definition in Kantian ethics. It operates in the sphere of moral obligation and what is morally required. In contrast, personal autonomy operates in the sphere of what is morally permissible, that is, what is neither required nor forbidden. This sphere includes some of the most important life decisions, usually including career, marriage, having children, making a home, becoming involved in politics, and so on. According to Diana Meyers, personally autonomous people decide to do what they really want to do. Autonomous conduct expresses the true or authentic self. In contrast, she says, heteronomous conduct expresses an apparent self, one instilled by socialization or made by "aping convention" (Meyers 1987, 619).

Diana Meyers has offered us a feminist analysis of personal autonomy. It provides a good test of the usual philosophic models of the relation between human action, social structure, and history, for she is determined to give an account that overcomes gender bias. The usual philosophical discussions of personal autonomy use men's lives as their model, though they do not often admit to doing so. Meyers dethrones these accounts, which she says take personal autonomy as an all-or-nothing phenomenon. She proposes three forms of autonomy, which involve competences and admit of degrees. "Programmatic autonomy" involves posing and answering the question, "How do I want to live my life?" "Episodic autonomy" involves asking, in a particular situation, "What do I really want to do now?" and acting on the answer. "Personal autonomy" is a function of the other two, and "it must be gauged along a number of dimensions"; even lives that, in many respects, are heteronomous may show a fragmentary autonomy (Meyers 1987, 626).

Diana Meyers wants to give an account of autonomy that offers a foundation for philosophical ethics that is respectful and takes women seriously. But she also believes her analysis can correct certain flaws in feminist theory, and so she develops her analysis out of a paradox she sees in some standard feminist positions.

One way of categorizing feminist positions is as difference theories or sameness theories. At least, Catharine MacKinnon categorizes them that way, and it's useful for some purposes (MacKinnon 1987). Difference theorists say that men and women are different, without making much of the fact that the difference is essentially one of power and authority in the definition of men and women. Difference theorists say men and women have different ways, but both are worthwhile. MacKinnon gives Carol Gilligan as an example of a difference theorist. I don't think she is, but we could construct a version of Carol Gilligan's account of moral reasoning that said women use a morality of care and relationship, and men use one of justice and rights, and both are important. That would be a difference theory.

Sameness theorists say men and women have the same human nature but because of unjust social arrangements, women lack opportunity to develop that nature fully. A feminist Lawrence Kohlberg might say that. Diana criticizes the sameness theorists because they aim at giving women "equal opportunity" to have a male-defined autonomy. She says that those sameness theorists valorize masculine traits and denigrate feminine ones— which is true.

A widespread feminist argument against these kind of sameness theorists is that the public sphere of characteristically male activities has been used to define human nature, human excellence, human morality, and human autonomy (Elshtain 1981). Science, politics, high art, and human civilization itself have been accomplished in the public sphere. Masculine characteristics include the definitive human ones of rationality, objectivity, and others considered requisite to those high human achievements. This is a stereotype. On this stereotype, men make history. In contrast, the domestic sphere, sometimes called women's sphere, has been dropped from history. On this stereotype, the feminine characteristics are shared with other animals: procreation, blind loyalty, emotion, love, and so on. I have to stress that we are talking stereotypes here, not empirical sociology or history or psychology.

Diana finds a paradox in sameness feminism and the search for equal opportunity. Accepting the sameness argument requires denigrating the domestic sphere, women's contributions and their traditional virtues. It requires denigrating the hundreds of millions of women in the world who live what she calls traditional lives.

Diana is a sameness theorist of a sort. She wants to achieve what we might call a unisex definition of human nature and a unisex definition of personal autonomy that incorporates both the masculine and the feminine. I don't mean she insists that men and women must live the same lives—not at all. It's a unisex view of autonomy, not a unisex view of lifestyle. I think she wants to show respect by granting that personal autonomy allows the choice of many different kinds of lives. One may exercise autonomy in all walks of life. I believe that the unisex definition would have to allow one to be autonomous in living the life of a traditional woman as well as in living the life of a nontraditional one. After all, personal autonomy cannot require that all women become career women.

This is an important point, and to make it clear, I have to change Diana's terminology somewhat. She seems to use the term, "traditional woman," to name someone who lives a traditional life and is heteronomous. I'd like to separate the two characteristics and make a distinction between women who live traditional lives heteronomously and women who live traditional lives autonomously. One reason the separation is necessary is to avoid putting career women on a pedestal. We don't want to have the hierarchy from heteronomy to autonomy defined at the top by career women. In the end, making the distinction will lead me to the conclusion that like other sameness theories, Diana's analysis of personal autonomy doesn't take adequate account of power and authority, even though she offers major improvements on many philosophical accounts of autonomy.

As I see it, she makes her new analysis by using a paradigm case: the movement from being a traditional woman who is personally heteronomous to becoming a woman who is personally autonomous. She allows us to recognize degrees of personal autonomy in this movement by defining three different sorts of personal autonomy. First, there is episodic autonomy in which one considers what she really wants to do in some situation and does it. Women leading traditional lives certainly exercise episodic autonomy on occasion. Second, there is programmatic autonomy in which one poses and answers questions; for example, How do I want to live my life? Do I want children? What sort of job do I want? Some women seem to answer these questions in ways that lead them to traditional lives. Episodic and programmatic autonomy are autonomy competences, and achieving them requires developing autonomy skills. Competences and skills allow of degrees, and a traditional woman may be more or less autonomous in these respects.

Diana's third kind of autonomy is the sort involved in having access to the authentic self. This is a process of development as much as a process of insight, and she says the authentic self emerges as one exercises autonomy competences. This means the authentic self is a process rather than a product—this idea is very fruitful.

Diana's schema allows us to see that "traditional women" do have autonomy skills, and it allows us to discern partial autonomy in many people's lives. There's quite a lot I like about her analysis. There are certain puzzles in her solution to the feminist paradox, however. Some of my basic puzzles concern the traditional woman. I want to ask, How do we recognize the traditional woman?

One way Diana gives us is that the traditional woman fits feminine stereotypes. This troubles me because those feminine stereotypes were constructed out of the self-same model that constructed the valorized masculine stereotypes. Those valorized male stereotypes are the ones that are class, race, and age biased as well as gender biased. Most women don't fit them. Children don't fit them. Many lower-class men, and men of minority groups and "developing nations," don't fit them. They are stereotypes, not empirical descriptions. The stereotypes define a hierarchical world of higher-class, white-male dominance in ways that justify that dominance at the same time that they help create the dominance. Feminine stereotypes are defined within the official description of that hierarchical world. Feminine stereotypes may not fit the life and self of the traditional woman as she lives it, as she herself understands it. What is the relationship between the stereotype and traditional women's lives?

The puzzle intensifies when we consider the autonomous and heteronomous women separately. When we do that, the very notions of autonomy and heteronomy become suspect. Diana's new, evolutionary model of the authentic self applies to people who are on the road to autonomy. Autonomy is a goal in a creative process in which men and women acquire skills, exercise competences, and so on. The authentic self itself is created out of the process. But what about the heteronomous self? What about the so-called heteronomous, traditional woman? Diana says that the reason that woman fits feminine stereotypes is that she has not overcome her feminine socialization. Presumably the autonomous, traditional woman has overcome her socialization but she chooses to live a traditional life. Does the autonomous traditional woman fit the stereotypes? What exactly are the stereotypes, and how do they relate to these women's lives? Diana doesn't discuss the traditional woman in these terms. But if we take the movement from the heteronomous traditional woman to the autonomous traditional woman as a paradigm, we may be able to get some answers from her very interesting analysis of autonomy.

Let's consider episodic autonomy first. Diana says a person asks, "What do I really want to do?" and acts on the answer. Episodic autonomy rests on a certain folk model of human action that presupposes an underlying psychological reality. Human individuals have intentions, emotions, thoughts, motives, virtues, and vices that bring about their actions and are important to the meaning and explanation of their actions. On this folk model, human individuals have intentions and motives that cause or otherwise bring about their actions.

Presumably both sorts of traditional women live similar lives. In the case of episodic autonomy, the difference between the heteronomous and the partially autonomous women lies in their inner states, which are the springs of the action. The woman who exercises episodic autonomy has a certain sort of rationality—Diana says that her convictions and feelings have previously been examined and endorsed. But she says that the traditional woman mindlessly apes convention, or acts out of her upbringing and socialization. We've here made a movement from talking of stereotypes to talking of convention and socialization.

In Diana's use, the socialization model explains both the inner, psychological reality that must be overcome and the outer social reality that must be overcome. The model is clear in the case of career women. Diana says that because of feminine socialization, their autonomy competency is less well developed so that the undertow of socially instilled gender stereotypes sometimes impedes their professional advancement so that they cannot fathom and resolve the conflict between their internalized image of womanliness and their career aspirations. And so her political conclusion is that feminists should work to change feminine socialization.

Now I won't deny that women have feminine images they need to overcome, nor will I deny that feminists should work to change feminine socialization. People talk that way, using folk models and folk terms, and we manage to do things and change things using those folk terms and folk models. Saying feminists should work to change feminine socialization may sometimes be good advice. I'm concerned here with philosophical and sociological models, not with folk models. I want a philosophical and sociological answer to how the autonomous traditional woman is different from the heteronomous one. Diana answers in terms of feminine socialization and a model of individual, internal psychology.

Let's look at the socialization model. The socialization story is that newcomers (whether infants or immigrants) undergo a process of socialization in which they internalize the norms. The socialization produces an internalized commitment, which is externalized in behavior. According to the story, anthropologists can observe the behavior and they then quite objectively describe norms, institutions, and in general, the culture or social structure. The human group is seen as a culture or a social structure and a system of social roles.

In this view of society, it looks as though the traditional woman can be objectively described—the stereotype would presumably be outlined by feminine norms and roles in the culture. It looks as though the autonomous traditional woman can be distinguished from the heteronomous one even if they do the same things—one apes convention in doing it, the other one is reflective and planning. This story supposedly holds for men as well, and people of the various classes, races, ethnic groups, religions, ages, and so on. We have a uniform account of heteronomy and autonomy, not simply a unisex account.

Several reifications are involved in the "norms and socialization" model of human group life: the reification of individuals, the reification of psychological states, and the reification of norms and social structures. It may sound curious to speak of the reification of human individuals, since they seem to be the most obviously real and obviously observable items in any society. The socialization approach reifies individuals by taking them as discrete entities with an internal mechanism built into them by socialization (or by biology and socialization). Socialization explains the internal structure of individuals at the same time it explains how the aggregate of individuals in a group come to behave in a coordinated manner—a manner different from the one that operates in some other groups. If we're all heteronomous, we mindlessly ape convention and act in a coordinated manner like wind-up dolls with the same innards. If we're all autonomous, we overcome socialization and alter our internal mechanisms. I don't know how Diana would explain our coordinated behavior then. It requires a different sociological model.

I have a sociological model that I use. It's associated with the sociological tradition of symbolic interactionism. I can't set it out here, of course. It offers a criticism of the socialization model, and it shows a picture of human beings creating and maintaining their social structure as they make their lives and their histories.

One defining feature of human group life is that social actors define one another and their environments—they act on the basis of the meanings they give and the meanings they suppose others are giving. This is "symbolic interaction." One striking feature of human group life, however, is that not everyone has the same power or authority to define what is going on, or to have their preferred definition taken as the "public definition." One way in which control is exercised and power is maintained is through managing how people define the world. Because human beings act on the basis of meanings, this "controlling definitions" isn't simply a matter of language. This is a central thesis of symbolic interactionism. It is also a central thesis of many feminist theories, and an explanation of how male dominance operates.[2]

In this sort of interactionist view, the masculine and feminine stereotypes are labels used in defining hierarchical social relationships. We can't define the traditional woman in terms of the labels without taking the side of those who are more powerful and have authority. On a model like this, we can no longer contrast autonomy and heteronomy, nor can we talk as Diana does about the traditional woman or changing feminine socialization. Instead, we talk about hierarchies and labels, and about authority and power. Instead we talk about how social structures are systematically created and maintained so that some people regularly come out on top of important hierarchies—class, age, race, and gender are some of them—and others regularly come out low down on those hierarchies. We do this in detailed terms by looking at what happens, by observation and interview—interactionist sociology is a micro-sociology that uses anthropological field methods.

The labeling process is one way in which the hierarchical social relationships are created and maintained. It describes one way in which human action and social structure are related. This a different way of seeing Diana's feminist paradox.

Nor can we explain the heteronomous traditional woman in terms of her socialization, her internalization of the feminine stereotype. Instead we must see her in interaction with others in the process of giving meaning to what is happening. She has her own understanding of what is going on. She contributes to the definition of the situations she is involved in. But the official definitions—the ones that operate in justification, the ones that get weight in the media, the law courts, the schools, the academic journals—are those formulated by people higher up in the hierarchies.

The interactionist model gives us a way to investigate the relationship between the traditional woman and the social structure within which she acts. Diana does not frame her discussion in terms of this relationship, nor do the analytic philosophers who take autonomy of various sorts to be important. The socialization model seems to make the question moot, so that many philosophers focus on the individual, not the relationship between human activity and social structure and history. But if we focus on the individual and not on the individual in the relationship, we ignore the fact of power and authority.

To describe the traditional woman, who lives out her life heteronomously, we must face the question of the relation between human action and human social structure. It is a question of how the existing social structure is created and maintained by women (and men and children) in their choices, actions, and life plans.

As a woman leaves tradition behind to become "the new woman," the form of the question seems to change. We begin to ask, "How are the existing structures overcome?" I see that as asking a question about human action and human history, for it requires knowing how the existing social structure is to be changed. We face two philosophical (or sociological) questions: How does our action create and maintain the social structure? And how does it change the social structure? These are classic questions in philosophy and some of the social sciences. The usual philosophic analyses of autonomy and heteronomy ignore these questions.

As a philosopher and a feminist I believe that it is very important to understand Diana's feminist paradox in terms of the relationship between human activity and social structure. On the political side, women cannot gain personal autonomy without the existing social organization being changed—even if they live traditional lives. This means that we cannot discuss personal autonomy without discussing the social and political structure at the same time, integrated with the evolution toward personal autonomy. More generally, we cannot discuss how it is that members of any subordinate group come to have personal autonomy without discussing change in social structure. With Diana's version of personal autonomy—it includes feminine virtues as well as masculine ones—it looks as though even members of dominant groups must work to change social structure to gain personal autonomy as well.

As academics, as members of a professional class, we are members of dominant groups. Most of us here at these sessions of the American Philosophical Association are educators or in training to be educators, which means we take an important part in the process of maintaining and justifying definitions of people and life. We know that. That is why Diana is trying to make a respectful analysis of autonomy. The fact that our work plays the part it does play means that it is immensely important that we develop analyses and methods of teaching and writing that are respectful of people's humanity and respectful of the truth of the world we live in. This is not easy, given our training and our personal investments in our research and the fact that we need to keep our jobs to keep food on the table. It takes tremendous courage and a good dose of autonomy. But finding our own authentic selves requires, necessitates, that we understand our own places in the hierarchies of community, nation, and world. Respecting others requires that we do our work with an honest understanding of the way that our work creates and maintains the social structure. The individualistic model of autonomy and the socialization model of human group life will not let us see our place. It mystifies our place. For our own sakes, and for the sake of showing respect to all human beings, we must put aside those models.

## Notes

1. Meyers 1989 distinguishes a variety of kinds of autonomy.
2. For symbolic interactionism see Becker 1973 and Blumer 1969, and for the relevance to deviance and social problems, see Becker 1973 and Spector and Kitsuse 1977, and a myriad of others. For feminism, see classic sources in Rich 1979, Merchant 1980, and a myriad of others.

# *12*

## Making Knowledge

*WITH ELIZABETH POTTER*

(1988)

It is in the knowledge of the genuine conditions of our life that we must draw our strength to live and our reason for acting.

—Simone de Beauvoir, *The Ethics of Ambiguity*

When we academic researchers describe ourselves as feminists, we use a word that has many meanings. "Feminist" carries the political meaning it had in 1970: We are members of the women's movement. It carries a professional meaning: We are academic feminists who do research within disciplines and work in professional organizations. It carries one or another theoretical meaning: For example, we are self-conscious members of the class of women under patriarchy. And it carries practical meanings: For example, we are members of NOW, or we fight *for* the ERA and abortion rights, and *against* racism, or we open our homes to battered women, or we live our lives as lesbian separatists.

The initial meaning of "feminist" in an anthology on a feminist restructuring of knowledge is the professional meaning: We are feminist academics. This is the initial meaning but not the final meaning; we do not separate it from others in our lives and our work. The relations of these different meanings must somehow be understood as we set about restructuring knowledge by rethinking the dominant intellectual traditions, by integrating the work of feminist scholars, and by moving toward a restructuring. Our concern is with selection within academic disciplines, in the sciences and the humanities.

Feminist approaches can best be understood by contrasting them with traditional, "objective" approaches to the production of knowledge. In the traditional approaches, there is one knowledge, valid for all and biased in no one's favor. Objectivity is supposed to be guaranteed by proper criteria and methods, continually corrected for gender, class, racial, and other biases. Behind the feminist critiques lies our recognition that traditional selections are not independent of the values of those who make them. The selections that feminists criticize are made by people who have the authority to make them and thus to produce the knowledge their selections shape. Feminist critiques ultimately point to the hierarchical structure of cognitive authority that allows the perspective of some to determine the shape of knowledge for all.

Feminist transformations of scholarly knowledge have followed in large measure from new criteria and methods of selection, as the articles collected in Hartman and Messer-Davidow (in press) show. Recently, however, feminist academics have begun to examine their own class and race biases. These biases pose a particularly acute problem because academic feminists share their class positions, as professional producers of knowledge, with the males they criticize. Philosophers Maria Lugones and Elizabeth V. Spelman point out this problem in feminist theory (1983): While feminist philosophers have uncovered the upper-class androcentrism of traditional philosophical theories, they have often failed to recognize the upper-class, white "Anglo" perspectives represented in their own theorizing. Just as upper-class, white, heterosexual, male perspectives dominate traditional knowledge, so too upper-class, white, heterosexual female perspectives dominated feminist inquiry. As feminist scholars, we must continuously correct in ourselves what we have criticized in others, and that requires developing methods enabling feminist inquirers to be sensitive to power differentials in their interactions with the people they study.[1]

Over a decade ago, Dorothy Smith spoke to feminist sociologists of the need for a "reflexive" sociology for women (1979). She argued that the academic professions are part of the capitalist superstructure. Social scientists, she said, support bourgeois ideology when they construct abstract theories of society. She criticized sociologists' efforts to place themselves, as knowers, on an "archimedian point" outside society and thereby turn women (and others) into objects, not subjects. In the "reflexive" sociology she called for, the knowers are situated in the society they study, and women and others appear not as objects of the professional knower's study but as knowers themselves. Thus do the theorizers become subjects of study and the subjects of study become potential theorizers. . . .

How are feminists of the academy to do this when our work, like ourselves, is marked by a tension between privation and privilege, oppression and liberation, the reproduction of old structures and the creation of new ones? When culture and power are inseparable. When science and power are inseparable as well. Feminists working within disciplines exercise power—power that arises from our class positions—to bring about changes within culture and science. To do reflexive work, we must come to terms with our class position. It is a position that both empowers us and separates us from other women. One of the main goals in this chapter is to take a look at our class position, the position of professionals who work within disciplines making knowledge.

## KNOWING THAT

Denise Frechet notes that modern science began with "a mechanistic view of the world, in which every event, determined by initial conditions, is knowable with precision independently of the observer." Current science, she says, questions the world "as though it were governed by a universal theoretical plan," an approach that echoes the need of the scientist to dominate, to reduce the diversity of phenomena to a fundamental identity, to manage the uncontrollable by promulgating an all-encompassing law. The "validity" of a scientific theory is thought to be further reinforced by its expression in a flawless language: mathematics. This reduction of complex phenomena to simpler laws requires a distinction between significant and insignificant aspects of phenomena and a distinction between the people who are allowed to judge decisions scientific and those who are deemed only to have opinions). "Yet another type of cleavage," she adds, "is that between 'neutral' scientific information and its evaluation or application in the outside world" (Frechet, in press).

The model that Frechet describes says that, ideally, knowledge is certified by reliable methods. For all their differences, the processes of certification in the humanities and the sciences have important similarities: Both have disciplinary methods, canons, and modes of criticism or falsification designed to compel agreement. The abstract form of the knowledge they produce is quite similar. Among philosophers, the logical positivists offer the clearest example of this model of knowledge, although with a few modifications such knowledge persists among "postpositivists" (including some feminist philosophers).

In the logical positivist view, the ideal sort of knowledge is essentially linguistic and propositional knowledge—"knowing that" rather than "knowing how" or "knowing a person or place." It is expressed in true propositions: Truth, for the positivists, is a semantic concept in as much as it is a property of sentences. The sentences of natural science seem to offer the best (if not the only) examples of knowledge, so one of the positivists' major aims is to distinguish scientific propositions from the empirically meaningless pronouncements of metaphysicians, poets, moralists, and priests. The sentences of science are deemed empirically meaningful because they can be confirmed or falsified by observations. In this model, metaphysics, poetry, morality, and the Bible are not meaningless *tout court*; their words and sentences (can) have emotive meaning, but they do not pass the scientific test of meaningfulness. To be seriously meaningful, the terms in a proposition must have reference to things in the world; and to be true, a proposition must correctly describe the things to which its terms refer. Moreover, to be meaningful, a proposition must be at least falsifiable; that is, we must be able to test it against observations. "The dial registers 3.5" is meaningful because it can be verified or falsified by looking at the dial; "abortion is permissible" fails to have any but emotive meaning, since it is merely the expression of a positive feeling about abortion.

The logical positivists selected definitions of meaning, truth, and knowledge, so as to exalt the products of scientists and downgrade the products of poets, folk savants, and popes, to say nothing of mothers and fathers. But it is the products that are exalted, not—except indirectly and at a great distance—the work that professional scientists actually do. The appeal to professional distinctions between philosophy as a "conceptual" endeavor and sociology or anthropology as "merely empirical endeavors" allows positivists to focus on abstract "scientific knowledge" or "scientific laws" rather than on, say, the journal publications of workers in the hives of science departments, or their political struggles for tenure, grants, and prizes.

The positivist analysis is an abstract, philosophical model that has had considerable influence among working scientists. It rests on two assumptions important to feminist inquiry. The first one is captured in its abstract method of justification; according to the model, it doesn't matter who a scientist is. Robert Merton refers to this rule as "the norm of universalism in science": No one has special access to scientific truth. Given the proper training, any individual—man or woman; white, black, or brown; worker, capitalist, or aristocrat—can produce knowledge or know the truth produced scientifically (Merton 1949). The norm of universalism in turn assumes that all human individuals are epistemically alike in as much as we all share the fundamental criteria of truth and reason, as they are exhibited in Western science.

By portraying the justification of a scientific hypothesis as the work of the individual scientist, the positivist model presents knowledge as an individual affair. This is "epistemological individualism," the view that knowledge is a species of belief and that beliefs are states of individuals. It is an unexamined outcome of "methodological individualism," a theory that only individuals are real and suited for scientific observation. It naturally gives rise to the view that scientific knowledge is advanced by the lone scientist dutifully following established procedures as he formulates his hypotheses, designs and performs his experiments, and publishes his results (Scheman 1983). His gender, race, and class; his personal history; his values and politics; his position within the profession; the place of the professions in society—all these appear to be irrelevant to the knowledge he "discovers." Agency is transformed into the mental activity of individual knowers grasping the one objective truth. The agent has propositional knowledge: He "knows that" something is true.

This notion of science was established and is maintained in our schools and colleges. In the schools, individual students listen, do their homework, and receive grades. The standard stories in the standardized texts support the individualistic model. For example, the satisfying story that often appears in introductory biology texts begins with Aristotle, moves on to Linnaeus, and describes the geologists who, "far more than biologists . . . paved the way for evolutionary theory." Inevitably, it mentions Lamarck and his "primitive idea" of evolution by the inheritance of acquired characteristics; and almost as inevitably, it provides an accompanying picture of giraffes stretching their necks. After a few words on the economist Malthus and the great geologist Lyell, the story culminates with the "Darwin-Wallace" theory of evolution by natural selection. At this point, the pre-text of history stops, and the text of science begins. For some years now, biology texts have been standardized within the publishing industry by using a characteristically wooden and impersonal language, pat formats, and strikingly similar styles of drawing and diagram. They are massive and weighty books, sewn-bound in hearty hardcover suited to hold "certified" knowledge and designed to last a lifetime (or to sell for the use of next year's class).

These histories and the model they present of knowers and knowledge are not cynically constructed for the consumption of outsiders. Many scientists believe them—even brilliant ones who understand the importance of history, like zoologist Ernst Mayr, who discusses why naturalists Charles Darwin and Alfred Russel Wallace found the solution to evolution while the great zoologists of the time failed.

The naturalist . . . is constantly confronted by evolutionary problems. No wonder that this is what he is most interested in; no wonder that his constant attention to this problem places him in a much better position to ask the right questions and to find answers and solutions than the experimental biologist. Finally, Darwin and Wallace were not amateurs, but, as naturalists, highly trained professionals. This fails to answer, however, why great systematists and comparative anatomists of the nineteenth century were so blind. There are probably multiple reasons for their failure. In the case of Owen and Agassiz, it was unquestionably too strong a conceptual commitment to alternate interpretations; in the case of leading German zoologists like J. Muller, Leuckart, and so on, it might have been a counterreaction to the unbridled speculation of the Naturphilosophen. (Mayr 1982, 424–25)

Mayr's procedure here is interesting. He makes a natural event of scientific discovery itself. That is, the events occur as discovery events: They originate in the psychological or mental processes that precede the discoveries, and they conclude in the revelation of objective regularities or processes in nature. Darwin and Wallace face nature in a way that leads them to ask the "right questions. The failure of Owen and Agassiz, Muller and Leuckart, is explained by their irrationality—their commitments, and counterreactions.

Mayr of course picks out Darwin and Wallace in retrospect, they are the figures who wrote treatises that later investigators took to be important to their own work. Mayr explains their success in terms of scientific rationality that he reifies. He understands this rationality in a fairly subtle way, but he reifies it and contrasts it with the nonrational procedures that are responsible for others' failures. Mayr reifies nature as well when he explains that the distinction between what Darwin and Wallace said and what the others didn't say is explained in terms of how well it captured reality and approached the truth. Thus, discovery counts as a step in the scientific progress toward truth, an indication that today's professional scientists continue the task of drawing the veil from the face of Nature.

These histories of discoveries subsume the work of scientists into the work of members of an abstract community engaged in extending human knowledge. The scientific community crosses cultures and periods to join together Bacon, Newton, Darwin, Einstein, and Watson and Crick. For this community of scientists, nature is *there*, as if nature were the same for all people in all times, as if the properly scientific questions asked of nature would be questions anyone would ask to find the truth; as if our relationship to nature were only cognitive; as if we were individuals sharing ideas and propositional knowledge. Disciplinary distinctions, let alone social and personal ones, are epistemologically irrelevant because scientists merely divide the work of knowing the great mosaic of Nature.

Many feminists have criticized the traditional analysis of science. For example, Denise Frechet argues, quite correctly, that the traditional paradigm of objective knowledge and science is male biased. But in doing so, she retains the usual roster of "great men" and their great ideas, by which science has been traditionally defined in the West. Relying on Nancy Chodorow's theory of mothering, she explains gender biases in terms of individual scientists' selves, created in them by child-rearing practices in which women mother. She retains the traditional premise that the fundamental forces in making knowledge lie in individual thought and emotion (here, molded by socialization). As a result, male scientists are seen as members of an abstract class of (presumably) all males, described in terms of the internal structure of the essential self they share. Here we find, not the traditional assumption, but a "dualistic universalism" of the two abstract classes of men and women. It allows feminist academics to take our places as members of the class of women under patriarchy, and it allows us to ignore crucial differences among women and among men.

The central fault of the traditional approach was that it obscured higher-class, male dominance—indeed, concealed it—by ignoring the concrete, social, and historical place of the groups of people who made knowledge. Frechet's criticism allows us to ignore our own social and historical place as makers of knowledge. And yet Frechet's sort of criticism, and the mothering theories on which it is based, have opened the eyes of many women—they express what many of us intuitively feel. And yet, they retain parts of the traditional model, which have been seriously criticized by feminists and which must be overcome, for scholarly and for political reasons.

Feminist scholars (and many others) have been moving away from the traditional paradigm of knowledge toward a more sociological, historical, and political approach. In doing so, we face squarely the fact that academic feminists are, after all, academically trained, and we share our class positions, as knowledge workers, with the predominantly white, higher-class men we criticize. Reflexive work, in its fuller sense, requires a deep understanding of that class position. It requires understanding something about the social organization of professionalization in the United States, the historical process of professionalization through which knowledge came to be produced as it is, the process through which we came to know how to produce it.

## KNOWING HOW

In *The Death of Nature* (1980), Carolyn Merchant pictures the rise of modern science in the scientific revolution as a movement from viewing our cosmos as an organism to viewing it as a machine. The dominant metaphor binding together cosmos, society, and self changed from organism to machine. From being an active teacher and parent, nature became a mindless, submissive body (190). Nature was known. Nature was manipulated. Nature was managed. The knower, the manipulator, the manager, was man. Using science and technology, man came to know how to do these things.

The death of nature that Carolyn Merchant describes was a long, slow process of changing the ways many people lived and worked. Out of this process came our present ways of doing sciences and humanities: Intellectual work became employment and, in the academy, it was divided into disciplines with special content and methods. This relationship to nature and the human world through the sciences and humanities is a way of making knowledge and a way of knowing how to do it—a social organization of knowledge. Professions and disciplines are important to that social organization of knowledge.

As we use the term, disciplines are social worlds organized around topics and methods of inquiry—roughly speaking, a social world is a group of people sharing forms of communication, symbolization, activities, sites, technologies, and organizations. Through disciplines, we divide intellectual labor and organize work on research problems. Disciplines are sources of skill and technology for other organizations, including businesses, universities, and the professions. (See Clarke and Gerson 1990; Gerson 1983; Strauss 1978.) Our concern here is with academic disciplines in which members make their livings as members of professions.

The notion of a profession has been widely debated. Howard Becker has identified some of the normative characteristics: A profession is an occupation having a monopoly on a difficult, and important body of knowledge, in part by requiring lengthy training to master that knowledge and certification to practice it. While the training and certification are generally organized across the profession, the body of knowledge is specialized within the discipline. Elliot Freidson says that a profession offers ways of building, controlling, and regulating markets for a class of technical services: a way of organizing an occupational labor market (Freidson 1982; 1986). One way that we organize knowledge in the United States is through professions.

The academic professions were born and the modern departmental structure of colleges and universities was made after the Civil War, as the United States became an industrialized, urban nation. The new view among some of the elite was that what the nation needed for leadership was not the old-style gentlemen who shared social and moral values in a stable society but trained experts who could guide social change. The new man of learning was not so much a man of culture as a specialized expert (Sloan 1980).

Around the turn of the century, there was a proliferation of scholarly professions—a birth of multiple disciplines in what eventually became the sciences, social sciences, and humanities. Lawrence Vesey discusses "the plural organized worlds of the humanities," saying that like other areas of knowledge, the humanities underwent "intellectual segmentation" between 1865 and 1920, dividing fields into kingdoms and principalities—classics, modern languages, history, philosophy, art, music, each subdivided into even smaller specialties. The same process happened in the natural sciences, and though we might in both cases mark some difference in subject matter, the massive overlaps indicate that content was not the main source of the divisions. For this was intellectual work in particular workplaces, and organizationally there was standardization. Vesey says,

> Here one encounters all the phenomena linked to the much discussed concept of professionalization, and indeed the arrival of firmly planted notions of structural hierarchy and bureaucratic procedure in all respects. The kingdoms may have been separate and diverse, but nearly all of them came to be governed by the same kind of rules. (Vesey 1979, 51)

The rules were those of professional organization, professional media, and academic department. In the beginning, Vesey says, the leaders and followers in these academic professions in the main became, "members of a single, quite well defined, cultivated elite." But as the twentieth century wore on, being an academic professional became more a career than a calling.

One of the important features of this new social organization of knowledge was the autonomy of those who make knowledge. Normatively, professionals are free of lay control (except through laws and licensing), for they are supposed to be subject to self-policing according to their codes of ethics. Within disciplines, researchers are autonomous in the sense that they are supposed to be free to do research on any topic, subject to the criteria set within their disciplines. Until recently, many of the academic disciplines were predominantly male, and the knowledge produced was androcentric. Autonomy has been a source of gender bias in research, but it has also proved to be a source of feminist power to overcome gender bias.

In *Advocacy and Objectivity* (1975), Mary Furner discusses how the social sciences developed as professions, achieving job security, academic freedom, and influence on the laws and policies affecting people's lives. These gains were made, Furner argues, at the price of limiting autonomy and the academic freedom to dissent within a fairly restricted range of views and forfeiting claims as professionals to advocate controversial social policies. In reviewing academic freedom cases in economics, Furner points out:

> In order to survive professionally, economists had to find ways of repressing partisanship and presenting an appearance of unity and objectivity to the public. Gradually moderates forged a kind of working alliance that sacrificed extremists . . . to scholarly values that highly self-conscious professionals considered more important: professional security and the orderly development of knowledge in their disciplines. (7)

Perhaps one of the most celebrated cases in the history of the struggle to define academic freedom was that of Edward Alsworth Ross, fired in 1900 from Stanford at the demand of Mrs. Leland Stanford herself. Ross was, Furner tells us, career-minded, but he was involved in left politics. Although he did not join any socialist organizations, he was the friend of laborers and socialist politicians and publicly expressed views such as support for free silver and public ownership of monopolies including the railroads. Since Leland Stanford's fortune derived from his railroad investments, Ross's views were directly at odds with the family's interests.

Ross was fired in November 1900, and his dismissal set off a spate of resignations by those social scientists at Stanford "who could afford the gesture" (and by Arthur Lovejoy in Philosophy) as well as a furor in the academic world. Despite strong support from the profession, immediate efforts to find Ross another equally desirable position resulted only in a "five-year detention" at the University of Nebraska. At last, in 1906, Ross took a chair of sociology at Wisconsin and held it for thirty years. Academic freedom cases such as this one produced mixed results, as Furner reports. Academics gained more by autonomy, relief from external pressure to tailor the product of their work, knowledge, to favor interested parties, but forfeited the possibility of legitimately advocating radical social change on pain of being unprofessional "reformers" or "radicals." The definition of knowledge that developed in response to the academic freedom cases that concerned advocacy is one that underscores "objectivity." The case histories themselves reveal that, in no small part, the term "objective" means "nonadvocating." An objective scholar is one who does not advocate controversial views; in fact, he is supposed not to advocate any views at all. Objective, scholarly work suppresses the agency of the scholar. We find this suppression not only in the social sciences but in the natural sciences and the humanities as well. Philosophy provides a good example of the latter.

The author disappears from the philosophy text, giving, in the words of Arthur Danto, "a noble vision of ourselves as vehicles for the transmission of an utterly impersonal philosophical truth" (Danto 1985, 67). These impersonal reports also sacrifice the identities not only of the philosophers but also of the people whose "positions" philosophers debate. Instead of taking seriously what people mean in their social contexts, philosophers construct "positions" (the skeptic's position, the liberal feminist position), or arguments (the empiricist argument on the foundations of knowledge, the pro-life argument); the professional benefits of mastering the impersonal literary form include presenting papers, winning tenure, and perhaps even serving as the president of the American Philosophical Association.

In fact, few philosophers are able to devote the major part of their time to writing papers for journals; instead, nearly all academic philosophers spend most of their time teaching. The existence of a philosophy profession depends on the existence of philosophy departments that, in turn, depend not only on teaching but also on courses that set the subject matter of the field, serve as introductions and prerequisites, and offer standard questions for preliminary examinations as well as definitions of fields of competence for job applicants.

Foundational to philosophy course offerings are the roughly matched pair, History of Ancient Philosophy and History of Modern Philosophy. These two are among the most canonical of canonical courses in philosophy departments in the United States; they are required of undergraduate majors and covered in graduate qualifying examinations.[2] Bruce Kucklick has traced the construction of the Modern canon in his paper "Seven Thinkers and How They Grew" (1984). The selection of these masters was instrumental in the creation of the profession of philosophy: It allowed philosophy to define its subject matter, claim a history, and conceive of itself as an independent field of knowledge suited for departmental status in institutions of higher education. Kucklick refers to this history as "victors' history" and claims that elevation to the canon "depends on disorder, on luck, on cultural transitions . . . on scholarly power plays, and on the sheer glacial inertia of the institutions of higher education." In fact, "the canon has been frozen in conjunction with the relegation to the university of the learning of all philosophical material" (137). It is a canon that sets the problems for scholarly discussion and fundamentally structures the content of the field by selecting contrasting "tropes" such as rationalism vs. empiricism and monism vs. dualism. The "dualisms" feminst philosophers criticize were installed in this canon as well: mind vs. body and culture vs. nature. The canon persists in many departments, courses, and particularly in introductory texts. Over the past generation, it has been severely criticized and now shares the stage with other concepts, problems, and texts.

The construction of a canon is a process of selection by the few for the many, and it occurs within a complex, patterned set of practices. As they link to restructure knowledge within the academy, feminists must work within the patterned practices. Therein lie our opportunities as well as the dangers we face. . . .

Across the academic disciplines, feminists have shifted from assumptions about reality to the ways reality is constructed, and they have shown that gender is a crucial category of analysis. Feminists have used the patterns and practices of their disciplines to make the changes, and we have succeeded in changing some of the patterns and practices themselves. For example, women's studies cuts across the "separate and diverse kingdoms" of the disciplines, and women's-studies programs, courses, journals, and anthologies, and women's-studies professional organizations are multidisciplinary. Women's studies offers fertile intellectual soil even for feminists who do most of their work within their home disciplines. It can serve as an institutional basis for legitimating courses, journals, conferences, and research, as well as funding for projects that use gender as a category of analysis.

We have had our successes within the academic professions, but how have we fared in changing the role they play in making knowledge?

## Knowing Our Places

Angelika Bammer (in press) sets a familiar feminist dilemma: How are we to go about the business of dismantling the masters' houses while we are trying to get computers for the offices we have set up inside them? This dilemma faces all those who work for social change by boring from within institutions. To dismantle from within requires us not only to locate ourselves within institutions but also to wield their forms of power and authority for our purposes. But to dismantle institutions from within also requires us to maintain our feminist relationship to all women. Can we, who reside in them, use these institutions to transform patriarchal hierarchies? The danger is cooptation. The danger in using the masters' tools is that we may do to other women what we have accused men of doing to all women.

The danger exists because, as feminist academics, we have a class position—we work within the professional classes charged with making knowledge and educating the populace in a society marked by class, race, age, ethnic, religious, and other differences. Bammer fears that class has become merely "a category among others that feminist critics learned to invoke in the litany of oppressions we recited." She asks us to consider what class, as a historical construct and a lived experience, has to do with the work of feminist literary critics—or indeed with the work of feminists in any discipline (Bammer, in press). How can we feminist academics create and maintain a sisterly relationship to all women when our relationships to many women are marked by class dominance, and racial, age, and ethnic dominance as well? Our dilemma can only be resolved in political action, by making new relationships in a revitalized women's movement, one in which feminists move together to reshape the institutions of society, including the academy. But as we await that historic moment, there are questions that concern our work and our places now.

What is our place as feminists among the academics?

What is our place as academics among feminists?

And a wider question,

What is our place as feminist academics among women?

Each woman's answers to these questions differ according to whether she lives in Cambridge, Massachusetts; Shreveport, Lousiana; Las Vegas, Nevada; Pierre, South Dakota; or Los Angeles, California. They differ according to whether she works in an elite women's college, a Catholic university, a technical school, or a prestigious research institution. They differ according to the community she moves in within her family and neighborhood, and her town or city, county and state. They differ according to a multitude of demographic markers—race, class, age, marital status, single parent, and whether she is lesbian or heterosexual. Women's answers differ because the opportunities open to us differ. "Our place" is both historical construct and lived experience. But some circumstances are shared by all of us. As academics, we have institutional warrant to produce knowledge and to engage in professional practices. But as feminists, we need to re-affirm and re-create the political warrants that governed our work in earlier years.

What is our place as feminists among the academics?

Feminist research shows the places we have made for ourselves in the disciplines. . . . The history of women's studies shows the places we have made not only in research but institutionally, in departments, programs, institutes, and academic organizations. But to call ourselves *academic feminists* indicates that we have political connections and responsibilities. What is the warrant for calling this work feminist? Who defines what makes some academic work feminist and other work not feminist (or even antifeminist)? We know who grants our authority to speak as academics. Who grants our authority to speak as feminists? We are led to the second question.

What is our place as academics among feminists?

Some feminist academics believe it is their responsibility to articulate a feminist theory that will serve as a basis for a feminist revolution (on analogy with the responsibility that Marxist intellectuals are supposed to have in making theory for a socialist revolution). Because feminist academics are, as women, members of the revolutionary class, the question of our place as academics among the feminists seems moot. For example, Sandra Harding argues that the condition of women who are feminist "inquirers" just is the condition of women.

> Women feminists remain women no matter what they do. . . . Thus the "problem of intellectuals" and of "vanguardism" . . . should be less probable within feminism, or at least less intense than in these other scientific movements for social change. Does it make a difference to the path a revolution takes if the social group that articulates revolution and the group that is to make the revolution are the same? (1986, 242)

Harding admits that, given the crucial differences among women, we cannot expect a unified feminist theory at this time. But the question of our place as academics among feminists might be rephrased: Should we think of ourselves as theorists of revolution at all? Are we, sitting at our computers in our offices, the ones to articulate how to dismantle the masters' houses?

Once upon a time, less than a generation ago, the place of feminist intellectuals was in the movement. When we worked with activist groups in the 1960s and 1970s, we were part of a mass political struggle. We helped to write position statements that analyzed the historical moment in which a revolutionary group found itself and that set forth strategies to bring about social change. When these position statements spoke of "all women," they were making rallying calls for political unity and defining the directions that strategy and reform should take. They were not statements about "objective knowledge of true propositions about all women." They described a constituency to be organized, not a category to be described. They were in the mode of "knowing how," not "knowing that."

In those times, feminist intellectuals, including academics, were accountable to others with whom they formed political alliances, and that accountability enabled us to take our stands within our institutions. The knowledge we helped produce did not arise primarily from our activities as professionals but from our participation in a mass struggle for social change. We could work in the tension between advocacy and objectivity because we were responsible to and supported by the feminists with whom we worked in the movement, and our analyses could be tested by their success in the political struggle. Relationships to other feminists were made within the political alliances. Relationships to other women (not simply feminists) were made within this political context.

What is our place as feminist academics among women?

The feminist insistence on a connection with all women signaled that politically, feminism was not simply an alliance of organizations fighting for the interests of their members (as, for example, the reproductive rights or consumer-rights alliances have come to be). It was a mass movement with a basic premise that women's liberation requires self-determination for all women. It carried a commitment to the end of dismantling patriarchal oppression so that women could find self-determination. More important, perhaps, was the commitment to use only means that respect other women and their varied experience. Sisterhood was the model, and the double commitment was the moral and the political basis of the movement. The model and the commitment give us a way, even today, to test our places and our work.

There are certain intellectual analyses that have been influential among feminists inside and outside the academy. For example, Denise Frechet explains traditional knowledge in terms of the social construction of the selves of the male founders of modern science. Female selves are said to be constructed differently. This sort of theory sets out essential characteristics that women share, and so it justifies female academics in making knowledge in the name of all women. One serious difficulty faces academic feminists because gender is not the only significant category in the construction of our selves. Can women of one age, race, class, ethnicity, and so on, speak for women who are different from them in those ways?

This difficulty has been widely recognized, particularly on grounds of racial or ethnic difference. Consider Maria Lugones. She speaks in a Hispanic voice from "the viewpoint of an Argentinian woman who has lived in the US for sixteen years, who has attempted to come to terms with the devaluation of things Hispanic and Hispanic people in 'America.'"

> None of the feminist theories developed so far seem to me to help Hispanas in the articulation of our experience. We have a sense that in using them we are distorting our experiences. Most Hispanas cannot even understand the language used in these theories—and only in some cases the reason is that the Hispana cannot understand English. We do not recognize ourselves in these theories. They create in us a schizophrenic split between our concern for ourselves as women and ourselves as Hispanas, one that we do not feel otherwise. Thus they seem to us to force us to assimilate to some version of Anglo culture, however revised that version may be. They seem to ask that we leave our communities or that we become alienated so completely in them that we feel hollow. (Lugones and Spelman 1983, 576)

Lugones's complaints would be echoed by many other women—including not only women of non "Anglo" races but also pro-life women, senior citizens, business women, religious women, children, recent women immigrants, physically disabled women, teenagers, working-class women, and even academic women who come by some miracle from the lower classes to be knowledge workers in the professional classes.

The "litany of oppressions" that Bammer criticizes selects the categories on the basis of an abstract rather than a lived politics of oppression. As a litany, "gender, class, race" is recited a priori from unassimilated political struggles. The political struggle for feminists is to find appropriate methods of selection within our disciplines, methods that overcome not only gender bias but all the other biases that distort the knowledge we make. In all of the disciplines, this endeavor requires us to understand historical construction and lived experience. It requires us most of all to see that through our sisterly actions, we must continually make our political connections to feminists and to all women.[3]

Few of us today write position papers. Many of us teach new bodies of knowledge that feminist academics have made. In the process, some new ties have been made between women in the academy and women outside. For example, the National Institute for Women of Color and the Institute for Women's Policy Research have offered ways for women of the academy to serve other women. But for the most part, we have had to leave the mass movement for a professional individualism that embodies the "epistemological individualism" and the "universalism" of the old model. This professional individualism guides us as we select and teach what our students will learn. Too often, we present papers at meetings using the male forms of address that we criticized in years past and an academic language that most women cannot understand. Academic survival forces us to pursue our individual career success. In the crush of duties, we are often pushed to treat other women in the workplace as secretaries, custodians, cooks, waitresses, or students rather than as sisters. Times have changed, and sisterhood is not as powerful as it once was. The change in our place is due to the successes and the failures of the women's movement—we may make history, but, as Marx said, we do not make it in circumstances of our own choosing.

We make history, but we also have a history. Our past is one of mass movements, including the recent "second wave." Our past shows in our research. If we are to be self-reflexive, we must be so in our academic work *and* in our lives outside the academy. Feminist practice can permeate the boundaries between classrooms and communities, research and lived experience, academic and everyday knowers. Feminist inquiry must be based on understanding our own places in our communities and societies. It is a heritage we must enact in our lives so we may pass it on to those who will make history when we are gone.

## Notes

This paper was originally written for *(En)gendering Knowledge* (Hartman and Messer-Davidow, in press), a multidisciplinary anthology of papers by feminists in the natural and social sciences and the humanities. I have deleted some discussions of other papers in that volume, deletions marked by a series of dots: ". . . ." Elizabeth Potter and I thank the editors of that volume for their literary, intellectual, and scholarly help. We also thank the participants in our talk at the New England Women's Studies Association in May 1987 at Trinity College. Portions of the introduction on Dorothy Smith are taken from Addelson 1984.

1. The point is that as academic feminists, we all would do well to follow the example of feminist ethnographers who recognize that they occupy the more powerful position and need to appreciate the characteristics of their female subjects that are antipathetic to their own white, middle-class, feminist sensibilities.

2. The great thinkers covered in Ancient Philosophy include the Presocratics, such as Thales, Parmenides and the Pythagoreans, and Plato and Aristotle. In Modern Philosophy, the canon includes Descartes, Spinoza, Leibniz, Locke, Berkeley, Hume, and Kant.

3. In Chapter 6 I argue that the methods of finding the categories should be both empirical and political.

# A Postscript of Thanks

These chapters were written over a period of seventeen years. The usual academic acknowledgments are given in footnotes to each of the papers, but by their nature, those footnotes cannot acknowledge some of the most important help that I was given during that long, difficult time.

First of all, there is help of a material sort. Smith College and its philosophy department gave me support from the beginning—support of a type one doesn't usually expect from an academic institution. I was given leaves when I asked for them, and I was given sabbaticals on a generous schedule. I have had support services (an office, computer services, student assistants, WATS line) the luxury of which can be appreciated only by those who freelance and have to pay their own bills. The department was always tolerant of my political work, even when the work seemed outrageous and I was dogmatic, patronizing, or otherwise hard to get along with. We (as a department) encouraged and supported feminist courses and teaching methods, and so did the college.

I worked with the Smith College Project on Women and Social Change from 1978 to 1981, under a grant from the Mellon Foundation, which allowed us support services, contact with visiting scholars, and paid leave from our college duties. That grant offered me opportunities I would not have had otherwise.

I was awarded a fellowship for the 1978–79 school year by the National Endowment for the Humanities. That grant gave me a year off to write a book on ethics using interviews with members of the organization as a basis. I could not write a book at that time, but many of the papers in this collection did grow out of that year of research and writing.

Over the years, I have had a number of student assistants—all of them active feminists—who not only helped with typing, photocopying, and library searches, but who contributed their ideas and their discoveries of new feminist work. My list includes Mira Ainbinder and Alisa Klein and Alison Friedman, who worked on getting this collection into shape. The assistants who worked with me on the individual papers over the years include Susan Parker, Amy Hines, and Shawn Pyne. The many students who helped with ideas and references include Elaine Cohen and Pamela Armstrong.

The help that I received from some others is less easy to explain in traditional terms. I wrote "Nietzsche and Moral Change" (Chapter 2) during the early spring of 1972, when I was meeting with Holly Graff to coach her for her preliminary examinations. Holly was the only person who had a grasp of what I was trying to do in that paper, and I simply could not have written it without talking it through with her. We would first discuss sample prelim questions she had written, then after that we would talk about what I had written on the paper. She could hear what I was trying to say when no one else could. She was also one of the two people in my professional circles who understood my political work with the organization.

The other person who has understood my political and philosophical commitment is Judy Wittner. I met Judy in 1980, when I was a visiting lecturer in the sociology department at Northwestern, teaching courses with Howard Becker. Since that time we have been close friends, and our ongoing conversations merge into one flow our political work, our scholarly work, and our lives and families. Judy has always heard what I was trying to say, and she has helped me more than I can tell with her support, her enthusiasm, her sensitivity, her criticisms, her insights, her vision . . . and her knowledge of the literature.

There are others whom I mention in notes to the chapters, but whose help has been more substantial than those notes can indicate. I am particularly grateful to Howard Becker, Arlene Daniels, and Joseph Schneider.

I have worked with my daughters Catherine Casey Pyne and Shawn Pyne from the time they were teenagers. It really began when they were children, and we stood together in a peace march, watching the legionnaires throw eggs in our direction. We shared various kinds of political work on and off—but they never worked as I did with the organization. They were always generous and understanding, though the hardships they had to put up with because of my career and political work were terrible. We have also worked together writing intellectual pieces, and that has been a great happiness. But none of that says how much I have learned from them and their experience and knowledge and how much the chapters in this book owe to their criticism, insights, and vision. I have relied on their knowledge of our society and its institutions. They are present in all of the chapters in this collection.

I dedicated this collection to my parents, their forebears and their children, grandchildren, and great-grandchildren. Now, in the prime of life, I want to thank another part of my family—the part I married into a decade ago. Like many others who fought through the 1960s and 1970s, I had to find a way to put the pieces together after the Movement ran its course. I am more thankful than I can say to Richard and his family for their gentleness and patience and love. I could not have done my work without it.

# References

Ackelsberg, Martha. 1976. "The Possibility of Anarchism." Ph.D. diss., Department of Politics, Princeton University.

Ackelsberg, Martha, and Kathryn Pyne Addelson. 1987. "Anarchist Alternatives to Competition." In Valerie Miner and Helen Longino, eds., *Competition: A Feminist Taboo?* New York: Feminist Press.

Addams, Jane. 1907. *Democracy and Social Ethics.* New York: Macmillan.

Addelson, Kathryn Pyne. 1984. "Introduction." *Women and Politics* 3, no. 4 (Winter).

———. 1985. "Doing Science." *Proceedings of the Philosophy of Science Association,* Summer.

Alinsky, Saul. 1969. *Reveille for Radicals.* New York: Vintage Books.

Anscombe, Elizabeth. 1981. *Ethics, Religion, and Politics.* Minneapolis: University of Minnesota Press.

Ardener, Edwin. 1975a. "The Problem Revisited." In Shirley Ardener, ed., *Perceiving Women.* New York: John Wiley and Sons.

———. 1975b. "Belief and the Problem of Woman." In Shirley Ardener, ed., *Perceiving Women.* New York: John Wiley and Sons.

Argyris, Chris. 1977. "The Impact of Formal Organization on the Individual." In David S. Pugh, ed., *Organization Theory.* Baltimore: Penguin Books.

Aubert, Vilhelm. 1965. *The Hidden Society.* Totowa, N.J.: Bedminster Press.

Baier, Annette. 1986. "Trust and Antitrust." *Ethics* 96 (January).

Baldwin, Roger, ed. 1970. *Kropotkin's Revolutionary Pamphlets.* New York: Dover Publications.

Ball, Donald W. 1967. "An Abortion Clinic Ethnography." *Social Problems* 14 (Winter): 293–301.

Bammer, Angelika. In press. "Mastery." In *(En)gendering Knowledge.* See Hartman and Messer-Davidow, in press.

Bart, Pauline B. 1980. "Seizing the Means of Reproduction." In Helen Roberts, ed., *Women, Health, and Reproduction.* London: Routledge and Kegan Paul.

Baynes, Kenneth; James Bohman; and Thomas McCarthy, eds. 1987. *After Philosophy: End or Transformation?* Cambridge, Mass.: MIT Press.

Becker, Howard S. 1966. *Social Problems: A Modern Approach.* New York: John Wiley and Sons.

———. 1970. *Sociological Work: Method and Substance.* Chicago: Aldine.

———. 1973. *Outsiders: Studies in the Sociology of Deviance.* New York: Free Press.

———. 1977. "Whose Side Are We On?" *Sociological Work.* New Brunswick, N.J.: Transaction Books.

———. 1986. *Doing Things Together.* Evanston, Ill.: Northwestern University Press.

Bellah, Robert, 1982. "Social Science as Practical Reason." *Hastings Center Report* 12, no. 5:32–39.

———. 1985. "The Humanities and Social Vision." In *Applying the Humanities.* See Callahan, Caplan, and Jennings 1985.

Bellah, Robert, et al. 1985. *Habits of the Heart: Individuals and Commitment in American Life.* Berkeley: University of California Press.

Berger, Peter L., and Thomas Luckmann. 1967. *The Social Construction of Reality.* Garden City, N.Y.: Anchor Books.

Bernstein, Richard. 1983. *Beyond Objectivism and Relativism: Science, Hermeneutics, and Praxis.* Philadelphia: University of Pennsylvania Press.

Blasi, Augusto. 1980. "Bridging Moral Cognition and Moral Action: A Critical Review of the Literature." *Psychological Bulletin* 88, no. 1.

Blumer, Herbert. 1967. "Society as Symbolic Interaction." In Jerome G. Manis and Bernard N. Meltzer, eds., *Symbolic Interaction.* Boston: Allyn and Bacon.

————. 1969. *Symbolic Interactionism: Perspective and Method.* Englewood Cliffs, N.J.: Prentice-Hall.

Boller, Paul F. 1981. *American Thought in Transition.* Washington, D.C.: University Press of America.

Bondi, Richard. 1984. "The Elements of Character." *Journal of Religious Ethics* 12, no. 2 (Fall).

Bookchin, Murray. 1971. *Post Scarcity Anarchism.* Berkeley, Calif.: Ramparts Press.

Boston Women's Health Book Collective. 1976. *Our Bodies, Ourselves.* 3d ed. New York: Simon and Schuster.

Bottomore, Tom, and Robert Nisbet, eds. 1978. *A History of Sociological Analysis.* New York: Basic Books.

Braverman, Harry. 1974. *Labor and Monopoly Capital.* New York: Monthly Review Press.

Brecker, Jeremy. 1974. *Strike!* Greenwich, Conn.: Fawcett.

Bringuier, Jean-Claude. 1980. *Conversations with Jean Piaget.* Chicago: University of Chicago Press.

Bruner, Jerome. 1986. *Actual Minds, Possible Worlds.* Cambridge, Mass.: Harvard University Press.

Bunch, Charlotte. 1974. "The Reform Tool Kit." *Quest: A Feminist Quarterly* 1, no. 1 (Summer).

Callahan, Daniel. 1982. "Tradition and the Moral Life." Carol Levine and Robert M. Veatch, eds. *Hastings Center Report* 12, no. 6.

Callahan, Daniel, and Sissela Bok, eds. 1980. *Ethics Teaching in Higher Education.* New York: Plenum Press.

Callahan, Daniel; Arthur L. Caplan; and Bruce Jennings, eds. 1985. *Applying the Humanities* (Hastings Center Series in Ethics). New York: Plenum Press.

Carnap, Rudolf. 1956. "The Methodological Character of Theoretical Concepts." In Herbert Feigel and Michael Scriven, eds., *Minnesota Studies in the Philosophy of Science,* vol. 1. Minneapolis: University of Minnesota Press.

Carter, April. 1971. *The Political Theory of Anarchism.* London: Routledge and Kegan Paul.

Cates, Willard, and Roger W. Rochat. 1976. "Illegal Abortion in the United States: 1972–74." *Family Planning Perspectives* 8 (March/April): 86–92.

Caws, Peter. 1972. "Reform and Revolution." In Virginia Held, Kai Nielsen, and C. Parsons, eds., *Philosophy and Political Action.* New York: Oxford University Press.

Chafe, William. 1977. *Women and Equality.* New York: Oxford University Press.

Chodorow, Nancy. 1978. *The Reproduction of Mothering: Psychoanalysis and the Sociology of Gender.* Berkeley: University of California Press.

Chickering, Arthur W. 1981. *The Modern American College.* San Francisco: Jossey-Bass.

Clarke, Adele, and Elihu Gerson. 1990. "Symbolic Interactionism in Social Studies of Science." In Howard Becker and Michal McCall, eds., *Symbolic Interactionism and Cultural Studies.* Chicago: University of Chicago Press.

Cole, Jonathan. 1979. *Fair Science: Women in the Scientific Community.* New York: Free Press.

Cole, Jonathan, and Stephen Cole. 1973. *Social Stratification in Science.* Chicago: University of Chicago Press.

Collingwood, R. G. 1946. *The Idea of History.* Oxford: Oxford University Press.

Daniels, Arlene Kaplan. 1975. "Feminist Perspectives in Sociological Research." In *Another Voice. See* Millman and Kanter 1975.

————. 1979. "Advocacy Research: Providing New Wares for the Free Marketplace of Ideas." *Sociology's Relations with the Community.* Calgary: University of Calgary Colloquium Proceedings.

————. 1985. "Good Works and Good Times: The Place of Entertainment in the Work of Women Volunteers." *Social Problems* 32, no. 4 (April).

————. 1988. *Invisible Careers: Women Civic Leaders from the Volunteer World.* Chicago: University of Chicago Press.

Daniels, Arlene Kaplan; Teresa Odendahl; and E. Boris. 1985. *Working in Foundations: Career Patterns of Women and Men.* New York: Foundation Center.

Danto, Arthur. 1965. *Nietzsche as Philosopher.* New York: Macmillan.

————. 1980. "Analytic Philosophy." *Social Research* 47, no. 4:615–16.

————. 1985. *Narration and Knowledge.* New York: Columbia University Press.

Davidson, Donald. 1982. "On the Very Idea of a Conceptual Scheme." In Michael Krausz and Jack W. Meiland, eds., *Relativism, Cognitive and Moral.* Notre Dame, Ind.: University of Notre Dame Press.

de Beauvoir, Simone. 1948. *The Ethics of Ambiguity.* New York: Philosophical Library.

Debro, Julius. 1970. "Dialogue with Howard S. Becker." *Issues of Criminology* 5, no. 2 (Summer).

DeVault, Marjorie. 1982. "Women's Invisible Work: Mrs. Ramsay's Craft." Paper presented at a conference on Virginia Woolf, College of St. Catherine, St. Paul, Minn., October 22–23.

————. 1984. "Women and Food: Housework and the Production of Family Life." Ph.D. diss., Department of Sociology, Northwestern University.

————. 1987. "Doing Housework: Feeding and Family Life." In Naomi Gerstel and Harriet Engel Gross, eds., *Families and Work.* Philadelphia: Temple University Press.

Dworkin, Andrea. 1977. *Our Blood.* New York: W. W. Norton.

Dye, Nancy Schrom. 1979. "Cleo's American Daughters: Male History, Female Reality." In *The Prism of Sex. See* Sherman and Beck 1979.

Ehrenreich, Barbara, and Deirdre English. 1979. *For Her Own Good: 150 Years of Experts' Advice to Women.* Garden City, N.Y.: Anchor Press/Doubleday.

Ehrlich, Carol. 1977. "Socialism, Anarchism and Feminism." *Second Wave,* Spring/Summer.

Eisenstein, Zillah. 1977. *Capitalist Patriarchy and the Case for Socialist Feminism.* New York: Monthly Review Press.

Elshtain, Jean B. 1981. *Public Man, Private Woman: Women in Social and Political Thought.* Princeton, N.J.: Princeton University Press.

Engelhardt, H. Tristram Jr., and Daniel Callahan, eds. 1976. *Science, Ethics, and Medicine.* Vol. 1 of *The Foundations of Ethics and Its Relationship to Science.* New York: Hastings Center.

Feinberg, Joel. 1985. *Reason and Responsibility.* Belmont, Calif.: Wadsworth.

————, ed. 1973. *The Problem of Abortion.* Belmont, Calif.: Wadsworth.

Ferguson, Kathy. 1978. "Liberalism and Oppression: Emma Goldman and the Anarchist Feminist Alternative." In Michael J. Gargas McGrath, ed., *Liberalism and the Modern Polity.* New York: Marcel Dekker.

Feyerabend, Paul. 1962. "Explanation, Reduction, and Empiricism." In Michael Radner and Stephen Winokur, eds., *Minnesota Studies in the Philosophy of Science,* vol. 4. Minneapolis: University of Minnesota Press.

————. 1970. "Against Method." In Michael Radner and Stephen Winokur, eds., *Minnesota Studies in the Philosophy of Science,* vol. 4. Minneapolis: University of Minnesota Press.

Fingarette, Herbert. 1967. *On Responsibility.* New York: Basic Books.

Flanagan, Owen J., and Jonathan E. Adler. 1983. "Impartiality and Particularity." *Social Research* 50, no. 3 (Autumn).

Flexner, Eleanor. 1971. *Century of Struggle.* New York: Atheneum.

Frankena, William K. 1963. *Ethics.* Englewood Cliffs, N.J.: Prentice-Hall.

Frechet, Denise. In press. "Toward a Post-Phallic Science." In *(En)gendering Knowledge. See* Hartman and Messer-Davidow, in press.

Freidson, Elliot. 1970. *Professional Dominance: The Social Structure of Medical Care.* Chicago: Aldine.

————. 1982. "Occupational Autonomy and Labor Market Shelters." In Phyllis L. Stewart and Muriel G. Cantor, eds., *Varieties of Work.* Beverly Hills: Sage Publications.

————. 1986. *Professional Powers: A Study of the Institutionalization of Formal Knowledge*. Chicago: University of Chicago Press.

Friedan, Betty. 1974. *The Feminine Mystique*. New York: Dell.

Furner, Mary. 1975. *Advocacy and Objectivity: A Crisis in the Professionalization of American Social Science*. Lexington: University Press of Kentucky.

Gandhi, Mohandus. 1957. *An Autobiography: The Story of My Experiments with Truth*. Boston: Beacon Press.

Gerson, Elihu M. 1983. "Scientific Work and Social Worlds." *Knowledge: Creation, Diffusion, Utilization* 4, no. 3 (March).

Gibson, Mary. 1977. "Rationality." *Philosophy and Public Affairs* 6, no. 3 (Spring): 193–225.

Gilligan, Carol. 1977. "In a Different Voice: Women's Conceptions of Self and of Morality." *Harvard Educational Review* 47, no. 4:481–517.

————. 1979. "Woman's Place in a Man's Life Cycle." *Harvard Educational Review* 49, no. 4 (November).

————. 1981. "Moral Development." In *The Modern American College*. See Chickering 1981.

————. 1982. *In a Different Voice: Psychological Theory and Women's Development*. Cambridge, Mass.: Harvard University Press.

————. 1983. "Do the Social Sciences Have an Adequate Theory of Moral Development?" In Norma Haan et al., eds., *Social Science as Moral Inquiry*. New York: Columbia University Press.

————. 1984a. "Remapping Development: The Power of Divergent Data." In Leonard Cirillo and Seymour Wapner, eds., *Value Presuppositions in the Theory of Human Development*. Hillside, N.J.: Erlbaum Associates.

————. 1984b. "Remapping the Moral Domain: New Images of Self in Relationship." Paper presented at conference, Reconstructing Individualism, Stanford Humanities Center, February 18–20.

————. 1987. "Moral Orientation and Moral Development." In *Women and Moral Theory*. See Meyers and Kittay 1987.

Gilligan, Carol, and Lawrence Kohlberg. 1971. "The Adolescent as a Philosopher: The Discovery of the Self in a Postconventional World." *Daedalus* 100:1051–86.

Gilligan, Carol, and John Michael Murphy. 1979. "Development from Adolescence to Adulthood: The Philosopher and the Dilemma of the Fact." In Deanna Kuhn, ed., *New Directions for Child Development: Intellectual Development Beyond Childhood*. San Francisco: Jossey-Bass.

Gilligan, Carol; Georgia Blackburne-Stover; and Mary Field Belenky. 1982. "Moral Development and Reconstructive Memory: Recalling a Decision to Terminate an Unplanned Pregnancy." *Developmental Psychology* 18, no. 6:862–70.

Glen, Kristin Booth. 1978. "Abortion in the Courts: A Laywoman's Historical Guide to the New Disaster Area." *Feminist Studies*, January, 1–26.

Goffman, Erving. 1961. *Asylums: Essays on the Social Situation of Mental Patients and Other Inmates*. Garden City, N.Y.: Doubleday.

Goldman, Emma. 1969. "Anarchism: What It Really Stands For." In Richard Drinnon, ed., *Anarchism and Other Essays*. New York: Dover Publications.

Green, Philip. 1981. *The Pursuit of Inequality*. New York: Pantheon Books.

Grimke, Sarah M. 1972. *Letters on the Equality of the Sexes and the Condition of Women*. In *Feminism*. See Schneir 1972.

Guerin, Daniel. 1970. *Anarchism*. New York: Monthly Review Press.

Gusfield, Joseph. 1967. "Moral Passage: The Symbolic Process in Public Designation of Deviance." *Social Problems* 15, no. 2.

————. 1981. *The Culture of Public Problems: Drinking, Driving, and the Symbolic Order*. Chicago: University of Chicago Press.

————. 1984. "On the Side." In *Studies in the Sociology of Social Problems. See* Schneider and Kitsuse 1984.

Hanson, Norwood Russell. 1958. *Patterns of Discovery.* Cambridge: Cambridge University Press.

Haraway, Donna. 1978. "Animal Sociology and a Natural Economy of Body Politic." Parts 1 and 2. *Signs* 4:21–60.

————. 1979. "The Biological Enterprise: Sex, Mind, and Profit from Human Engineering to Sociobiology." *Radical History Review,* Spring-Summer special issue, 206–37.

Harding, Sandra. 1986. *The Science Question in Feminism.* Ithaca, N.Y.: Cornell University Press.

Harding, Sandra, and Merrill B. Hintikka, eds. 1983. *Discovering Reality: Feminist Perspectives on Epistemology, Metaphysics, Methodology and Philosophy of Science.* Boston: D. Reidel.

Harrison, Beverly. 1983. *Our Right to Choose: Toward a New Ethic of Abortion.* Boston: Beacon Press.

Harsanyi, John C. 1976. *Essays on Ethics, Social Behavior, and Scientific Explanation.* Dordrecht, Holland: D. Reidel.

Hart, H. L. A. 1961. *The Concept of Law.* Oxford: Clarendon Press.

Hartman, Joan E., and Ellen Messer-Davidow, eds. In press. *(En)gendering Knowledge: Feminists in Academe.* Knoxville: University of Tennessee Press.

Hartmann, Heidi. 1981. "The Unhappy Marriage of Marxism and Feminism: Towards a More Progressive Union." In Lydia Sargent, ed., *Women and Revolution.* Boston: South End Press.

Hartsock, Nancy. 1974. "Political Change: Two Perspectives on Power." *Quest: A Feminist Quarterly* 1, no. 1 (Summer).

Haskel, Thomas L. 1977. *The Emergence of Professional Social Science.* Urbana: University of Illinois Press.

Hauerwas, Stanley. 1977. *Truthfulness and Tragedy.* Notre Dame, Ind.: University of Notre Dame Press.

————. 1980. "Abortion: Why the Arguments Fail." In *A Community of Character. See* Hauerwas 1981.

————. 1981. *A Community of Character: Toward a Constructive Christian Social Ethic.* Notre Dame, Ind.: University of Notre Dame Press.

Hauerwas, Stanley, and Alasdair MacIntyre. 1983. *Revisions.* Notre Dame, Ind.: University of Notre Dame Press.

Hubbard, Ruth; Mary Sue Henifin; and Barbara Fried. 1982. *Biological Woman: The Convenient Myth.* Cambridge, England: Schenkman.

Hughes, Everett C. 1984. *The Sociological Eye.* New Brunswick, N.J.: Transaction Books.

Jaggar, Alison M. 1983. *Feminist Politics and Human Nature.* Totowa, N.J.: Rowman and Allanheld.

Jarvie, I. C. 1984. *Rationality and Relativism: In Search of a Philosophy and History of Anthropology.* London: Routledge and Kegan Paul.

Jencks, Christopher, et al. 1972. *Inequality.* New York: Basic Books.

Kanter, Rosabeth M. 1977. *Men and Women of the Corporation.* New York: Basic Books.

Kaufmann, Walter. 1968. *Nietzsche: Philosopher, Psychologist, Antichrist.* New York: Vintage Books.

Kittay, Eva Feder, and Diana T. Meyers, eds. 1987. *Women and Moral Theory.* Totowa, N.J.: Rowman and Littlefield.

Kleiber, Nancy, and Linda Light. 1978. *Caring for Ourselves: An Alternative Structure for Health Care.* Vancouver: School of Nursing, University of British Columbia.

Kohlberg, Lawrence. 1969. "Stage and Sequence: The Cognitive-Developmental Approach to Socialization." In David A. Goslin, ed., *Handbook of Socialization Theory and Research.* Chicago: Rand McNally.

————. 1971. "From Is to Ought." In *Cognitive Development and Epistemology. See* Mischel 1971.

————. 1981. *The Philosophy of Moral Development.* San Francisco: Harper and Row.

————. 1982. "A Reply to Owen Flanagan and Some Comments on the Puka Goodpaster Exchange." *Ethics* 92, no. 3 (April): 513–28.

Kohlberg, Lawrence, and R. Kramer. 1969. "Continuities and Discontinuities in Childhood and Adult Moral Development." *Human Development* 12:9–120.

Kornegger, Peggy. 1975. "Anarchism: The Feminist Connection." *Second Wave,* Spring.

Kropotkin, Peter A. 1913. *The Conquest of Bread.* London: Chapman Hall.

Kucklick, Bruce. 1984. "Seven Thinkers and How They Grew: Descartes, Spinoza, Leibniz, Locke, Berkeley, Hume, Kant." In *Philosophy in History. See* Rorty, Schneewind, and Skinner 1984.

Kuhn, Thomas. 1970. *The Structure of Scientific Revolutions.* 2d ed. Chicago: University of Chicago Press.

Ladd, John. 1970. "Morality and the Ideal of Rationality in Formal Organization." *The Monist* 54, no. 4.

————. 1975. "The Ethics of Participation." In J. Roland Pennock and John W. Chapman, eds., *Participation in Politics.* New York: Atherton-Leber.

————. 1978. "Legalism and Medical Ethics." In John W. Davis, Barry Hoffmaster, and Sarah Shorten, *Contemporary Issues in Biomedical Ethics.* Clifton, N.J.: Humana Press.

Lee, Nancy Howell. 1969. *The Search for an Abortionist.* Chicago: University of Chicago Press.

Lehning, Arthur, ed. 1974. *Michael Bakunin: Selected Writings.* New York: Grove Press.

Lemert, Edwin. 1951. *Social Pathology: A Systematic Approach to the Theory of Sociopathic Behavior.* New York: McGraw Hill.

Leval, Gaston. 1975. *Collectives in the Spanish Revolution.* London: Freedom Press.

Lofland, Lyn. 1975. "The 'Thereness' of Women: A Selective Review of Urban Sociology." In *Another Voice. See* Millman and Kanter 1975.

Lugones, Maria, and Elizabeth V. Spelman. 1983. "Have We Got a Theory for You: Feminist Theory, Cultural Imperialism, and the Demand for the Women's Voice." *Hypatia: Journal of Feminist Philosophy* 1, no. 1. Published as special issue of *Women's Studies International Forum* 6, no. 6.

Luker, Kristin. 1975. *Taking Chances: Abortion and the Decision Not to Contracept.* Berkeley: University of California Press.

————. 1984. *Abortion and the Politics of Motherhood.* Berkeley: University of California Press.

MacIntyre, Alasdair. 1984. *After Virtue.* 2d. ed. Notre Dame, Ind.: University of Notre Dame Press.

MacKinnon, Catharine A. 1987. *Feminism Unmodified: Discourses on Life and Law.* Cambridge, Mass.: Harvard University Press.

Macklin, Ruth. 1985. "Standards in Philosophy." In *Applying the Humanities. See* Callahan, Caplan, and Jennings 1985.

Malcolm X. 1986. *The Autobiography of Malcolm X.* New York: Grove Press.

Martin, Mike. 1989. *Everyday Morality: An Introduction to Applied Ethics.* Belmont, Calif.: Wadsworth.

Matza, David. 1969. *Becoming Deviant.* Englewood Cliffs, N.J.: Prentice-Hall.

Mayr, Ernst. 1982. *The Growth of Biological Thought.* Cambridge, Mass.: Harvard University Press.

Merchant, Carolyn. 1980. *The Death of Nature: Women, Ecology, and the Scientific Revolution.* San Francisco: Harper and Row.

Merton, Robert K. 1949. *Social Theory and Social Structure.* Glencoe, Ill.: Free Press.

Merton, Thomas. 1974. *A Thomas Merton Reader.* Edited by Thomas P. McDonnell. Garden City, N.Y.: Image Books.

Meyers, Diana. 1987. "Personal Autonomy and the Paradox of Feminine Socialization." *Journal of Philosophy* 84, no. 11 (November).

———. 1989. *Self, Society, and Personal Choice.* New York: Columbia University Press.

Mill, John Stuart. 1951. *Utilitarianism.* Everyman Edition.

———. 1972. *The Subjugation of Women.* In *Feminism.* See Schneir 1972.

Millman, Marcia, and Rosabeth Moss Kanter, eds. 1975. *Another Voice.* Garden City, N.Y.: Anchor Press/Doubleday.

Mills, C. Wright. 1956. *The Power Elite.* New York: Oxford University Press.

———. 1963. *Power Politics and People: The Collected Essays.* Edited by Irving Louis Horowitz. New York: Ballantine Books.

Milton, Kay. 1979. "Male Bias in Anthropology." *Man, Journal of the Royal Anthropological Institute, London,* 14:40–54.

Mischel, Theodore, ed. 1971. *Cognitive Development and Epistemology.* New York: Academic Press.

Mullins, Nicholas C. 1973. *Science: Sociological Perspectives.* New York: Bobbs-Merrill.

Murphy, John M., and Carol Gilligan. 1980. "Moral Development in Late Adolescence and Adulthood: A Critique and Reconstruction of Kohlberg's Theory." *Human Development* 23, no. 2:77–104.

Newton, Lisa. 1988. *Ethics in America: Source Reader.* Englewood Cliffs, N.J.: Prentice-Hall.

Nietzsche, Friedrich. 1966. *Beyond Good and Evil.* Translated by Walter Kaufmann. New York: Vintage Books.

———. 1968a. *Thus Spake Zarathustra.* In Walter Kaufmann, ed., *The Portable Nietzsche.* New York: Viking Press.

———. 1968b. *The Will to Power.* Edited by Walter Kaufmann. New York: Vintage Books.

———. 1969. *On the Genealogy of Morals.* Edited by Walter Kaufmann. New York: Vintage Books.

Noddings, Nel. 1984. *Caring.* Berkeley: University of California Press.

Oleson, Alexandra, and John Voss, eds. 1979. *The Organization of Knowledge in Modern America.* Baltimore: Johns Hopkins University Press.

Pearsall, Marilyn. 1986. *Women and Value.* San Diego: Wadsworth.

Perry, William. 1968. *Forms of Intellectual and Ethical Development in the College Years.* New York: Holt, Rinehart and Winston.

Petchesky, Rosalind Pollack. 1984. *Abortion and Woman's Choice: The State, Sexuality, and Reproductive Freedom.* New York: Longman.

Piaget, Jean. 1948. *The Moral Judgment of the Child.* Glencoe, Ill.: Free Press.

———. 1971. *Structuralism.* New York: Harper and Row.

Polkinghorne, Donald. 1987. *Narrative Knowing and the Human Sciences.* Ithaca, N.Y.: State University of New York Press.

Popper, Karl. 1965. *Conjectures and Refutations: The Growth of Scientific Knowledge.* New York: Basic Books.

———. 1966. *The Open Society and Its Enemies.* New York: Harper Books.

Quine, Willard Van Orman. 1963. *From a Logical Point of View.* New York: Harper and Row.

———. 1969. *Ontological Relativity and Other Essays.* New York: Columbia University Press.

Rains, Prudence. 1971. *Becoming an Unwed Mother.* Chicago: Aldine.

———. 1975. "Imputations of Deviance." *Social Problems* 23 (October): 1–11.

Rajchman, John, and Cornel West, eds. 1985. *Post-Analytic Philosophy.* New York: Columbia University Press.

Rawls, John. 1971. *A Theory of Justice.* Cambridge, Mass.: Harvard University Press.

Rescher, Nicholas. 1978. *Scientific Progress.* Pittsburgh: University of Pittsburgh Press.

Reskin, Barbara R. 1978. "Sex Differentiation and the Social Organization of Science." *Sociological Inquiry* 48:3–4.

Rich, Adrienne. 1979. *On Lies, Secrets, and Silence: Selected Prose, 1966–78.* New York: W. W. Norton.

Rock, Paul. 1979. *The Making of Symbolic Interactionism.* Totowa, N.J.: Rowman and Littlefield.

Rorty, Richard. 1979. *Philosophy and the Mirror of Nature.* Princeton, N.J.: Princeton University Press.

———. 1982. *Consequences of Pragmatism (Essays: 1972–1980).* Minneapolis: University of Minnesota Press.

Rorty, Richard; Jerome B. Schneewind; and Quentin Skinner, eds. 1984. *Philosophy in History.* Cambridge: Cambridge University Press.

Rowbotham, Sheila. 1974. *Hidden from History.* London: Philo Press.

Rubin, Lillian B. 1976. *Worlds of Pain.* New York: Basic Books.

Sarvis, Betty, and Hyman Rodman. 1974. *The Abortion Controversy.* New York: Columbia University Press.

Scheffler, Israel. 1967. *Science and Subjectivity.* Indianapolis: Bobbs-Merrill.

Scheman, Naomi. 1983. "Individualism and the Objects of Psychology." In *Discovering Reality. See* Harding and Hintikka 1983.

Schneider, Joseph. 1985. "Defining the Definitional Perspective on Social Problems." *Social Problems* 32:214–27.

Schneider, Joseph, and John Kitsuse. 1984. *Studies in the Sociology of Social Problems.* Norwood, N.J.: Ablex.

Schneir, Miriam, ed. 1972. *Feminism: The Essential Historical Writings.* New York: Vintage Books.

Sennett, Richard, and Jonathan Cobb. 1973. *The Hidden Injuries of Class.* New York: Vintage Books.

Sherif, Carolyn Wood. 1979. "Bias in Psychology." In *The Prism of Sex. See* Sherman and Beck 1979.

Sherman, Julia A., and Evelyn Torton Beck, eds. 1979. *The Prism of Sex.* Madison: University of Wisconsin Press.

Singer, Marcus G. 1961. *Generalization in Ethics: An Essay in the Logic of Ethics, with the Rudiments of a System of Moral Philosophy.* New York: Alfred A. Knopf.

Singer, Peter. 1979. *Practical Ethics.* Cambridge: Cambridge University Press.

Sloan, Douglas. 1980. "The Teaching of Ethics in the American Undergraduate Curriculum, 1876–1976." In *Ethics Teaching in Higher Education. See* Callahan and Bok 1980.

Smetana, Judith. 1982. *Concepts of Self and Morality.* New York: Praeger Special Studies.

Smith, Dorothy. 1979. "A Sociology for Women." In *The Prism of Sex. See* Sherman and Beck 1979.

———. 1987. *The Everyday World as Problematic: A Feminist Sociology.* Boston: Northeastern University Press.

Spector, Malcolm, and John Kitsuse. 1977. *Constructing Social Problems.* Menlo Park, Calif.: Cummings.

Stacey, Judith. 1988. "Can There Be a Feminist Ethnography?" *Women's Studies International Forum* 11, no. 1:21–27.

Stacey, Judith, and Barrie Thorne. 1985. "The Missing Feminist Revolution in Sociology." *Social Problems* 32, no. 4 (April).

Sterba, James. 1984. *Morality in Practice.* Belmont, Calif.: Wadsworth.

Stone, Katherine. 1973. "The Origins of Job Structures in the Steel Industry." *Radical America,* November/December.

Strauss, Anselm. 1978. *A Social Worlds Perspective.* Vol. 1 of Norman K. Denzin, ed., *Studies in Symbolic Interaction.* Greenwich, Conn.: JAI Press.

———. 1987. *Qualitative Analysis for Social Scientists.* Cambridge: Cambridge University Press.

Sumner, L. W. 1981. *Abortion and Moral Theory.* Princeton, N.J.: Princeton University Press.

Thayer, Frederick. 1973. *An End to Hierarchy! An End to Competition!* New York: New Viewpoints.

Thompson, E. P. 1968. *The Making of the English Working Class.* Hammondsworth, England: Penguin Books.

Thomson, Judith Jarvis. 1971. "A Defense of Abortion." *Philosophy and Public Affairs,* September, 47–66. Reprinted in *Today's Moral Problems. See* Wasserstrom 1979.

Turner, Simmie Freeman. 1978. "Nietzsche on Truth." Unpublished essay.

Velasquez, Manuel, and Vincent Barry. 1988. *Philosophy.* Belmont, Calif.: Wadsworth.

Vesey, Lawrence R. 1979. "The Plural Organized Worlds of the Humanities." In *The Organization of Knowledge in Modern America. See* Oleson and Voss 1979.

Wallman, Sandra. 1979. *Social Anthropology of Work.* New York: Academic Press.

Walzer, Michael. 1970. "The Obligations of Oppressed Minorities." *Commentary,* May.

Ward, Colin. 1973. *Anarchy in Action.* New York: Harper and Row.

Wasserstrom, Richard A. 1979. *Today's Moral Problems.* 2d ed. New York: Macmillan.

Whitbeck, Caroline. 1983. "The Moral Implications of Regarding Women as People: New Perspectives on Pregnancy and Personhood." In William Bondeson et al., *Abortion and the Status of the Fetus.* Boston: D. Reidel.

Winch, Peter. 1958. *The Idea of a Social Science.* London: Routledge and Kegan Paul.

———. 1964. "Understanding a Primitive Society." *American Philosophical Quarterly* 1:307–24. Reprinted in *Ethics and Action. See* Winch 1972.

———. 1972. *Ethics and Action.* London: Routledge and Kegan Paul.

Wolfe, Alan. 1989. *The Ties That Bind.* Berkeley: University of California Press.

Wolff, Robert Paul. 1977. *Understanding Rawls: A Reconstruction and Critique of a Theory of Justice.* Princeton, N.J.: Princeton University Press.

Woolgar, Steven, and Dorothy Pawluch. 1985. "Ontological Gerrymandering: The Anatomy of Social Problems Explanations." *Social Problems* 32:214–27.

Young, R. M. 1969. "Malthus and the Evolutionalists." *Past and Present* 43:109–41.

Zimmerman, Mary K. 1977. *Passage Through Abortion: The Personal and the Social Reality of Women's Experiences.* New York: Praeger.

# Index